I0688322

Alexander Dirom, William Mackie

An Inquiry Into the Corn Laws and Corn Trade of Great Britain,

and their influence on the prosperity of the Kingdom. With suggestions for the improvement of the corn laws.

Alexander Dirom, William Mackie

An Inquiry Into the Corn Laws and Corn Trade of Great Britain,
and their influence on the prosperity of the Kingdom. With suggestions for the improvement of the corn laws.

ISBN/EAN: 9783337183486

Printed in Europe, USA, Canada, Australia, Japan

Cover: Foto ©Suzi / pixelio.de

More available books at **www.hansebooks.com**

AN

INQUIRY

INTO THE

CORN LAWS AND CORN TRADE

OF

GREAT BRITAIN,

AND THEIR INFLUENCE

ON THE

PROSPERITY OF THE KINGDOM.

WITH SUGGESTIONS FOR THE IMPROVEMENT OF THE CORN LAWS.

By THE LATE ALEXANDER DIROM, ESQ.
OF MUIRESK, IN THE COUNTY OF ABERDEEN.

TO WHICH IS ADDED,

A SUPPLEMENT,

By MR WILLIAM MACKIE OF ORMISTON IN EAST LOTHIAN,

Bringing down the CONSIDERATION of the SUBJECT to the PRESENT TIME;
INVESTIGATING the CAUSE of the present SCARCITY; and suggesting MEASURES
for promoting the CULTIVATION of the WASTE LANDS; and for rendering the
PRODUCE equal to the INCREASING CONSUMPTION of the KINGDOM.

EDINBURGH:

Printed for WILLIAM CREECH;
And O. NICOLL, Pall Mall; and J. SEWELL, Cornhill; London.

1796.

TO THE RIGHT HONOURABLE

HENRY DUNDAS,

ONE OF HIS MAJESTY'S PRINCIPAL SECRETARIES OF
STATE, &c. &c. &c.

SIR,

On my return from the East Indies, in
the year 1792, I found the following Work in Manuscript, among my deceased Father's papers; with
a memorandum written, in the end of the year 1787,
a short time before his death, containing a recommendation to me to have it published.

Finding that my Father had obtained your
permission to dedicate his intended publication to
you; and it being congenial to your character to countenance a work, which has the prosperity of the
kingdom for its object, I am happy in thinking that
this Inquiry, whatever may be found to be its merit,
will still have the advantage of appearing under your
patronage; nor does it afford me less satisfaction to
have this opportunity of testifying the high respect,
with which I have the honour to be,

SIR,

Your much obliged, and

Most obedient humble Servant,

ALEX. DIROM.

Edinburgh, 10th March 1796.

PREFACE

BY THE EDITOR.

THE Author of the following Work, who lived to the age of fixty-three, devoted a confiderable part of his time to the ftudy and practice of agriculture*. To a profeffional knowledge of the law, he added extenfive literary acquirements; and, actuated by a ftrong zeal for the public good, undertook this inveftigation, which will appear to have been a work of much reflection and refearch.

The great object, which the author appears to have had in contemplation, was to exhibit fuch a view of the principles and effects of the Corn Laws, enacted at different periods in Great Britain, as might fhew that the Corn Trade, both as a manufacture, and an article of commerce, is, of all others, the firft in importance to the profperity of the kingdom. His ftatements, founded upon *facts*, tend to prove, that abundance of grain at home, and at a moderate price, cannot be obtained by *importation* from abroad, and can only be fecured by giving fuch liberal encouragement to *exportation*, as may render agriculture, or the raifing of corn, the favourite object of

---

* An account of the Author's practice in Agriculture will be found in Wight's State of Hufbandry in Scotland, Vol. 3. page 677, and page 719.

induftry in the kingdom. Thus, inftead of purchafing a confiderable part of our fubfiftence from foreign countries, we may, by falutary regulations in the Corn Laws, be enabled, not only to fupply ourfelves, but to render our country one of the principal granaries of Europe.

It is neceffary to remark, that this inveftigation includes only the Corn Laws, as far down as the year 1774, and the confideration of the fubject in general, to the year 1786. Since that period, feveral ftatutes, particularly that of 1791, by which all the former Corn Laws are repealed, have received the fanction of Parliament ; the expediency of which, it is hoped, may, in fome meafure, be alfo judged of from the principles fuggefted in the courfe of this Inquiry.

In order, however, to afford to the Public a continued chain of information, on a fubject fo difficult, and fo important, the Editor applied to Mr Mackie of Ormifton, in the county of Eaft Lothian, a man of extenfive knowledge in this line, as well as in practical agriculture*, to furnifh him with a review of the Corn Laws that have been enacted fince this Inquiry was written, and to bring down the confideration of the fubject to the prefent times. This has been done by Mr Mackie in Two Letters, which the Editor hopes will be found to be an ufeful and able Supplement to the Work.

---

* Mr Mackie is the author of two fmall Tracts, the one entitled, Difquifitions on the Influence of Soil and Climate, in Improving the nourifhing quality of Vegetabls ; the other, An Addrefs to the Landed Intereft in Great Britain, on the Prefent State of the Diftillery. Both printed for William Creech, Edinburgh, 1786.

CONTENTS.

SUPPLEMENT.

LETTER I.

LETTER II.

APPENDIX.

Nᵒ I.

Nᵒ II.

* The Supplement to the Inquiry, contains an account of the Exports and Imports of Grain from the year 1785 to 1793 inclusive.

CONTENTS.

INQUIRY

INTO

THE CORN LAWS, &c.

CHAP. I.

Of the General State of Nations, with respect to the alimentary support of Mankind; and more especially that of Great Britain.

THE ſtrength and power of nations being limited, or extended, according to the number and induſtry of their inhabitants, the attention of their reſpective governments ought to be directed to ſuch meaſures as have an immediate tendency to encourage *agriculture*; thereby giving riſe to an uſeful population, and enlarging that baſis which affords the moſt ſolid ſupport to *manufactures* and *commerce*.

On reverting to the ſtate of mankind, in the different ſtages of ſociety, we find that the inhabitants of a country, who ſubſiſt by hunting, can aſſociate only in ſmall numbers, on account of the great extent of land which the chace requires to ſup-

A

port a family; and of courfe, the population muft bear a fmall proportion to the extent of territory which they poffefs.

If, like the Tartars or Arabs of old[*], a nation be wholly employed in pafturage, its population will be in proportion to its herds, or, which is in effect the fame, in proportion to the number of cattle, which the territory occupied by fuch nation is capable to fupport.

Under mild and fruitful climates, where mankind are partly fupported by the fpontaneous productions of the earth, and obtain their fubfiftence with a fmall degree of labour, the population may be great, but the inhabitants will in general be feeble and enervated ; unaccuftomed to mental, as well as to bodily exertions, they are without refources upon emergencies ; their ftruggles in adverfity muft be weak ; and a barren feafon will either banifh or cut off a number of them, proportioned to the decreafe of the ufual quautity of food.

In communities fuch as Holland, Venice, Genoa, Geneva, and other republics, the Hanfe, and other free towns, whofe induftry is great, but whofe territory is of fmall extent, the inhabitants muft barter their labour in the different arts, or in commerce, for the productions of the lands of other nations ; depending therefore, in a great meafure, upon foreign countries for fubfiftence, their profperity can advance by only flow degrees, and their population will be proportioned to the fupply procured by their manufactures and commerce.

In Great Britain, and other extenfive countries under the

* Vide Genefis, c. 13. ver. 2, 5, 6.; and c. 33. ver. 13.

like climate, where the foil is capable of being made highly productive by labour, but without labour is nearly. barren, the exertion of the inhabitants is called forth, and is rewarded by abundant crops. The population, manufactures, and commerce of fuch nations, will increafe with the induftry and capital employed in Agriculture, and can be limited only by their territory.

Since the acquifition of the means of fubfiftence muft precede that of the conveniencies or the luxuries of life, fo the induftry which procures the firft, muft, in the order of time, as well as of importance, be prior to that which furnifhes the others. The true riches, therefore, of all countries, both primarily and ultimately, muft be derived from bodily labour, and the food of mankind, produced by that labour; population, and every occupation of mankind, being entirely fupported by, and dependant upon thefe main fources of national wealth.

It is evident, that a much greater number of people, can be reared and fupported in the fame extent of territory, by the productions of the vegetable, than poffibly can be by thofe of the animal world. Thus the Hottentots, who lived by hunting, having been preffed backward by the Dutch colonifts at the Cape of Good Hope, have decreafed in numbers at leaft proportioned to the territory of which they have been divefted ; yet, by the cultivation of the foil, the number of the Dutch colonifts, now comfortably fupported upon the fame fpace of land occupied by their predeceffors, exceeds the latter probably fifty times. The fame obfervation may be applied to North America.

A 2

Agriculture, or the art of raifing corn, having increafed population, and greatly contributed to extend the ftrength and
power of Great Britain, it may be worthy of the attention of
the community, to enquire into its rife, to contemplate its progrefs, to invefligate the caufes of its decline, as well as of its
profperity; and as far as poffible (*avoiding theory*) to point
out to the legiflature, from the experience of paft times, thofe
circumftances that have moft materially contributed to its fuccefs, or to its depreffion.

The period appears to be very diftant when agriculture was
firft introduced into Great Britain; for when the Romans invaded the fouthern parts of it, they found the fields full of
corn, and the inhabitants in poffeffion of trained horfes and
chariots of war, which they managed with great dexterity*.
And although the other parts of the ifland were inhabited by
people, who lived by pafturage or by hunting, and clothed
themfelves in the fkins of their cattle, or of their game, yet,
having been initiated by the Romans in the arts of civilized
life, they foon began to cultivate their fields, and to raife corn.

After the departure of the Romans, the inroads of the
Scots and Picts, the invafion and conqueft by the Saxons,
their heptarchy, and military appointments, were all unfavourable to agriculture; and the invafions and fucceffes of the
Danes, and the immenfe fums which they carried out of England, continued its depreffion†.

* Cæfar's Commentary, lib. 4. 28. and lib. 5. 10. Clarke's edit.
† Flor. Wigorn. Brad. Hift. Eng. vol. 1. p. 123.; Cartes Hift. of England,
vol. 1. p. 534; Hume's Hift. Eng. vol. 1. p. 93. &c.

The Norman conqueft, by the frefh diftreffes of war, and the change of property, retarded its recovery; and, except in the royal domains, or thofe of the dignified clergy, of the great barons, or of religious orders, agriculture for a long time after that period, appears to have been left to the feeble exertions of fuch people, as by their infirmities or age, or their inferior fituation in life, were not called for in war. By degrees, however, the Englifh and Norman families came to be fo much incorporated, that the diftinction was loft; the bold and independent fpirit of the Englifh Nobles again appeared, and the fields began again to receive cultivation.

It would appear that at fome diftant period, agriculture had been in a higher ftate of perfection in Scotland, than it now is, and that the country had been more populous than at prefent. The ftraight and equal ridges ftill appearing upon extenfive fields and high grounds, in every part of the country, which muft have been barren for many centuries; and even the penalties in fome of the old Scotch laws having been paid in wheat, feem to point out a more plentiful and populous era.

Malcolm II. gave great fupport to agriculture; but in the year of his death (1034) a few days after the fummer folftice, there were fevere frofts and deep fnow, which deftroyed the fruits of the earth, and a great famine enfued*.

In the beginning of the reign of Malcolm IV. a great famine raged over all Scotland, by which great numbers of men and cattle were deftroyed†.

* Buchanan's Hift. Scot, l. 6. *fub finem.*   † Ib. l. 7. 37.

But whatever progrefs agriculture may have made in Scotland, prior to the acceffion of William, in the year 1165, the war with England, the captivity of that prince, and the money paid for redeeming the fuperiority or vaffalage of his kingdom, which William had furrendered for his releafe, brought Scotland into fuch diftrefs, that, upon the acceffion of his fon Alexander II. in the year 1214, agriculture was found to have been almoft totally abandoned ; and the very firft law, made in his reign, was to oblige the inhabitants to labour and fow their lands*.

Under Alexander III. Scotland recovered, in fome degree, its agriculture and its confequence ; but the difputes that happened upon his death, and the war which enfued with England, diminifhed both afterwards for·many ages.

It is not, however, to a very diftant period we need apply to difcover at what time agriculture came to be fo far advanced in England, as to render *wheat* the chief article of fubfiftence. This could only be the cafe, when the quantity raifed became fo abundant as to bring the prices of that grain, one year with another, to be reafonable, and nearly equal. If fcarcity fhould now double the ordinary prices, it would produce dearth ; but if it fhould triple them, famine would follow. Therefore, fo long as we find the prices of wheat vary, ten, twenty, thirty, or forty times the current value of it, in years of ordinary plenty, we muft confider the culture of that grain to have been ftill in its infancy, and that mankind did not depend upon wheat as the chief part of their fupport. In the year 1244, the price of wheat was 2s. the

* Stat. Alex. II. c. 1.

quarter. In 1270, it was at L. 4, 16s. equal to L. 47 : 12 : 4
of prefent money; fo that, in fuch times, it would appear in
fmall quantities, and only at the tables of the rich. In 1288,
it was 1s. 6d. In 1317, it was at L. 2, 4s. before harveft,
and the fame year, after harveft, it fell to 6s. 8d. In 1349,
the price was 2s. In 1359, it was L. 1 : 6 : 8; and in 1361,
2s. the quarter. So late as the year 1557, wheat rofe from 8s.
the quarter, to L. 2 : 13 : 4. In 1562, it was at 8s. the quarter, and in 1574, at L. 2, 16s*.

CHAP. I.

We are difappointed, when we apply to the ftatutes of our
ancient legiflatures, to difcover the encouragement beftowed
upon agriculture; for that feems not to have occurred to them,
as a matter in any way neceffary: on the contrary, we find
many of the old laws of England and Scotland, inviting and
encouraging foreign merchants and others, to import corn

---

* The principles, upon which the ancient money of England, and of Scotland is converted into the prefent Sterling money, are explained in the Appendix, No I.; which
alfo contains a Table of the price of the quarter of wheat in England, at fuch periods
as it can be properly authenticated, from the year 1223 to 1784.

The authors are numerous who have made calculations of the progrefs of the value of money from the Conqueft to the prefent time; and to afcertain it has been found
a matter of the greateft difficulty. Mr Hume, in his Hiftory of England, vol. 1.
p. 228. calculates the money about the time of the Conqueft at 30 times the value of
the prefent money. He even goes the length to fay, that we may multiply the fums
mentioned by hiftorians, for fome reigns after the conqueft, by 100.

Bifhop Fleetwood, in his Chronicon Pretiofum, publifhed in 1707, fhews, that a
quarter of wheat, which in the year 1240 coft L. 4 : 13 : 9, would be equal to about
L. 50 of prefent money. In 1469 he reckons that L. 5 was equal to L. 40 of prefent
money, or as 1 to 8.

The calculations of our Author are lower than Bifhop Fleetwood's, but, upon
the whole, correfpond pretty nearly with them. They are made upon principles
more general, and more eafily applied than the Bifhop's, and appear, from other
manufcripts left by the Author, to have been adopted by him, after a long and pain-
ful inveftigation of the fubject. *Edit.*

and all kinds of provifions; and the inhabitants purchafed them, with their raw materials, of wool, leather, and lead, which they themfelves were then incapable of working up*.

Agriculture was for feveral centuries after the Conqueft, without reputation, and without fupport. The lands were chiefly in the hands of the clergy, or of the great barons; they were laboured by their villains or flaves, in proportion to whom, the number of hufbandmen or foemen was very fmall over all England†. The freemen, who occupied farms in the country, and they were but few, held no rank in fociety; and befides the depredations of the banditti, with whom the kingdom in thofe days was overrun, they were oppreffed by the greater legal depredation of *purveyance*. This originally comprehended the neceffary provifions, carriages, &c. which the neareft farmers were obliged to furnifh, at the current prices, to the Kings armies, and his houfes and caftles in time of war. It was called *the great purveyance*, and the officers who collected thofe neceffaries were called *purveyors*. The *fmaller purveyance* included the neceffary provifions and carriages for the King's houfehold, when living at home, or travelling through the kingdom, which the tenants in the King's demefne lands were obliged to furnifh gratis; and the like practice came to be adopted by the barons, and great men, in every tour which they thought proper to make in the country‡.

* Vide Magna Charta, K. John, cap. 50.
† Brady's Hift. of England, General Preface, p. 7. 8. &c.
‡ This cuftom exifts now in the *Eaft Indies*, where the feudal fyftem is in force. *Edit.*

These exactions were so grievous, and levied in so licentious a manner, that the farmers, when they heard of the court's approach, often deserted their houses, as if the country had been invaded by an enemy*.

Purveyance came to be a prodigious distress upon the subjects in both kingdoms, and was perhaps, for many centuries, the chief obstruction to the agriculture and improvement of Great Britain.

The abuse was extended so far, that hostlers, brewers, and victuallers, purchased the King's letters-patent, of the office of purveyor. The exactions were so grievous, and the office came to be so odious, 'that the heinous name of purveyor, ' was ordered by law to be changed into that of buyer †.'

Many laws were made for the reformation and regulation of purveyance, without effect. The distresses of the people of England, arising from this mode of oppression, are well painted in one of those reforming laws, 28 Hen. 6, entituled ' The ' penalty for taking any persons horses or cart, without the ' delivery of the owner, or some officer, or for taking money ' to spare them.'

An higher legal distress cannot well be imagined, than this old and ordinary method of purveyance ; nor a measure more injurious to the best interests of the kingdom.

* Hume's Hist. vol. 1. p. 242.   † 36 Ed. III. c. 2.

The practice was not confined to the neighbourhood of the King's houfehold, it was fpread over the whole kingdom; for when fuch powers are to be fold, purchafers would be found every where.

If a farmer had an hazardous crop to take in, if he had an appointment upon urgent bufinefs, if he had fixed a day for the marriage of a fon or daughter; it was then that his neighbour purveyor came, and laid hold of his horfes and carriages for the fervice of the King, and detained them until they were redeemed by a fine; and this fine would be proportionate to the anxiety, or the diftrefs of the farmer; for all fentiments of humanity or juftice were out of the queftion.

By this law, thofe letters-patent having been recalled, none fuch were afterwards iffued; but purveyance in other refpects continued to be executed in its ufual rigour.

In the 30th of Elizabeth, the Commons paffed a bill for regulating purveyance; but it was loft in the Houfe of Peers.

In the following feffion, they made a frefh attempt to remove that grievance; but the Queen exprefsly prohibited them to meddle with that branch of her prerogative.

The various modes of oppreffion by purveyance, fo late as the reign of James I. are pointed out by Bacon, in his fpeech delivered in the firft parliament of that king *.

* Hume's Hift. vol. 4. p. 641.

Another great diftrefs upon agriculture had arifen, and continued long, in the execution of the office of Clerk of the market.

The Clerk of the market was originally an officer in the King's houfehold, who had the charge of the King's meafures, and the cuftody of the ftandards for regulating the weights and meafures throughout the kingdom.

But the jurifdiction of this office had, by degrees, been extended over the whole markets of the kingdom, and by the general inequality of weights and meafures then in ufe, the Clerk of the market came to be invefted with powers in appearance legal, to opprefs the farmers, and other fubjects, at his pleafure.

The Crown had alfo been in the practice of letting the office to farm, for which, great fums of money were paid ; and, of courfe, it became neceffary to the leffees, for their own reimburfement and profit, to execute the unjuft powers committed to them with the utmoft rigour *.

* The Cutwal of the bazar, or market, in India, is exactly fuch an officer as is here defcribed. In fhort, the peafantry of that country, particularly under the native princes, labour under all the hardfhips that appear to have exifted in Great Britain fome hundred years ago. This being the cafe, may not benefit be derived, even in the government of the Britifh empire in India, from the inveftigation of this fubject, fo important in all countries? And might not the example of our government there, were they to redrefs all fuch grievances, have a happy influence in alfo directing the attention of the native princes, to objects of fuch confequence to the profperity of their people? *Edit.*

S·veral laws were made for removing this grievance without effect *, until the 16th Cha. I. when the jurisdiction of this officer was restricted to the verge of the court; and the powers of the officer, over the rest of the kingdom, were committed to the Mayor, or other Head-officer of the city, borough, or town-corporate; and to any Lord, Lords of liberty, liberties or franchises, his, or their deputy or deputies, or agents, according to their several liberties and jurisdictions †.

These circumstances, however, in the mean time served to deprefs the rising spirit of improvement; and, joined to the general ignorance of the proper methods of cultivation, induced the landholders to difufe tillage, and to throw their grounds into inclofures, for the fake of pafture, which contributed much to the depopulation of the kingdom, in thofe times, when there were not commerce and manufactures fufficient to employ the hands thrown out of hufbandry.

Camden obferves, that after the allowance given to export corn in the 5th of Eliz. agriculture received new life and vigour; but it is certain, during all that reign, and that of her fucceffor, England depended upon foreigners for bread. There was a regular importation from the Baltic, and from France; and when thefe failed, the bad confequences were very fenfibly felt by the nation. Sir Walter Rawleigh, in his

* 16 Ed. 2. c. 9.—14 Ed. 3. ft. 1. c. 12.—16 Rich. 3. c. 3.
† 16 Ch. 1. c. 19.

obfervations, computes that two millions went out of the kingdom at one time for corn *.

Nor did England ever fupply herfelf with corn, till after
the fyftem of corn laws, begun by King William in 1638,
were completed in 1700.

In Scotland, the iron rod of purveyors, was alfo exercifed
with great feverity. Their conduct in early times has been
trafmitted to us by an act of the Chamberlain Air (circuit
court) c. 17.

Agriculture has now become the chief manufacture of
Great Britain; it is that upon which all others depend, and
in which many more people are employed, than in any other
manufacture whatever.

The confequence of agriculture to the ftate, from the numbers of people employed in it, is highly increafed by the numerous and vigorous offspring which they produce, by whom
the wafte, made in the human fpecies by every other manufacture, is fupplied.

We find no manufacturer returning his fon to the plough,
while almoft every ploughman endeavours to breed up, at
leaft one of his fons, to what is vulgarly called a trade, as
giving him a higher rank in fociety. Prejudices remain long
after their caufes have ceafed; and perhaps this fentiment con-

* Hume's Hift. vol. 5. p. 127.

CHAP. I.

tinues to be impreſſed upon the bulk of mankind, from the mean ſtate in which our early farmers were placed.

By the encouragement of agriculture, we not only ſecure plenty, and moderate prices at home, and raiſe a new trade and employment for freſh numbers of people, by the exportation of our excreſcent ſtock; but we make ground, otherwiſe barren, to be fruitful; and the employment of one additional man, or the improvement of one acre of ground at home, is certainly of more conſequence to the community, than of an hundred ſuch in a colony.

It is from plenty alone, that cheapneſs and equal prices can proceed, and this plenty can only be procured by raiſing corn at home; for if we ſhall depend upon foreign importation, the ſupply and the prices muſt both be precarious.

It is generally believed, that the number of inhabitants in Great Britain is about eight millions; and we may ſuppoſe, that each perſon will conſume rather more than a quarter of wheat yearly; or of wheat and other grain to that value *.

* Maitland in his Survey of London, 2d edition, fol. 756, ſays, that the bakers unanimouſly agreed, that, including puddings, pies, and other paſtry ware, people in London over-head, conſumed 10 ounces of flour each day, which requires 5 buſhels, 2 pecks of wheat for each, yearly.

Mr Hume in his Eſſay on Antient Nations, Edin. Edit. 1752, page 235, ſays ‘ the ‘ portion of corn given every month, to every man of full years in Rome, was 5 ‘ modü.’ This Mr Hume computed at 1 qr. 2 buſhels yearly; but according to Dr Arbuthnot it amounted to 1 qr. 7 b. 1 p. yearly.

Eſſai ſur les Monies, printed at Paris in 1746, p. 51, in the notes ſays, ‘ It is not

Wheat is double the value of the inferior grain over-head *. To avoid multiplicity of computations, we shall rank malt as barley, and throw, upon the general confumption of the people, the grain confumed by horfes not employed in agriculture, and by hogs, poultry, ftarchmakers, &c.; and when it is confidered that a great number of the people live chiefly upon the inferior grain, we cannot, under all thefe circumftances, appropriate lefs than two quarters of the feveral forts of grain over-head, to the confumption of each perfon, upon

‘ thought too high an eftimation of the confumption of men, one with the other, to ‘ rate it at 3 fetiers a year; if there are thofe that eat lefs, there are a great many ‘ who confume more.’ Three fetiers are equal to 1 qr. 4 b. 3 p. London meafure. Corn Tracts, p. 188. 190.

Our foldiers when encamped, and prifoners of war, are allowed a pound and a half of brown bread, each day, which is equal to 9 bufhels of wheat yearly.

In the royal hofpitals of Chelfea and Greenwich, the allowance is one pound a day, of wheaten bread, which is faid to go farther than a larger quantity of brown bread, which requires 7 bufhels of wheat yearly.

Thefe computations are made from wheat of the beft quality.

People who labour hard, and who form the larger part of the community, will confume more than either of thofe portions; and the weaker that any grain is, it will require the greater quantity of it for fuftenance.

Wheat, as the fuperior, commands in a great meafure, in all feafons, the value or price of the inferior grain; and as its proportional value to the latter can be afcertained with certainty, we have made choice of the fuperior grain fingly, as the foundation of our computations in the prefent work.

Add to this that we could not find fo many authentic proofs of the prices of the inferior grain, at diftant periods, as of wheat; and that the different kinds of inferior grain, were not always comprehended in the fame law, the calculations will be infinitely more comprehenfible, when made from one object or datum, inftead of feven or eight

* Vide Explanatory Table, Appendix, No 8. art. 6.

an average yearly, for bread, beer, fpirits, &c. and of courfe the confumption of 8 millions of people, will be 16 millions of quarters of the feveral kinds of grain over-head yearly.

It will be afcertained that, for many years, Great Britain exported about 850,000 quarters of grain yearly; and we may therefore conclude, that, in thofe years of profperity, corn fufficient was raifed to fupport the inhabitants for near 14 months, befide the feed to be fown, at the rate of fomewhat more than 1,300,000 quarters monthly; for it may be admitted, that at leaft one month's provifion muft be kept on hand to bring in the new crop.

But even in fuch years, the produce is fo nearly balanced by the confumpt at home, that, independent of bad feafons, if by any miftake, or mifapplication of the laws, the hand of labour fhould, in a fmall degree, be withdrawn from agriculture, the confequences would be dreadful. From the ftrength of our commerce, we might ward off the blow for a fhort time, by the importation of foreign grain; but while that would impoverifh us by the payment of the price, it would increafe our wants, by trenching upon the remains of our own agriculture.

Yet if the people can be plentifully and cheaply fupported, and even the exportation mentioned kept up, it would be a vaft addition to the wealth and refources of the kingdom; but if, by any encouragement that the law can give, corn could be yearly raifed fufficient for 15 months provifion to the in-

habitants, an exportation of a million and a half of quarters
of grain, in years of ordinary plenty might be kept up, which
would be equal to a tenth part of the whole exports of the
kingdom : an immenfe fund of riches, and of employment to
numbers of people, more than at prefent exift in Britain would
from thence enfue ; and the importation of foreign grain
would always be unneceffary, unlefs after fome extremely
barren feafon.

Importation of foreign grain, although at fome times neceffary, is at all times ruinous, by the check it gives to our
agriculture, and fhould never be admitted but from neceffity,
and with great circumfpection.   In that event the prices muft
be high, and the market precarious ; becaufe our fupply then
depends upon the judgment, perhaps the caprice of other people;
and added to the prime coft and freight, &c. we are fubjected
to the payment of fuch taxes, as the prince from whofe ports
we are to be fupplied, fhall be pleafed to put upon it ; and
which may poffibly be increafed in proportion to our neceffities.   Befides, by importation, we employ the lands and labour of other nations, at the expence of yielding fo much of
our own, and fo far we cut off our own refources.

In every country, the quantity of feed fown, will always
be proportioned to the ufual demand for the crop ; and a nation accuftomed to raife more corn than it confumes, and to export the excrefcence, will feldom feel fcarcity or high prices ;
becaufe a fhort crop, which in other fituations might be hurt-

C

ful, will generally afford a fufficient fupply for home confumption, although exportation muft ftop.

All nations who have hands fufficient for the purpofe, wifh
to keep their raw materials at home, to be wrought up by
their own people, and to allow a free trade of the goods manufactured.

When 100 people are employed upon the fame fubject, if
10 of them are fufficient for one branch of it, and 90 are
required for the other, we may in general fuppofe the firft
to be the raw material, and the other the manufacture.

Corn being entirely the produce of labour, the land upon
which it grows may be faid to be the raw material, and of
100 people employed in bringing corn from the feed to the oven
or ftill, more than 90 are engaged in bringing it to market-
able grain; after which, fewer people are employed in it, than
are neceffary to cut and few up the woolen and linen cloths,
after they have received the laft hand of the manufacturer;
fo that corn, when brought to be dreffed grain, is a finifhed
manufacture in every fenfe of the word.

The generality of other manufactures are arbitrary, and
may be taken up or laid down at pleafure, poffibly without
much detriment to the nation; but agriculture muft be fupported, as it is the hinge upon which both our lives and actions
turn, and the ultimate and only certain refource of the ftate,
both for men and for money.

Almoſt every other manufacture, may be admitted to a free
trade ; but, as the trade of corn muſt at all times be limited
by, and ſubſervient to the neceſſities of the ſtate, it requires
the attention of a careful and foſtering parent. Our agriculture ought therefore to be guarded by the wiſeſt laws, and
the ſtricteſt execution of them, as the only certain means of
employing the greateſt number of people, and conſequently
of increaſing our population ; and it is the better entitled to
this attention, that the farmer and the landholder pay a full
proportion of all taxes impoſed, for promoting and protecting
the ſale of our other manufactures, both at home and abroad,
as well as for the growth of corn at home.

It is not eaſy to aſcertain, with certainty, the number of
people employed in the raiſing, manufacturing, tranſporting,
and ſale of corn ; but it may be computed with a great degree
of probability.

It is imagined that a farm, from which 100 quarters of
grain, of the ordinary production of the county in which it
is ſituated, can be ſold yearly, (after maintaining the farmer's
family, ſupporting his cattle, &c. and ſowing the ground for
another crop), will employ, at an average, 12 people, old and
young *.

* It is ſuppoſed that the farmer's family conſiſts of himſelf, his wife, and three
children at a medium ; that he acts as overſeer, that his wife manages the dairy, and
that they employ,

   2 men ſervants,
   1 maid ſervant,

In larger farms, where the foil is good, and the climate favourable, fewer people will be required ; and when the farms are fmaller, or the foil and climate lefs favourable, more will proportionally be neceffary.

To raife 13 millions of quarters of grain for fale, would, according to the above calculation, require the labour of 1,560,000 people, old and young ; and their maintenance, at the rate of two quarters to each perfon, being added to that quantity, will make up the general yearly confumpt of 16 millions of quarters.

But befide the farmers, who raife grain for fale, (without including millers, mealmen, factors, and others employed entirely in the corn trade), there muft be at leaft two hundred thoufand families of cottagers in Great Britain, who raife as much corn as ferves their own families only, and whofe land-rents are paid by other branches of their induftry ; and allowing 5 to each of their families, there cannot in all be fewer

> 1 herd,
> 1 hind or labourer for threfhing corn, &c, and
> 2 children to tend the leffer animals.

The cattle and live-ftock neceffary for work, or to be reared for profit, may be confidered to confift of at leaft,

> 4 work horfes, and a riding horfe, or
> 8 oxen in place of the 4 horfes, for work ;
> 6 cows and their production for three years, and about
> 50 fheep ; and that the farm will befides feed
> 8 hogs and two breeders, with poultry, &c.

than two millions and a half of people employed in huſbandry.

Deducting 5 millions of quarters of grain, for the maintenance of the farmers and cottagers (at the rate of two quarters to each perſon), from the 16 millions of quarters, which
we have reckoned to be the quantity required for the general
conſumpt of the kingdom, there remains 11 millions of quarters of grain, which is to be conſidered as the produce of the
lands, after ſupporting the people and cattle employed in raiſing
the corn, and ſowing the ground; or, in other words, a
quantity equal to the conſumpt of the 5 millions and a half
of people, who are not employed in huſbandry.

But it is to be obſerved, that the 11 millions of quarters
of grain, are raiſed by the million and a half of farmers; for
the cottagers, raiſing only as much grain as will ſupport their
own families, come not into the computation; ſo that every
perſon, old and young, employed in huſbandry, as a trade or
manufacture, is ſuppoſed to raiſe as much corn as will maintain himſelf, and nearly four other perſons, after ſupporting
the ſtock upon the farm, and labouring and ſowing the ground
for another crop.

We have taken up this calculation, as is already ſaid, from
the generally received opinion, that there are 8 millions of
people in Great Britain; but we are apt to believe that the
population conſiderably exceeds that number.

If this be the cafe, we do not pretend to alter the computation, by faying, that every perfon, old and young, employed in agriculture as a fcience or trade, could raife, upon an average, more grain than would fupport 4 other perfons befides himfelf, after defraying the other neceffities of the farm; for we believe that if 48 or 50 people, old and young, in proportion to the raifers, were to be billeted upon fuch a farm as we have mentioned, they and the people upon the farm would find full ufe for all the productions of it, after fupporting the cattle, &c. and fowing the ground.

But if there are more people, the numbers of the corn-raifers will be more alfo, in proportion to the number of the other members of the community, which will make no difference in the other parts of the calculation; and from every confideration we have had in view, and every judgment we can form, we are apt to imagine that there are at leaft 2 millions of people, old and young, employed in agriculture in Great Britain, befide the cottagers; and that the numbers of the other branches of the community are in proportion. This would make the population of the country amount to about 11 millions.

In ftating this number, we have, among other confideratio s, taken he taxes or public revenue, under review, amounting to 15 millions of pounds Sterling, all which muft be raifed from the induftry of the people at large *; for thofe

---

* This was written in the year 1786, when the public revenue rather exceeded fifteen millions. *Edit.*

parts of the community, who, by their birth, fortune, or employment, are not subjected to bodily labour, although equally neceſſary in ſociety, are not very conſiderable in number, when compared with the great body of the people.

Fifteen millions of pounds, to be paid yearly by eight millions of people, would amount to 37s. 6d. each perſon, or L. 9 : 7 : 6 out of each family, ſuppoſed to conſiſt of five perſons, which would appear rather impoſſible to be borne; but divided among 11 millions, it will only affect each about 23s. 6d. per annum, or L. 5 : 15s. from each family, which is more likely to be the caſe.

It has been ſaid, that the land tax, the window tax, the tax upon carriages, &c. do not affect induſtry; but that is without foundation : For land, without the induſtry of people, would be of little or no comparative value; nor is it of any conſequence whether the landlord or the tenant pays the land tax: For if it be paid by the tenant, he will pay proportionably leſs rent; and without the induſtry of the people, there would be neither cultivated land, nor windows, nor carriages to pay taxes. Every public burthen muſt be paid out of the common ſtock of induſtry, although ſome of the taxes may affect one claſs of people more than another.

In the unimproved ſtages of ſociety, there was no occaſion for public taxes; becauſe every member of the community contributed perſonally, both to public and private defence and accommodation. *

There are but four occupations natural to mankind, hunting, fishing, pasturage, and war for defence or retaliation; for agriculture is a trade or manufacture, and has been introduced by art.

The persons who were at the head of those occupations, were the makers of their own instruments, as well as the users of them; their children and relations were allowed to participate in their toils and in their pleasures, but those who served them were their slaves.

In well regulated communities, there must be subordination, but slavery is not necessary; on the contrary, every person is free, and a useful member of the society in his vocation, whatever it is, so long as he conforms himself to the rules of the society.

Men of superior birth, fortune, or merit, come naturally to be employed in the political line or department of government; the farmer raises bread for the community; the sailor and soldier defend it; the manufacturer, assisted by the labourer, works up its raw materials; the artisan by the division of labour, and the application of the mechanic arts, gives assistance to both; the merchant facilitates the exchange of its commodities with those of other nations: and thus every part of the community hangs by the other.

In the course of this inquiry it will appear, that from the Union, till the year 1763, is the period when agriculture, with

fome few exceptions, received the full protection of the laws.
If from the exports of grain from England and from Scotland,
during that time*, we may judge of the comparative quantities
raifed in each of the kingdoms, which may poffibly not be an
improper rule, we fhall find that England produces 15 times as
much corn as Scotland ; that, in general, the crops of England
confift of $\frac{8}{20}$ of wheat, and $\frac{12}{20}$ of inferior grain ; and that
the crop of Scotland has only $\frac{1}{18}$ of wheat, and $\frac{17}{18}$ of inferior
grain †.   In England the prevailing crop appears to be wheat
and barley ; and in Scotland barley and oats.

During the above profperous period, the average exportation from Great Britain for 10 years, from 1740 to 1750, was
848,660 quarters yearly.   In 1750 above a million and a half
of quarters were exported ; and, for feveral other years, the

* Vide Appendix, No 3.

† From the Reports of the rents or revenue of the bifhopricks and religious houfes in
Scotland, fo far as they were payable in grain, made up after the Reformation in the
year 1562, which have been very carefully collected by Maitland, in his Hiftory of
Scotland, it appears, that the quantity of grain amounted to 5078 bolls of wheat,
and 64,655 bolls of inferior grain.   Thefe proportions would point out the crop of
Scotland to confift of about $\frac{1}{13}$ of wheat, and $\frac{12}{13}$ of inferior grain.   But if it be confidered that the rents of the clergy were, in general, of the better kind of grain,
and that the exportation from Scotland was chiefly of the inferior grain ; if we take
the medium of the proportions of the grain paid to the clergy, and of that exported,
we may with great probability conclude that, in general, the crop of fuch land confifts of $\frac{1}{11}$ of wheat, and $\frac{10}{11}$ of inferior grain.

But again, taking the quality of the crop of both kingdoms under review, and computing the quarter of wheat at 40s. and that of the inferior grain, over-head at 20s. ;

D

annual importation was above a million of quarters. The average exportation for 50 years, from 1710 to 1760, was near 600,000 quarters yearly * ; and in the courfe of thofe years it will be found, that *the prices of grain gradually fell as exportation increafed ; and rofe again as exportation decreafed, and as the importation of foreign grain took place*†.

we fhall find, that in England the quarter of grain, ever-head, is worth 28s. and in Scotland only 21s. 4d. ‡ ; fo that in point of quality the crop of England is about ¼ of more value than that of Scotland ; and being 15 times more in quantity, the crop of that kingdom may be even 19 times the value of that of Scotland.

So powerfully and fteadily do climate and foil operate, that the fpecies of grain payable to the clergy of old, points out the general ftate of the crop of the feveral diftricts in Scotland at this day. Only, in examining this point, it muft be attended to, that the Archbifhoprick of St Andrew's comprehended all the territory fouth of the Forth, which was afterwards, in the year 1633, erected into the Bifhoprick of Edinburgh.

* Vide Appendix, No 2.

† Vide Appendix, No 4. & 5.

‡ Vide Explanatory Table, Appendix, No. 6. Art. 8.

CHAP. II.

*Of the caufes and effects of the feveral Corn Laws of Great Britain,
prior to the Revolution in the year 1688.*

FOR feveral centuries after the Conqueft, in order to maintain the laws of England, in force, it was thought neceffary to renew, or to confirm them, upon the acceffion of every
new fovereign. The laws themfelves too, though generally
made with great care and attention, receiving but little fupport from the executive power, fell often into difufe.

This accounts for the numerous confirmations of the Great
Charter, and the frequent re-enactions of the fame laws on
this and other fubjects, without any frefh meaning, to be
found upon the ftatute-book.

In thofe times, the rents of lands, poffeffed by tenants or
farmers, were chiefly payable in corn or cattle, or other pro-

ductions of the foil. The rules by which the rents were received, were very irregular; the meafures of grain varied,
they were taken heaped, and 9 bufhels were generally taken
for the quarter.

By the Great Charters of King John and Henry III, often
confirmed by fucceeding kings and parliaments, one weight
and one meafure had been appointed to be ufed over all England, but with very little effect. Of this we have fufficient
evidence from an act of the 25 Ed. III. by which the weights
and meafures were again attempted to be regulated; and by
which 8 bufhels ftricken, and no more, were appointed to be
received for the quarter of grain, ' *But faving the rents and*
' *farms, and all manner of franchifes, of the lords.*' With fuch
refervations it is not to be expected that the law could have
any effect.

1360.

Under fuch impofitions, with the oppreffion of purveyance,
and the depreffed fituation in life, wherein the farmers were
placed, it is not to be wondered that agriculture languifhed,
and that a numerous community depended upon foreign provifions for their fubfiftence.

It would be an ufelefs and a difagreeable labour, again
to harrow up the laws, and the habits, which checked the
productions of our own fields, and made foreign provifions
neceffary. We fhall now, with pleafure, leave them behind us, to enter upon a more agreeable inveftigation, and

endeavour to trace the steps by which agriculture emerged from obfcurity, and rofe to be the firft pillar of the ftate.

But before entering particularly into the corn laws; as foreftallers, regrators, and ingroffers, are frequently mentioned, it may be neceffary to make the reader acquainted with them.

For many years after the Conqueft, the greateft part of the trade or bufinefs of England, was carried on in markets and fairs; and a very confiderable part of the revenue of the crown arofe from the duties payable to the king upon the goods brought to them for fale*. The barons had alfo tolls at the fairs within their refpective jurifdictions.

When the farmers and merchants were bringing their corn, and other neceffaries, to be fold at the markets and fairs, people met them by the way, and purchafed their provifions, in order to retail them at a higher price. By thefe means the king and the lord of the manor loft the feveral duties payable to them, and the price was raifed upon the inhabitants, by leffening the quantity of provifions brought to market. Such were the original foreftallers, and thus both public and private intereft were united againft them, and fevere penalties were laid upon the practice †.

* Hume, vol. 1. p. 414.

† Ord. for Bakers incert. temp. c. 10. 25 Ed. 3. ft. 4. c. 3; 27 Ed. 3. c. 11, and 2 Rich. 2. ft. 1. c. 2.

But the defcription of a foreftaller was farther extended,
‘ to any perfon who fhould buy any merchandife or victual,
‘ coming toward any fair or market, or toward any city,
‘ port, creek, or road of England or Wales, from beyond fea,
‘ to be fold ; or who fhould make any bargain for having the
‘ fame, before the merchandife or victuals fhould be in the
‘ market to be fold ; or who fhould make any motion for en-
‘ hancing the price ; or fhould move any perfon coming to
‘ the market to forbear to bring the things to be fold *.

‘ A perfon who fhould by any means regrate, obtain, or get
‘ into his poffeffion, in any fair or market, any corn, wine,
‘ fifh, butter, cheefe, &c. that were brought to any market in
‘ England or Wales to be fold, and fhould fell the fame in any
‘ fair or market holden or kept in the fame place, or in any
‘ other fair or market within four miles thereof, fhould be
‘ holden and reputed a regrator †.

‘ A perfon who fhould ingrofs, or get into his hands, by
‘ buying, contract, or promife-making, any growing corn in
‘ the fields, or any other corn.or grain, butter, cheefe, fifh,
‘ or other dead victuals whatever, with intent to fell the fame
‘ again, fhall be holden and reputed an ingroffer‡.’   It is need-
lefs to add that fevere penalties were enacted againft the offenders.

* 5 & 6 Ed. 6. c. 14. § 1

† Ibid. § 2.

‡ Ibid. § 3.

Several parts of the laws againſt ingroſſing were, however, afterwards foftened, to facilitate the internal commerce of the kingdom, which will be noticed in their proper place.

In Scotland, laws to the fame purpofe were made againſt foreftallers and regrators; and although the word ingroſſer does not appear in the laws, the defcription of an ingroſſer, and the penalties upon the practice, are fully comprehended under the defcription of the foreftaller and regrator *.

Many antient laws had been made, inviting the importation of foreign provifions, and the exportation of Englifh grain had been prohibited †. So that while the exportation of the excrefcent part of our own produce was prohibited, and the importation of foreign grains encouraged, we cannot confider agriculture to have been cherifhed as a national object.

But a dawn of reafon began now to appear, and a law was made, authorifing all the king's fubjects to carry corn out of the kingdom, upon payment of the cuftoms and fubfidies ‡. Which law was confirmed this year, referving to the king and council to reftrain the exportation when they fhould judge that to be neceſſary ‖.

But this refervation had been conftructed into a prohibition

* Burrow Laws, c. 78. Cham. Air. c. 19. 20. 21. Ja. 5. Par. 4. c. 21. Par. 7. c. 98. and Ja. 6. Par. 12. c. 148.

† Abbrev. Imp. & Exp. Laws, vide Appendix, No 7.

‡ 17 Rich. 2. c. 7. ‖ 4 Hen. 6. c. 5.

to export grain without a licence, which had totally prevented the beneficial confequences expected from the firft law.

This mifapprehenfion of the law, or poffibly the high hand of executive power, making licences difficult, checked the early progrefs of agriculture, and brought diftrefs upon the whole kingdom.

1436.
This fufficiently appears from the preamble of the following law, by which liberty was given to perfons to tranfport grain to where they pleafed, without licence, except to the enemies of the king when wheat was at 6s. 8d. and barley at 3s. the quarter*. And thefe fums were rather above the middling prices, being equal, in the prefent money, to L. 2 : 4s. for the quarter of wheat, and 19s. 10d. for the quarter of barley.

1442.

1444.
This law had been found fo beneficial to the kingdom, and had produced fuch plenty of corn, that it was now confirmed, and continued for ten years, and foon after was made perpetual †; and the confequences were, that, fo far as we can now difcover, the price of grain did not fluctuate greatly for 40 years, and was very moderate ‡.

But ftill the laws inviting the importation of foreign grain continued in force; the trade was in the hands of foreign

* 15 Hen. 6. c. 2.
† 20 Hen. 6. c. 6. and 23 Hen. 6. c. 5.   ‡ Vide Appendix, No 1.

merchants, who carried their corn, and other provisions, from port to port, and secured the market before the English farmers could bring forward their produce.

And although thofe merchants may have loft upon the grain which they imported into England at this time, they gained upon the general courfe of the trade; becaufe they received, in return, wool, unfinifhed woollen cloth, and ready money, upon which they made great profit in their own countries, and thus were enabled to underfell the produce of our fields at home.

This appears to have been the cafe, even after this period, from two reftrictive and regulating laws of Richard III. * by the laft of which it appears, that the foreign merchants, who imported wines into England, had not only taken their payment, two thirds in woollen cloth, and one third in ready money, but had confiderably leffened the contents of their wine cafks, although fold under the former titles and contents.

The diftrefs upon hufbandry, occafioned by the continual importation of foreign grain, came at length to be attended to, and a preventative law was made; although we can learn from it nothing of the caufes, but, in general, that the labourers and occupiers of land had been grievoufly damaged by the importation of foreign grain, when corn at home was at a fmall price; and that therefore the importation of foreign

CHAP. II.

1463.

* 1 Rich. 3. c. 8. 13.

E

CHAP. II.

grain was prohibited, until the prices at home should exceed 6s. 8d. for the quarter of wheat, 4s. for rye, and 3s. for barley *; equal to L. 1 : 15 : 2, L. 1, 1s. and 15s. 10d. of present money.

These were the laws to which the agriculture of England may be said to have owed its origin ; and, although their purposes have been often defeated, by other laws, they are the foundation which still remains, and upon which a great fabric (at present out of repair) has been built, which, with moderate attention, may long continue to be the chief ornament and support of Great Britain.

Upon these laws the agriculture of England rested for near a century ; but it is to be lamented, that the want of execution rendered them, in a great degree, nugatory : The prohibition of the importation of foreign grain was never attended to, and the occupiers of land in England had still to struggle with the competition of grain from abroad, and the oppression of purveyance, and other grievances at home.

1552.

This is evident from an act of this year made against regrators, forestallers, and ingrossers ; by which the crime of forestalling is extended to persons buying victuals coming in ships from beyond the seas, to be sold in any market or fair, city, port, haven, creek, or road, as if no laws had subsisted by which such importation had been prohibited.

---

* 3 Ed. 4. c. 2.

Although a repreffion of the practices of foreftalling and
regrating might have been neceffary, it is difficult to difcover
a reafon for the enactment of ingroffing, at fo late a period
as the prefent reign, when commerce had made fome confiderable progrfs; and, by the fame law, no perfon at home
could tranfport corn from one part to another without a licence; neither could they purchafe corn, to be laid up in their
granaries for home fale, until the quarter of wheat· was at, or
under, 6s. 8d. (equal to 16s. 6d. of prefent money); malt
and barley at 3s. 4d. (8s. 3d.); oats at 2s. (4s. 11½d.); peafe
and beans at 4s. (9s. 11d.); and rye at 5s. (12s. 5d.) per
quarter *.

Thus the former fyftem of corn laws was totally overturned; for although thefe were the prices to which exportation
was limited, by the act of Edward IV. in 1463, the value of
money was materially changed; for, at the former period, there
were only 37s. 6d. in the pound of filver, and now there were
60s. and at the former period, money bore a very high and unlimited intereft, and now, it yielded only about 12 per cent.
per annum; fo that 6s. 8d. for a quarter of wheat in 1463,
was equal to L. 1 : 15 : 2; and, in the year 1552, it was only equal to 16s. 6d. as is already noticed; and the prohibition
to purchafe corn, to be laid up in granaries, or to carry it
coaftways, until it fhould fall to a price below the expence of
raifing it, muft neceffarily put a total ftop to all trade in corn,
and ruin the farmers; and all this was done at a time when
the price of grain had been uniformly low.

* 5 & 6 Ed. 6. c. 14.

It does not feem to have occurred to the legiflature at this time, that by keeping the corn at home in times of great plenty, the price muft be raifed, becaufe the farmers would not be able to continue their trade of raifing corn at a dif-advantage; fo that, how foon the ftock on hand was ex-haufted, fcarcity or famine would enfue; nor did it oc-cur, that by allowing an exportation of the excrefcent ftock, plenty would be enfured, by keeping an open market to the farmers, and thereby enabling them to carry on their bufi-nefs, and to raife more corn than was generally neceffary for home confumption; nor did they attend to the benefit that would arife to the kingdom, from the additional number of people that might be employed in raifing and exporting what corn could be fpared, and the fums of money that would be brought into the kingdom for the price of it.

They feem to have proceeded upon the principle, that the only way to preferve plenty, was to keep all the corn and o-ther provifions at home, and import as much as poffible from abroad, which experience has fully proved to be totally erro-neous.

1554.

The fame plan, however, was followed out, and enforced by another law of this year, which enacts, ' That whereas ' fundry good ftatutes and laws have been made within this ' realm, in the time of the Queen's highnefs moft noble pro-' genitors, that none fhould tranfport, carry, or convey, out ' of this realm, into any place in the ports beyond the feas, ' any corn, butter, cheefe, or other victuals, except only for

‘ victualling the towns of Calais, &c. upon divers great pains
‘ and forfeitures, in the fame contained : That notwithftanding
‘ many and fundry covetous and infatiable perfons, feeking
‘ their only lucres and gains, have and do daily carry and
‘ convey innumerable quantity, as well of corn, cheefe, but-
‘ ter, and other victuals, as of wood, out of this realm, to
‘ parts beyond feas, by reafon whereof the faid corn, victual,
‘ and wood, are grown into a wonderful dearth, and extreme
‘ prices, to the great detriment of the commonwealth of this
‘ your Highnefs’ realm, and your faithful fubjects of the
‘ fame.’

It was therefore enacted, that no manner of perfon or perfons fhould export any wheat, rye, barley, or other fort of
grain, growing within England ; or any malt made within the
fame ; or any beer, butter, cheefe, herring, or wood, without
having licence fo to do, under fevere penalties ; except when
the common price of corn, within England, fhould not exceed
for wheat 6s. 8d. (equal to 16s. 6d. of prefent money) ; rye,
4s. (9s. 11d.) ; and barley, 3s. (7s. 5d.) per quarter *.

Here it may be obferved, that notwithftanding the com-
plaint, of the high price of grain, in the preamble to this law,
the price of wheat this year, and feveral years before, had
been only 8s. the quarter, (equal to 19s. 10d. of prefent money); and the export prices were far below the medium prices,
in times of ordinary plenty.

* 1 & 2 Phil. and Mary, c. 5.

Such, however, was the policy of Edward VI. and of Philip and Mary; and it was foon after followed in Scotland by laws exprefsly prohibiting the exportation of all kinds of victuals, tallow, and flefh, under fevere penalties *.

Several favourable feafons happened to follow after this law had paffed, the importation of foreign grain was continued, and the price of wheat continued about 8s. the quarter; but the Englifh farmers came to be ruined, and agriculture began to be abandoned.

1554.

Laws are neceffary for the regulation of fociety; but they become inept when they either direct impoffibilities, or order people to labour in profeffions, by which they cannot earn a reafonable fubfiftence. The wife laws of Hen. VI. and Ed. IV. had fubfifted without repeal during the whole of the reigns of Hen. VII. and Hen. VIII. but without receiving any countenance or execution; and yet they, as well as Ed. VI. and Phil. and Mary, the latter of whom were the chief inftruments in crufhing hufbandry, made repeated laws to oblige people to labour and fow their lands †.

1562.

Thefe incongruities did not efcape the obfervation of the vigorous adminiftration of Elizabeth, although the defire to raife money fuperfeded the wifdom of the other inftitutions propofed for the benefit of the kingdom.

* Mary, par. 6. c. 42.—Ja. 6. par. 11. c. 55.

† 4 Hen. 7. c. 19.—7 Hen. 8. c. 1.—27 Hen. 8. c. 22.—5 & 6 Ed. 6. c. 5.—2 & 3 Phil. and M. c. 2.

Soon after her acceſſion, ſhe renewed the former laws for rebuilding houſes of huſbandry, and labouring the land, which had formerly been in culture, with more vigour; but, by another law, ſhe allowed the farmers to export their grain as merchandiſe, when the price of it was not high at home.

The former laws, obliging the proprietors or tenants to re-build the decayed houſes of huſbandry, and to return to tillage, had given the penalties to the king; but theſe were now given to the next heir, &c. of the perſon offending.

' It was enacted, that ſuch lands as had been put in tillage
' and eared in any one year, and ſo kept 4 years, ſince the 20th
' Hen. VIII. ſhould be again eared and put in tillage, accord-
' ing to the nature of the ſoil and cuſtom of the country, by
' the occupier thereof, upon pain that every offender ſhould
' forfeit 10s. an acre yearly, to the next in remainder or re-
' verſion, for the term of life, lives, or in tail, for which he
' might diſtrain; and in default, by the ſpace of one year,
' then he, in the reverſion or remainder in fee ſimple, ſhould
' have the ſame remedy; and in his default, to the imme-
' diate lord of the fee; and in his default, the Queen, or the
' Queen and the informer *.'

By the other law ' It was enacted, that it ſhould be lawful
' for all and every perſon and perſons, being ſubjects of
' the Queen's majeſty, her heirs and ſucceſſors, only out of

CHAP. II.

1562.

* 5 Eliz. c. 2.

' such ports and creeks, as by proclamation should be pub-
' lished and appointed, to load, carry, and transport any
' wheat, rye, barley, malt, peafe, or beans, unto any parts
' beyond the seas, to fell as a merchandife, in ships, crayers,
' or other veflels, whereof any Englifh born fubjects then
' shall be the only owners; fo that the price of the faid corn
' and grain, fo carried and tranfported, exceed not the prices
' hereafter following, at the times, havens, and places where
' and when the faid corn and grain shall be shipped and
' laden, viz. the quarter of wheat, at 10s. (equal to L. 1 : 8d.
' of prefent money); the quarter of rye, peafe, or beans, at
' 8s. (16s. 7d.); and the quarter of barley or malt, at 6s. 8d.
' (13s. 10d.) of current money of England *.'

This was a confiderable extenfion of the exportation prices;
and it appears by Camden and Sir Walter Rawleigh, both fa-
mous authors, and co-temporaries of Queen Elizabeth, that
from the year 1562, that great princefs having penetrated
into the caufes of odious monopolies, the exorbitant prices of
provifions, and artificial fcarcities, that impoverifhed and
devoured the nation, wifely took off the old prohibition of the
exportation of corn, leaving full liberty in that refpect; and
it is remarked by the fame authors, that the direct and immediate confequence of this wife meafure, was the increafe of
tillage, and the reduction of importation.

And Sir Walter, in his Remarks on Trade, prefented to

* 5 Eliz. c. 5. § 26.

James I. pofitively afferts, that for fome years preceding the
above period, the importation of corn had exceeded 45 millions of livres*.

CHAP. II.

But foon after a more vigorous effort was made to recover
the agriculture of England, by a law entitled, ' An act for
' the better increafe of tillage, and for maintainance and in-
' creafe of the navy and mariners of England.'

1570.

By this law it was enacted, ' That it fhould be lawful to
' every perfon and perfons, being fubjects of the Queen's ma-
' jefty, her heirs and fucceffors, and inhabiting within her
' highnefs realms and dominions, only out of fuch ports and
' creeks, where were, or fhould be refident, a cuftomer or
' collector of fubfidy, or tonnage and poundage, or one of
' their deputies, and not elfewhere, to load, carry, or tranfport
' any wheat, rye, barley, malt, peafe, or beans, into any ports
' beyond the feas, in amity with the realm, and not prohibited
' by any reftraint or proclamation; only to fell as a merchan-
' dife, in fhips, crayers, or other veffels, bearing crofs fails,
' whereof any Englifh born fubjects, inhabiting within her
' highnefs dominions, then fhould be the only owners, at fuch
' times as the feveral prices thereof fhall be fo reafonable and
' moderate, in the feveral counties where any fuch tranfporta-
' tion fhall be intended, as that no prohibition fhould be made,
' either by the Queen's majefty, her heirs or fucceffors, by

---

* Gen. Review of England from 1600 to 1662, p. 18. The book from which this
quotation is taken, having been written in French, the fum mentioned is called prefent money, but can mean only millions of livres.

F

' proclamation to be made in the shire town, or in any port
' towns in the county; or else by some order of the Lord Pre-
' sident and Council of the North, or the Lord President and
' Council in Wales, within their several jurisdictions; or of
' the justices of assize, at their sessions, in other shires, out of
' the jurisdiction of the said two presidents and councils; or
' by the more part of the justices of the peace of the county,
' at their quarter sessions, in this manner following, that is,
' The said lord presidents and councils for the shires, within
' their jurisdictions, the justices of assize at their several
' sessions in other shires, out of the said jurisdictions, belong-
' ing to the said councils in the North, and in Wales, yearly,
' should, upon conference had with the inhabitants of the
' county, of the cheapness and dearth of any of the said kinds
' of grain, within the counties, within the jurisdictions of the
' said councils, or in the other counties within the limits of the
' said justices of assize, by their discretion determine whether
' it should be meet, at any time, to permit any grain to be
' carried out of the realm, by any port within the said several
' jurisdictions or limits; and so should, in writing under their
' hands and seals, cause and make a determination either for
' permission or prohibition; and the same cause to be, by the
' sheriffs of the counties, published and affixed in as many
' accustomed market towns and ports, within the said shire,
' as they should think convenient, and in such manner as the
' Queen's majesty's proclamations were usually published and
' affixed; which determination of the said presidents and coun-
' cils in their jurisdictions, and of the justices of assize in their
' limits, should continue in force for the time, place, and

‘ manner therein expreſſed, until the ſaid preſidents and coun-
‘ cils ſhould otherwiſe order; or until the juſtices of aſſize, at
‘ their being in their ſaid circuits, in every of the ſaid coun-
‘ ties, ſhould alter or otherwiſe order the ſame, except the ſame
‘ ſhall be otherwiſe, in the mean time, altered or countermand-
‘ ed by the Queen's majeſty, her heirs or ſucceſſors; or by
‘ ſome order of the juſtices of the peace, in the counties ſitu-
‘ ated out of the juriſdiction of the ſaid two councils, in their
‘ quarter ſeſſions, to be holden in the mean time; or the greater
‘ part of them ſhall find the ſame determination of the juſtices
‘ of aſſize to be hurtful to the county, by means of dearth, or
‘ to be a great hindrance to tillage, by means of too much
‘ cheapneſs; and ſhould by their writings, under their hands
‘ and ſeals, make any determination to the contrary, either
‘ for permiſſion or prohibition of carriage of any kind of
‘ grain out of the realm; and the ſame determination ſhould
‘ cauſe to be, in like manner, publiſhed and affixed as above
‘ is ſaid. Which determination ſhould alſo continue in force,
‘ except the ſame ſhould be altered by the Queen's majeſty,
‘ her heirs and ſucceſſors; or until the juſtices of aſſize, at
‘ their being in their ſaid circuits, in every of the ſaid coun-
‘ ties afore to them limited, ſhould alter or otherwiſe order
‘ the ſame; who ſhould and might, upon new conference had,
‘ by their diſcretions, from time to time, alter and change the
‘ ſaid determinations, in the whole or in part, as to their diſ-
‘ cretions ſhould ſeem meet; and the ſame ſhould alſo cauſe
‘ to be publiſhed, as is before preſcribed.’

‘ Provided, neverthelefs, that neither any of the ſaid preſi-

' dents and councils, nor the faid juftices of affize, nor the
' faid juftices of peace, above-mentioned, fhould publifh any
' their determinations, above-mentioned, until the fame fhould
' be firft, by writing, notified to the Queen's majefty, or to
' her privy council; and by her majefty, or her privy council,
' fhould be liked or allowed.'

' Provided alfo, that the Queen's majefty, her heirs and fuc-
' ceffors, fhould have and receive, by the cuftomers and offi-
' cers of her ports, for the cuftom or poundage of every quar-
' ter of wheat, to be tranfported by force of this ftatute,
' twelve-pence; and of every quarter of other grain, eight-
' pence.   And of every quarter of wheat that fhould be,
' by any fpecial licence thereafter to be granted, tranfport-
' ed out of the realm, and not by force of this ftatute,
' two fhillings; and of every quarter of other grain, fixteen-
' pence, &c.'

' Provided alfo, that her Majefty, her heirs and fucceffors
' might, at all times, by writ of proclamation, to be publifhed
' generally in the whole realm, or in the counties of the realm
' where any port towns were, command that no perfon fhould,
' by virtue of this act, tranfport, or carry out any manner
' of grain, to any parts out of her dominions, either generally
' out of any port of the realm, or particularly out of any
' fpecial ports, to be in the fame proclamation named; and
' that it might not be lawful, for any perfon, to carry out
' any fuch grain, contrary to the tenor of the fame proclama-

' tion, upon such pains as by the laws of the realm are, and
' have been provided *.'

Here the corn trade appears to have been scientifically con-
sidered ; and if the plan laid down had been properly digested
and modified, and the duties upon exportation removed, there
can be no doubt of the act having produced the most beneficial consequences to the kingdom ; but the judges, to whom
this most important business was committed, had no certain
rule to direct their procedure ; they were not allowed to determine, by the price of grain at the time of their yearly inquiry, which is the only certain index of plenty or scarcity,
but merely upon a conference with the people of the country,
to judge, whether it would be hurtful to the kingdom, by
means of dearth, or be a great hindrance to tillage, by too
much cheapness, to allow of exportation of grain ; than which,
nothing could be more vague and uncertain.

But whatever consideration may have been given to the
framing of this act, the laying a duty of 20 *per cent. ad valorem*,
upon grain to be exported, by licence, and 10 *per cent.* upon
grain to be exported by the statute, was equal to a prohibition, and gave full scope to the importation of foreign grain,
which was still received without the payment of any duty.
So difficult it is, in all situations, to judge, or point out the
propriety of conduct, where revenue or public interest is concerned.

* 13 Eliz. c. 13.

CHAP. II.   In Scotland, the prohibition to export grain to foreign parts, was continued, under fevere penalties *.

We can only judge of the effects of the above law of England, from the prices of grain that followed it; and from thence we cannot think they had been favourable, as we find the price of a quarter of wheat, in the year 1574, to have been L. 2 : 16s. equal to L. 5 : 15 : 8 of prefent money; and in 1587, no lefs than L. 3 : 4s. equal to L. 6 : 12 : 8 †.

It is to be regretted, that the legiflatures, of every country, do not, at all times, when they make laws, give the fpecific and true reafons of the enactions, that people of the fame age, and more efpecially thofe of after generations, may profit by their experience, and be enabled to judge of the expediency of the inflitutions, from their confequences; whereby poflerity may have it in their power to follow the tract, or to avoid the danger.

1593.   In the prefent cafe we have no fuch guide.   The corn laws were now again revifed; but it would appear to have been done rather in bad humour.   We find them taken notice of in an act, entitled, ' An act for the revifing, continuance, ex-
' planation, and perfecting of divers ftatutes ‡.'

By this act it appears, that government had abandoned the

* Ja. 6. Par. 11. c. 55.   † Vide Appendix, No 1.
‡ 35 Eliz. c. 7.

impracticable fcheme of obliging people to labour their land, whether they could live by that occupation or not; and the act for this purpofe, paffed in the 5th of the prefent reign, was now repealed; and it appears, from other circumftances, that the plan laid down by the act of the 13th, was laid afide, although the act itfelf is neither repealed nor mentioned; for we find the refolutions of the legiflature changed by the 23d fection of this act, in the following words: ' Provided alfo,
' and be it further enacted by the authority of this prefent
' parliament, that when the price of corn and grain exceedeth
' not the rates hereafter following, at the times, and havens,
' and places where and when the fame corn and grain fhall be
' fhipped or loaded, viz.—the quarter of wheat at 20s.; the
' quarter of rye, peafe, and beans, at 13s. 4d.; the quarter of
' barley or malt, at 12s. current Englifh money : That then it
' fhall be lawful, to all and every perfon or perfons, being fub-
' jects of her Majefty, her heirs and fucceffors, to load, carry,
' or tranfport any of the faid corn or grain, in fuch manner
' and form as in the faid act made for the maintenance of the
' navy, (5 Eliz. c. 5.) is limited and appointed; and that the
' Queen's majefty, her heirs and fucceffors, fhall have and re-
' ceive, by the cuftomers and officers of her ports, for the
' cuftom or poundage of every quarter of wheat to be tranf-
' ported by force of this ftatute, 2s. and of every quarter of
' any other grain, 16d.: Which faid feveral fums, fo to be
' had, or taken as cuftom or poundage, to be in full fatisfac-
' tion of all manner of cuftom or poundage, for the faid corn
' or grain, by any conftitution, order, ftatute, law, or cu-

' ftom, heretofore made, ufed, or taken, for tranfporting of
' any fuch manner of corn and grain.'

By this act exportation was allowed when wheat was at
20s. the quarter (equal to L. 2 : 1 : 4 of prefent money); rye,
peafe and beans, at 13s. 4d. (L. 1 : 7 : 8); and barley and malt,
at 12s. (L.1 : 4 : 10); which is juft double the prices at which
exportation was allowed by the former law of the 5th of this
reign : But at the fame time the duties payable upon grain exported by force of the ftatute, were doubled, which, joined
to an unlimited importation, without the payment of any
duty whatever, became equal to a prohibition, rendered the
act nugatory, and kept the price of grain at an extravagant
height; for we find that a quarter of wheat, in the year 1594,
fold at L. 2 : 16, equal to L. 5 : 15 : 8 ; in 1595, at L. 2 : 13 : 4,
equal to L. 5 : 10 : 2 ; in 1596, at L. 4, equal to L. 8 : 5 : 4 ;
and in 1597, at L. 4 : 12s. equal to L. 9 : 10s. of prefent
money *.

Things, however, remained in that fituation until this
year, when, upon the acceffion of James I. a number of ftatutes were revifed, fome of them continued and others repealed, without affigning any reafon for fo doing ; and, among
other matters, it was enacted, That ' when the prices of corns
' or grains exceeded not the rates following, at the times, havens,
' and places, where and when the fame corn or grain fhall be

---

* Vide, Appendix, No 1.

‘ shipped or loaded, viz. the quarter of wheat at 26s. 8d. (e-
‘ qual to L. 2 : 13 : 4 of present money) ; the quarter of rye,
‘ pease, and beans, 15s. (L. 1 : 10) ; the quarter of barley and
‘ malt, 14s. (L. 1 : 8) of current English money ; that then it
‘ should be lawful for all and every person and persons, being
‘ subjects of the King's majesty, his heirs or successors, to tranf-
‘ port of his own, and to buy and transport, any of the said
‘ corns and grains, into any parts beyond seas, in amity with
‘ his Majesty, to sell as merchandise, in ships, crayers, or other
‘ vessels, whereof any English born subject or subjects then
‘ should be the owner, or owners, any law, usage, or statute to
‘ the contrary notwithstanding : And that his Majesty, his
‘ heirs and successors, should have and receive, from the cus-
‘ tomers and officers of the port, for the custom or pound-
‘ age of every quarter of wheat, to be transported by force
‘ of this statute, 2s. ; and of every quarter of other grain, 16d.
‘ in full of all manner of custom and poundage : Provided
‘ always, that the King's majesty, his heirs and successors,
‘ might at all times, by his or their writ of proclamation, to
‘ to be published generally in the whole realm, or in any
‘ the counties of the realm, where any port towns are, com-
‘ mand that no person should, by virtue of this act, tran-
‘ port or convey, any manner of grain out of his Highness'
‘ dominions generally, or out of any special port to be in the
‘ same proclamation particularly named, for such time as
‘ should therein be limited and appointed : And it should not
‘ be lawful for any person to carry out any such grain, con-
‘ trary to the term of the same proclamation, upon such pains

G

‘ and forfeitures, as by the laws and ſtatutes were and had
‘ been provided in that behalf *,’

It is not eaſy to diſcover the reaſons for enacting the laws
of the reign of James I. Many of them give none ; the preamble to others are often unſatisfactory ; and, with reſpect to
corn and huſbandry, they are totally ſilent.

Beſides, the deſire to raiſe a revenue from corn, pervaded,
and in a great meaſure defeated the beneficial intentions of
the whole of the corn laws, for 130 years prior to the commencement of the 17th century.

In the preſent caſe, the prices of grain, at which exportation was permitted, were conſiderably extended, and were very high ; but we cannot conſider this extenſion to have proceeded from any benefit already felt from exportation, under
the former law ; for ſo long as that was loaded with a duty of
10 *per cent.* and importation permitted without duty, we cannot imagine that any conſiderable quantity of grain had been
exported ; and, as the former duties upon exportation were by
this law ſtill continued, perhaps we are not in the wrong if
we believe, that the preſent extenſion or enlargement of the
exportation prices, proceeded, in ſome meaſure, from a view
to raiſe a revenue from corn, by giving a larger ſcope to the
exportation of it.

A writing, publiſhed in 1621, by Sir Thomas Culpeper, in-

* 2 Ja. 1. c. 25. § 26. 27.

forms us, that at that time the French with their corn, and
the Dutch with that of Poland, fupplied the Englifh markets,
and that the national corn was continually below its true value. ' At prefent,' fays Culpeper, ' whilft corn and the other
' merchandifes which the earth produces, are at a low price,
' the fpade and the plough are forfaken ; the poor find little
' employment, and wages are extremely low. If the proprie-
' tors of lands could find their account in minding them,
' there would foon be many more people employed in their
' cultivation than there now are, and wages would be better.
' Every man, bleft with health and ftrength, would not be
' poor, except through extreme lazinefs*.'

In another revifing act of this reign, 58 ftatutes are recapitulated by their titles only ; and continued, except in fo far
as they had been altered in that feffion of parliament.

In this law † there are the following fections relative to corn,
' Provided alfo, and be it further enacted by the authority of
' this prefent parliament, that when the prices of corn and grain
' exceed not the rates hereafter following, at the times, havens,
' and places, when and where the fame corn and grain fhall
' be bought, fhipped, or loaded, viz.—the quarter of wheat
' at 32s. ; the quarter of rye at 20s. ; the quarter of peafe and
' beans at 16s. ; the quarter of barley or malt at 16s. ; of cur-
' rent Englifh money : That then it fhall and may be lawful,
' for all and every perfon and perfons, being fubjects of the

1623.

---

* Corn Tracts, p. 174. † 21 Ja. 1. c. 28. § 3. 4.

‘ King's majefty, his heirs and fucceffors, to carry and tranf-
‘ port his own, and to buy to fell again in markets, and out
‘ of markets, and to keep and fell, or carry and tranfport
‘ any of the faid corn or grain, from the places where
‘ they fhall be of fuch prices, into any parts beyond the feas,
‘ in amity with his Majefty, as merchandife, in fhips, crays,
‘ or other veffels, whereof any Englifh born fubject or fub-
‘ jects then fhall be the owner or owners, or the fame to car-
‘ ry and fell in other places within this realm, or dominions
‘ thereof, any law, ufage, or ftatute to the contrary hereof
‘ notwithftanding : And that the King's majefty, his heirs
‘ and fucceffors, fhall have and receive by the cuftomers and
‘ officers of his ports, for the cuftom or poundage of every
‘ quarter of wheat, to be tranfported by force of this ftatute
‘ out of this realm, 2s. ; of every quarter of other grain,
‘ 16d. : Which faid feveral fums fo to be had or taken as cu-
‘ ftom or poundage, fhall be in full fatisfaction of all manner
‘ of cuftom or poundage, for the faid corn or grain, by any
‘ conftitution, order, ftatute, law, or cuftom heretofore made,
‘ ufed, or taken, for tranfporting of any fuch manner of corn
‘ or grain.

‘ Provided always, and be it enacted by the authority of
‘ this prefent parliament, that the King's majefty, his heirs
‘ and fucceffors, may at all times, by his or their writ of pro-
‘ clamation, to be publifhed generally in the whole realm, or
‘ in any of the counties of the realm, where any port towns
‘ are, command that no perfon fhall by virtue of this act,
‘ tranfport or convey, any manner of grain, out his Highnefs’

‘ dominions generally, or out of any fpecial ports, to be in
‘ the fame proclamation particularly named, for fuch time
‘ as fhall therein be limited and appointed : And it fhall
‘ not be lawful for any perfon to carry out any fuch grain,
‘ contrary to the tenor of the fame proclamation, upon fuch
‘ pains and forfeitures, as by the laws and ftatutes of this
‘ realm are, and have been, provided and ordained in that
‘ behalf, this act, or any thing therein contained to the con-
‘ trary, notwithftanding.’

The extention of the export prices, by this law, was very
great, for 32s. for wheat, was equal to L. 3 : 4s. of prefent
money; 20s. for rye, was equal to L. 2 ; and 16s. for barley
and malt, peafe and beans, was equal to L. 1 : 12s.; and
all thefe fums are very near double the medium prices of
the prefent time, in years of ordinary plenty : fo that the
act appears clearly to have been made for an extenfion of the
revenue.

By this law too, the penalties of ingroffing were removed,
fo long as the prices of grain did not exceed thofe fpecified in
the law ; and indeed, the laws againft ingroffing were fuch as
behoved to put a total ftop to all trade in corn, whether internal or external, until they were foftened or abolifhed.

Soon after the acceffion of Charles I. we find an act, by   1627.
which 56 ftatutes were revifed, and recapitulated by their
titles ; and fo much of thefe ftatutes as were not then altered
or explained, were ordained to remain in force.

In this law, without any preamble or reafon given, the 3d and 4th fections of the act 1623, above copied, are ingroffed, verbatim, in the 24th and 25th fections *.

But although the export prices were literally the fame, they were very different in fact; for, in the year 1624, the yearly intereft of money having been reduced from 10 to 8 *per cent.* 32s. for a quarter of wheat, which in 1623 was equal to L. 3 : 4s. was, in 1627, equal to only L. 2 : 11 : 2 of prefent money; and the prices of other grain in proportion.

The long interval of parliament, after the feffion in which the above law was paffed, and the confufions which foon followed the meeting of the next parliament, in 1640, probably prevented any further attention to this matter, during the remainder of this reign.

1660.

Although by connecting the corn laws with revenue, the wife inftitutions of the reign of Elizabeth, and her two immediate fucceffors, had been, in a great meafure, defeated, agriculture had been otherwife treated by the laws as an object of high importance; not only on account of the numbers employed in it, and the intrinfic value of its produce, but alfo for the fupport that would be given to the navy, by the exportation trade, which would arife from it; but upon the refloration of Charles II. it was thoughtlefsly abandoned as a mere object of revenue.

* 3 Cha. I. c. 5. ſ 24. 25.

Without taking any particular notice of agriculture, or giving any reason for the alteration of the corn laws, we find the following section in the act of tonnage and poundage: ' And be it further enacted, by the authority aforesaid, that ' it shall and may be lawful, immediately after passing of this ' act, for any person or persons, to ship, carry out, and tran- ' sport, by way of merchandise, these several sorts of goods ' following, that is to say, gun-powder, when the same doth ' not exceed the price of L. 5 the barrel; and wheat, rye, ' peafe, beans, barley, malt, and oats, beef, pork, bacon, but- ' ter, cheefe, candles, when the same do not exceed in price, ' at the ports from whence they are laden, and at the time of ' their lading, these prices following, that is to say, wheat, ' the quarter, 40s. ; rye, peafe, and beans, the quarter, 24s. ; ' barley and malt, the quarter, 20s. ; oats, the quarter, 16s. ; ' beef, the barrel, L. 5 ; pork, the barrel, L. 6 : 10 ; bacon, ' the pound, 6d. ; butter, the barrel, L. 4 : 10 ; cheefe, the ' hundred, L. 1 : 10 ; candles, the dozen pounds, 5s. ; paying ' the refpective rates appointed by this act, and no more ; any ' former law, ftatute, prohibition, or cuftom to the contrary, ' in any wife, notwithftanding *.'

So that corn came to be juft enlifted in the fame roll with other articles, upon which duties were made payable.

The prices limited for the exportation of wheat, being 40s. was equal to L. 2 : 8s. of prefent money ; 24s. for the quarter

---

* 12 Cha. II. c. 4. § 11.

of rye, peafe, and beans, was equal to L. 1 : 8 : 10; 20s. for the quarter of barley and malt, was equal to L. 1 : 4s.; and 16s. for the quarter of oats, was equal to 19s. 2d. And by this law the duties, payable upon exportation, were 20s. (equal to L. 1 : 4s.) for the quarter of wheat; 10s. (equal to 12s.) for the quarter of rye, peafe and beans, barley, malt, and buck wheat; and 6s. 8d. (equal to 8s.) for the quarter of oats: which behoved to operate equally to a prohibition.

By the rates inward, adjoined to the fame law, the importation duties were fixed as follows:

For the quarter of wheat, when the price, at the place of importation, did not exceed 44s. (equal to L. 2 : 12 : 10), the fum of L. 2 (equal to L. 2 : 8s.); and when it exceeded that price, 6s. 8d. (equal to 8s.)

For the quarter of rye, when the price, at the place of importation, did not exceed 36s. (equal to L. 2 : 3 : 2), the fum of L. 1 : 6 : 8, (equal to L. 1 : 12s.); and when it exceeded that price, 5s. (equal to 6s.)

For the quarter of beans, barley, and malt, when the price, at the place of importation, did not exceed L. 1 : 6 : 8, (equal to L. 1 : 12s.), the fum of L. 1 : 6 : 8, (equal to L. 1 : 12s.); and when it exceeded that price, 5s. (equal to 6s.) of prefent money.

So that until the price of wheat was above L. 2 : 12 : 10, of prefent money, per quarter, and of other grain in proportion, the importation high duties were, in like manner, equal to a prohibition; and the exportation being, in fact, prohibited, the

prices would foon rife, and prepare the country for importation, at the low duties.

And this accordingly happened; for, in 1660, the quarter
of wheat fold at L. 2 : 16 : 6, equal to L. 3 : 7 : 9, of prefent
money; in 1661 it rofe to L. 3 : 10s. equal to L. 4 : 4s.; and,
in 1662, to L. 3 : 14s. equal to L. 4 : 8 : 10, of prefent
money*.

Thefe laws, befides raifing grain to an extravagant height,
had ruined many of the farmers; agriculture declined; and
a great part of the lands lay without tillage.

Thefe circumftances induced the parliament again to take
the corn laws under their confideration; and, from the preamble to a law of this year, made for the encouragement of
trade, the ruinous fituation of hufbandry is clearly pointed
out. It mentions, ' Forafmuch as the encouraging of tillage
' ought to be, in an efpecial manner, regarded and endeavour-
' ed; and the fureft and effectualeft means of promoting and
' advancing any trade, occupation, or myftery, being by ren-
' dering it profitable to the ufers thereof; and great quantities
' of land, within this kingdom, for the prefent, lying in a
' manner wafte, and yielding little, which might thereby be
' improved to confiderable profit and advantage (if fufficient
' encouragement were given for the laying out of coft and
' labour on the fame), and thereby much more corn pro-

1663.

* Vide Appendix, No. 1.

H

' duced, greater numbers of people, cattle, and horses em-
' ployed, and other lands rendered also more valuable *.'   It
was therefore enacted as follows :

' Be it enacted by the King's most excellent majesty, with
' the advice and consent of the Lords spiritual and temporal,
' and the Commons in this present parliament assembled; and
' by the authority thereof, be it enacted, That from and after
' the first day of September 1663, and from thence-forward,
' when the prices of corn and grain, Winchester measure, do
' not exceed the rates hereafter following, at the havens and
' places where the same shall be shipped and laden, viz. The
' quarter of wheat, 48s. (equal to L. 2 : 17 : 7 of present
' money); the quarter of buck wheat, barley, or malt, 28s.
' (equal to L. 1 : 13 : 7); the quarter of oats, 13s. 4d. (equal
' to 16s.); the quarter of rye, pease and beans, 32s. (equal to
' L. 1 : 18 : 5) current English money; that then it shall be
' lawful for all and every person and persons, to ship, load,
' carry, and transport, any of the said corns or grains, from
' the havens and places where they shall be of such prices,
' unto any parts beyond the seas, as merchandise, any law,
' statute, or usage, to the contrary notwithstanding; paying
' such rates for the same, and none other, as are to be paid
' when the same might have been transported by one act passed
' this present parliament, entitled, ' A subsidy granted to the
" King of tonnage and poundage."

' And it is hereby further enacted, by the authority afore-

---

* 15 Cha. II. c. 7. § 1. 2. 3. 4.

‘ faid, that when the prices of the aforefaid corns and grains
‘ *do not* exceed the rates above-mentioned, refpectively, Win-
‘ chefter meafure, at the havens and places, into which any of
‘ them fhall be imported, from any parts beyond the feas,
‘ there fhall be paid for the cuftom and poundage of every
‘ quarter of wheat, 5s. 4d. (equal to 6s. 5d. of prefent money);
‘ and for every quarter of rye, 4s. (equal to 4s. 10d.) ; and
‘ for every quarter of barley or malt, 2s. 8d. (equal to 3s. 2d.);
‘ for every quarter of buck wheat, 2s. (equal to 2s. 5d.) ; for
‘ every quarter of oats, 1s. 4d. (equal to 1s. 6d.) ; and for
‘ every quarter of peafe and beans, 4s. (equal to 4s. 10d.) of
‘ prefent money.

‘ And it is hereby further enacted, by the authority forefaid,
‘ that when the prices of corn or grain, Winchefter meafure,
‘ do not exceed the rates following, at the markets, havens,
‘ or places where the fame fhall be bought, viz. The quarter of
‘ wheat, 48s. ; the quarter of rye, 32s. ; the quarter of barley
‘ and malt, 28s. ; the quarter of buck wheat, 28s. ; the quar-
‘ ter of oats, 13s. 4d. ; the quarter of peafe or beans, 32s. ;
‘ that then it fhall be lawful for all and every perfon and per-
‘ fons (not foreftalling and felling the fame in the fame mar-
‘ ket, within three months after buying thereof) to buy in
‘ open market, to lay up and keep in his or their granaries or
‘ houfes, and to fell again, fuch corn or grain, of the kinds
‘ forefaid, as without fraud or covin fhall have been bought
‘ at or under the prices before expreffed, without incurring
‘ any penalty ; any law, ftatute, or ufage to the contrary not-
‘ withftanding.’

H 2

CHAP. II.

We have every reafon to think, from the preamble to this law, that the encouragement of trade in general, and agriculture in particular, was its chief object; and there can be no doubt but thefe were the intentions of the legiflature; and yet, by the infertion of a fingle monafyllable, probably done infidioufly in the ingroffing, and afterwards paffing unobferved, the whole law was reduced to a mere folecifm in terms.

By this law the exportation prices were extended beyond the former bounds; but the exported grain was ftill loaded with near 50 *per cent.* of duties, which was equal to a prohibition.

Upon the other hand, the high importation duties were taken off; and when the prices of grain did *not* exceed the fame rates limited for exportation (or, in other words, when grain was at the loweft price), importation was allowed, upon payment of about 9 *per cent.* of duties *ad valorem;* being much lower than the low duties fixed by the act of tonnage and poundage.

The word *not*, in the importation claufe of the law, perverts the meaning of the whole. It never could have been the intention of the legiflature to permit importation at low duties, until grain had rifen above the exportation prices; for until that rife, the prohibition to ingrofs was taken off, and the fame reafons operated in both cafes.

We can hardly place this to inattention; and we are the
more inclined to this opinion, that by a law of the fame year
paffed in Scotland, where the policy of England was very
much attended to, and often followed, although importation
of grain had been, by the laws of that kingdom, before this
period, permitted without limitation or duties, they now permitted the exportation of grain, when it did not exceed certain
prices; but they laid a duty of about 40 *per cent. ad valorem*,
upon all grain to be imported, when the prices were under
thofe ftipulated by the act *.

An abftract of this Scots law may be ufeful and entertain-
ing. It proceeds thus: ' Our Sovereign Lord, confidering how
' neceffary it is for the encouragement of the tillage of this
' country, which is fubject to fo much toil and expence,
' though the improvement thereof be moft advantageous to
' the whole kingdom, that liberty be granted for the exporta-
' tion of corns, after the natives are fufficiently provided for;
' Therefore the King's majefty, with the advice and confent
' of his eftates in parliament, ftatutes and declares, That it
' fhall be lawful to export corns, of all forts, when they are
' under the prices following, at the ports or refpective places
' of exportation, viz. Ilk boll of wheat, under L. 12 (equal to
' L. 1 : 4s. of prefent money); bear and barley, under L. 8
' (equal to 16s.) the boll; oats and peafe, under 8 merks,
' (equal to 10s. 8d.) the boll; notwithftanding of any former
acts, laws, or practife to the contrary, they paying the ufual

* Cha. II. par. 1. feff. 3. c. 12. 14.

‘ cuftom and bullion as formerly (6d. of prefent money per
‘ boll) ; with this provifion, that when the Lords of his Ma-
‘ jefty's fecret council fhall judge it neceffary, for the good of
‘ the kingdom, and preventing of dearth, they may difcharge
‘ the exportation of victual, of all forts, for fo long a time as
‘ they fhall think fit. As alfo for the improvement of the
‘ pafturage of this kingdom, and for encouragement of the
‘ breeders of the beftial thereof, It is ftatute and ordained,
‘ with advice and confent forefaid, that the exportation, by
‘ fea, of all forts of beftial, either nolt, fheep, or fwine, and
‘ barrelled flefhes, of all fort, fhall be free of cuftom, bullion,
‘ and all other impofitions, for the fpace of nineteen years
‘ next, after the date hereof.

‘ The eftates of parliament, confidering what great fums
‘ of money are carried out of the kingdom, by perfons im-
‘ porters of corn hither from Ireland ; who, having fold their
‘ corns, export the money, without bartering any of the com-
‘ modities of this kingdom, whereby the whole nation, thofe
‘ near adjacent parts of the kingdom, are much impoverifhed
‘ of money; and that it is juft and reafonable that the faid
‘ corns fhould bear cuftom, toward the increafe of his Majefty's
‘ revenue, proportionally with other imported commodities ;
‘ efpecially when the corns of this kingdom are fold at eafy
‘ rates : Therefore the King's majefty, with advice and con-
‘ fent of his eftates of parliament, doth hereby impofe L. 3
‘ Scots (equal to 6s. of the prefent money) of cuftom, upon ilk
‘ boll, Linlithgow meafure, of corn imported into this king-
‘ dom, from Ireland, after the firft day of September next :

‘ And appoints 30s. Scots (equal to 3s. Sterling) to be raifed
‘ upon ilk boll already imported, and not yet retailed, con-
‘ form to an act of the committee of eftates, made there anent
‘ anno 1660.   But left the more indigent fort of people might
‘ be prejudiced, by heightening the prices of faid corns in the
‘ time of dearth, under pretence of the faid cuftom : Therefore
‘ the King's majefty, with advice and confent forefaid, doth
‘ hereby give power to the Lords of his privy council, to re-
‘ mit and difcharge the exacting of the faid cuftom, when
‘ they fhall find the prices of the victual of this kingdom,
‘ meal and barley refpective, to exceed L. 8 the boll ; and ap-
‘ points the Lords of his exchequer to caufe put this act to full
‘ execution, and caufe the forefaid cuftom be exactly levied ;
‘ with power to them to allow fuch fees to the collectors
‘ thereof as they fhall think fit.’

CHAP. II.

Here the Scotch parliament clearly took the lead in the liberal and wife exercife of their powers, for the encouraging of
agriculture, and thereby procuring plenty and cheapnefs of
provifions of all kinds.

They permitted the exportation of all forts of grain, when
the prices at home were moderate, upon payment of a fmall
duty ; and, as long as the prices remained in that fituation,
the duties payable upon importation were equal to a prohibition : and they gave unlimited powers to export cattle, and
barrelled flefhes of all kinds, without the payment of any
duty : While, in England, importation was permitted, when the
price of corn at home was at the cheapeft rate, upon payment

of a low duty; and the duties upon exportation, when the price of corn was in the fame fituation, amounted to a prohibition.

1669.

And the parliament of Scotland, upon re-confidering the fubject, and finding the exportation of corn had been obftructed, by the duty payable upon the fame, they now removed all duties, except a merk the chalder (equal to 1s. 4d. prefent money), payable upon corn exported, when the prices at home did not exceed thofe ftated in the above law, anno 1663 *. And for preventing any debates that might arife anent the refpective prices of victual, when the fame were under or above the rates expreffed in the faid act, they recommended to, and authorifed the Lords of the privy council to determine the fame; and declared, that it fhould be lawful to his Majefty's fubjects to export corns of all forts, unlefs by a proclamation or public intimation from the faid Lords of council they be prohibited and difcharged to do the fame.

1670.

The conftant drain upon England, for payment of the price of the great quantities of grain imported, brought on a revifion of the corn laws; and by a law now paffed, entitled, An act for improvement of tillage and the breed of cattle, for the common good and welfare of the kingdom, it was enacted, That it fhould be lawful for every perfon, native and foreigner, at any time, to tranfport, as merchandife, all forts of corn, although the prices exceeded the rates in the act of

* Cha. II. par. 2. feff. 1. c. 14.

the 15th of the prefent reign ; paying for the fame the rates contained in the act of tonnage and poundage. And when the prices of corn, at the places where the fame fhould be imported, fhould not exceed the rates following, there fhould be paid for cuftom thefe rates, viz. For every quarter of wheat, when the fame fhould not exceed 53s. 4d. (equal to L. 3 : 4s. of prefent money), the fum of 16s. (equal to 19s. 2d.) ; when the fame fhould exceed 53s. 4d. and not exceed L. 4 (equal to L. 4 : 16s.), there fhould be paid 8s. (equal to 9s. 7d.) ; for every quarter of rye, when the fame did not exceed 40s. (equal to L. 2 : 8s.), the fum of 16s. (19s. 2d.) ; for every quarter of barley, malt, or buck wheat, when the fame did not exceed 32s. (equal to L. 1 : 18 : 5), the fum of 16s. (19s. 2d.) ; for every quarter of oats, when the fame did not exceed 16s. (19s. 2d.), the fum of 5s. 4d. (equal to 6s. 5d.) ; and for every quarter of peafe and beans, when the fame did not exceed 40s. (L. 2 : 8s.), the fum of 16s. (19s. 2d.) : And when the prices of corn fhould exceed the rates forefaid, there fhould be paid the former cuftom and poundage. Suppofed to have been intended by the act 1663 to be 5s. 4d. (equal to 6s. 5d.) for wheat ; 4s. (equal to 4s. 10d.) for rye, peafe, and beans ; 2s. 8d. (equal to 3s. 2d.) for barley and malt ; and 1s. 4d. (equal to 1s. 6d.) for oats *.

This law was certainly intended to encourage the exportation of Englifh corn ; and to check, if not to prohibit, the importation of foreign grain.

* 22 Cha. II. c. 13. § 1. 2.

I

But exportation was effectually prevented by the high duties continued upon it; and, similar to the operation of the word *not* in the former law, the check intended for importation was rendered nugatory, by having no rule laid down for afcertaining the price of grain, at the time or place of importation; fo that this trade continued to be carried on upon payment of the low duties, agriculture languifhed, the merchants found their account in feeding the people with foreign grain, and the prices continued high; the average price of the quarter of wheat, for the ten years preceding this date, having been L. 2 : 8 : 10, equal to L. 2 : 18 : 8 of prefent money.

A farmer knows little about laws; he feldom hears of them; if he did, he probably would not underftand them, or if he did underftand them, his cry is at too great a diftance to be heard; but he feels his fituation, when he finds himfelf unable to maintain his family, and pay his landlord, by the raifing of corn. By thefe laws, the poorer farmers came to be ruined, the richer were weakened, and obliged to turn their attention from corn to cattle, fheep, or any other object by which they could fupport their families; the price of corn rofe upon the manufacturers and labourers, and an importer of foreign grain came be a great man, raifed upon the ruins of the landholders, the farmers, and the manufacturers.

This picture, may, with great propriety, be held up to the prefent day.

The landholder, however, comes to feel in his turn; his tenants fail, and his rents are not paid. Neceffity calls forth exertion, he difcovers the caufe of the evil, and his fituation enables him to apply for redrefs.

Thefe operations, however, are generally very flow. We have feen a fingle monofyllable pervert the meaning and beneficial intentions of a very material law, and remain for feven years without alteration; and, in the prefent cafe, things remained as they were now placed, during the remainder of this thoughtlefs reign, which continued for 15 years after the prefent period. The price of grain of courfe continued high; the average price of a quarter of wheat, for the 20 years, from 1660 to 1680, having been L. 2 : 9 : 9, equal to L. 2 : 19 : 9, of prefent money.

Upon the acceffion of James II. the evafion of the duties payable upon grain imported, and the diftrefs brought upon England by the immenfe importation of foreign grain, were brought before the parliament of that kingdom, and the following law was made, entitled, ' An additional act for the ' improvement of tillage *.'

' Forafmuchas (by an act made in the 22d year of the reign ' his late Majefty, of ever bleffed memory, entitled, 'An act for ' the improvement of tillage, and the breed of cattle,' it is, ' amongft other things provided and enacted, that from and

CHAP. II.

1685.

---

* 1 Ja. 2. c. 19.

I 2

' after the 29th day of June 1670, and from thence forward,
' certain rates should be paid for the custom and poundage of
' foreign corn and grain, imported into this kingdom, accord-
' ing to the prices of English corn, at the towns, havens, and
' places, when and where the same should be imported, as
' by the said act particularly appeareth :

' And inasmuch as no provision was made by the said act,
' for ascertaining and determining the said prices, by reason
' whereof several great quantities of foreign corn and grain
' have been imported, without paying the respective duties by
' the said act appointed, contrary to the true intent and mean-
' ing of the said act :

' Now for supplying the said defect) be it enacted, by the
' King's most excellent majesty, by and with the advice and
' consent of the Lords spiritual and temporal, and the Com-
' mons in this present parliament assembled, and by authority
' of the same, That from and after the feast of St Michael the
' archangel, next, and from thence forward, it shall and may
' be lawful to, and for all and every the justices of the peace
' for the several and respective counties, within his Majesty's
' kingdom of England, dominion of Wales, and town of
' Berwick upon Tweed, wherein foreign corn or grain shall or
' may be hereafter imported ; and they and every of them
' are hereby enjoined and required, at their next respective
' quarter-sessions, after Michaelmas and Easter-day yearly, by
' the oaths of two or more honest and substantial persons of
' the respective counties, being neither merchants nor factors

The landholder, however, comes to feel in his turn; his tenants fail, and his rents are not paid. Neceffity calls forth exertion, he difcovers the caufe of the evil, and his fituation enables him to apply for redrefs.

Thefe operations, however, are generally very flow. We have feen a fingle monofyllable pervert the meaning and beneficial intentions of a very material law, and remain for feven years without alteration; and, in the prefent cafe, things remained as they were now placed, during the remainder of this thoughtlefs reign, which continued for 15 years after the prefent period. The price of grain of courfe continued high; the average price of a quarter of wheat, for the 20 years, from 1660 to 1680, having been L. 2 : 9 : 9, equal to L. 2 : 19 : 9, of prefent money.

Upon the acceffion of James II. the evafion of the duties payable upon grain imported, and the diftrefs brought upon England by the immenfe importation of foreign grain, were brought before the parliament of that kingdom, and the following law was made, entitled, ' An additional act for the ' improvement of tillage *.'

' Forafmuchas (by an act made in the 22d year of the reign ' his late Majefty, of ever bleffed memory, entitled, 'An act for ' the improvement of tillage, and the breed of cattle,' it is, ' amongft other things provided and enacted, that from and

---

* 1 Ja. 2. c. 19.

I 2

‘ after the 29th day of June 1670, and from thence forward,
‘ certain rates fhould be paid for the cuftom and poundage of
‘ foreign corn and grain, imported into this kingdom, accord-
‘ ing to the prices of Englifh corn, at the towns, havens, and
‘ places, when and where the fame fhould be imported, as
‘ by the faid act particularly appeareth :

‘ And inafmuch as no provifion was made by the faid act,
‘ for afcertaining and determining the faid prices, by reafon
‘ whereof feveral great quantities of foreign corn and grain
‘ have been imported, without paying the refpective duties by
‘ the faid act appointed, contrary to the true intent and mean-
‘ ing of the faid act :

‘ Now for fupplying the faid defect) be it enacted, by the
‘ King’s moft excellent majefty, by and with the advice and
‘ confent of the Lords fpiritual and temporal, and the Com-
‘ mons in this prefent parliament affembled, and by authority
‘ of the fame, That from and after the feaft of St Michael the
‘ archangel, next, and from thence forward, it fhall and may
‘ be lawful to, and for all and every the juftices of the peace
‘ for the feveral and refpective counties, within his Majefty’s
‘ kingdom of England, dominion of Wales, and town of
‘ Berwick upon Tweed, wherein foreign corn or grain fhall or
‘ may be hereafter imported; and they and every of them
‘ are hereby enjoined and required, at their next refpective
‘ quarter-feffions, after Michaelmas and Eafter-day yearly, by
‘ the oaths of two or more honeft and fubftantial perfons of
‘ the refpective counties, being neither merchants nor factors

‘ for the importing of corn, nor anyways concerned nor in-
‘ terefted in the corn fo imported; and each of them having
‘ a freehold eftate of L. 20 *per annum*, or a leafehold eftate of
‘ L. 50 *per annum*, above all charges and reprizes, and being
‘ fkilled in the prices of corn, (which oath all and every the
‘ faid juftices are hereby empowered to adminifter) and by
‘ fuch other ways and means as to them fhall feem fit, to ex-
‘ amine and determine the common market prices of middling
‘ Englifh corn and grain, of the refpective forts in the faid act
‘ mentioned, as the fame fhall be commonly bought and fold,
‘ in the faid refpective counties into which any foreign corn
‘ or fhall be imported, and to certify the fame, with two fuch
‘ oaths made as aforefaid, in writing annexed, unto his Ma-
‘ jefty’s chief officer and collector of the cuftoms for the time
‘ being, refiding in the faid refpective ports or havens, where
‘ the faid corn and grain fhall be imported, to be hung up in
‘ fome public place in the cuftom-houfe, to which all perfons
‘ may refort, for their information.

‘ And it is hereby farther enacted, by the authority afore-
‘ faid, that from and after the feaft of St Michael the arch-
‘ angel, next, the cuftom and duty of foreign corn and grain,
‘ imported into any of his Majefty’s faid dominions of Eng-
‘ land, Wales, and town of Berwick upon Tweed, appointed
‘ by the faid act to be paid, fhall be collected and paid accord-
‘ ing to the prices contained in fuch refpective certificates as
‘ aforefaid, and not otherwife ; any thing in this act, or in
‘ any other law or ftatute, contained to the contrary notwith-
‘ ftanding.

CHAP. II.

‘ Provided always, and be it further enacted by the autho-
‘ rity aforefaid, That all that by virtue of this act is to be
‘ done by the juftices of the peace, at their quarter-feffions,
‘ in their feveral counties, fhall be done and performed in like
‘ manner in the city of London, in the months of October
‘ and April yearly, by the mayor, aldermen, and juftices of
‘ peace there ; and that the perfons making fuch oath fhall be
‘ no corn-chandler, mealman, factor, merchant, or other per-
‘ fon interefted in fuch corn fo to be imported ; but fhall be
‘ fome fubftantial houfe-keepers, living in Middlefex or Sur-
‘ rey, qualified as aforefaid.’

In Scotland, the importation of victual from Ireland had
been prohibited under fevere penalties ; but referving power to
the Lords of the privy council to admit of it, for fuch times as
they fhould think fit, when the price within the kingdom was
at or above L. 8 Scots, (equal to 16s. of prefent money) for
beer and meal; and L. 10 (equal to 20s.) for wheat, per boll*.
And now a total prohibition to import victual from Ireland
was enacted, and all victual that fhould be imported from
thence was ordered to be funk and deftroyed †.

1686.

The average price of a quarter of wheat in England, for the
ten years from 1650 to 1660, was L. 2 : 9 : 6, equal to L. 2 : 19 : 5
of prefent money ; from 1660 to 1670, it was L. 2 : 8 : 10, equal

---

* Cha. 2. par. 2. feff. 3. c. 3.

† Ja. 7. par. 1. feff. 3. c. 14.

to L. 2 : 18 : 8 ; from 1670 to 1680, it was L. 2 : 10 : 8, equal
to L. 3 : 0 : 10 of prefent money; and the average price of
the quarter of wheat, from 1631 to 1685, inclufive, was L. 2
4s. 3d. equal to L. 2 : 13 : 1 of prefent money.

The reader will be farther enabled to judge of the unfavourable fyftem of the corn laws, which we have reviewed in
this chapter, by the fcale we fhall annex of the prices fixed
by thofe laws, for the exportation and importation of wheat,
from the year 1360 to 1688 *.

It is very fingular, that the benefit which muft arife to e-
very nation, from raifing as much corn as poflible, and exporting fuch parts of it as the home confumption does not require, fhould have been fo long mifapprehended in Great Britain. The example of their neighbours, who wifely exchang-
ed their excrefcent ftock of corn, for the raw materials and
money of England and Scotland, fhould have pointed out the
benefit of that trade ; for had it not been profitable they would
not have continued it for fo many centuries.

This importation trade cut many ways againft the moft material interefts of Great Britain. Our agriculture decayed,
a great part of the lands lay without tillage, population
confequently decreafed, the public revenue fuffered a proportional diminution, and our remaining manufacturers came to

* Vide, Appendix, No 6.

CHAP. II.

be fed at a very high price, with the productions of the lands of other nations, often our enemies, who drew immense profits therefrom, and drained our country of its wealth.

CHAP. III.

Of the causes and effects of the several Corn Laws of Great Britain, subsequent to the Revolution in the year 1688.

HAVING traced the corn laws of Great Britain, for near five hundred years prior to the Revolution; and having, to the best of our ability, recognised the wisdom, and pointed out the errors or defects of those laws, it is with pleasure we now approach to that period, when the same daring and enlightened spirit, that could dart through and reform the errors of government, appears to have cut asunder those chains, in which the agriculture of these kingdoms had been fettered for so many ages.

This happy change was not effected by amending or reforming the old laws, or simply, by lessening the duties upon grain exported; but boldly, by relinquishing every idea of revenue from corn raised at home, and establishing a new system, which would both invigorate agriculture, and give a new spring to trade and navigation.

K

In a numerous, and well regulated fociety, the efficiency of laws points out, to the legiflature, the ftudy, the care, and the attention, with which they ought to be conftructed.

Their operations are immediate, the confequences are foon felt; and the effects of thofe laws, which we are now about to inveftigate, will, it is hoped, afford inftruction to future generations, as well as to the prefent.

1688.

Soon after the acceffion of William and Mary, the following law was made, entitled, ' An act for encouraging the ex
' portation of corn.'

' Forafmuch as it hath been found by experience, that the
' exportation of corn and grain into foreign parts, when the
' price thereof is at a low rate in this kingdom, hath been a
' great advantage, not only to the owners of land, but to the
' trade of this kingdom in general:

' Be it therefore enacted, by the King's and Queen's moft
' excellent majefties, by and with the advice and confent
' of the Lords fpiritual and temporal, and of the Commons
' now affembled in parliament, and by the authority of the
' fame, That when malt or barley, Winchefter meafure, is and
' fhall be at 24s. per quarter (equal to 28s. 10d. of prefent
' money), or under; rye, at 32s. (equal to 38s. 5d.) per quar-
' ter, or under; and wheat, at 48s. (equal to L. 2 : 17 : 7) a
' quarter, or under; in any port or ports of this kingdom, or
' dominion of Wales; every merchant or other perfon, who

CHAP. III.

' fhall put on fhip board, in Englifh fhipping, the mafter and
' two thirds of his mariners, at leaft, being their majefties
' fubjects, any forts of the corn aforefaid, from any fuch
' ports, where the rates fhall not then be higher than as afore-
' faid, with intent to export the faid corn to parts beyond the
' feas, every fuch merchant, or other perfon, fhall bring a certi-
' ficate, in writing, under his or their hands, containing the
' quantity or quality of corn, fo fhipped, to the farmers, com-
' miffioners, collectors, or other perfons appointed, or to be
' appointed, for the time being, to collect the duties and rates,
' arifing by cuftoms within any fuch port ; and, upon proof
' made of any fuch certificate, by one or more credible perfon
' or perfons, upon their oaths, which oaths the faid commif-
' fioners, or other perfons, are hereby authorifed and required
' to adminifter ; and upon bond given, by every fuch mer-
' chant, or other perfons, in the fum of L. 200 at leaft, for
' every 100 tons of corn fo fhipped, and fo proportionably,
' that the faid corn (danger of the feas excepted) fhall be ex-
' ported into parts beyond the feas, and not be again landed
' in the kingdom of England, dominion of Wales, the iflands
' of Guernfey and Jerfey, or town of Berwick upon Tweed :
' Every fuch merchant, fo fhipping off any of the aforefaid
' corn, and giving certificate and bond as aforefaid, fhall have
' and receive from fuch farmers, commiffioners, and collectors,
' or other perfons, in any port refpectively, where the fame
' corn fhall be fo fhipped, for every quarter of barley or malt,
' ground or unground, 2s. 6d. (equal to 3s. of prefent money);
' for every quarter of rye, ground or unground, 3s. 6d. (equal
' to 4s. 2d.) ; for every quarter of wheat, ground or un-

‘ ground, 5s. (equal to 6s.); which fum or fums, every fuch
‘ commiſſioner, farmer, or other perfons, are hereby autho-
‘ rifed and required, upon demand by fuch exporter, to make
‘ prefent payment of accordingly; without taking or requi-
‘ ring any thing for cuſtom ; or any fee or reward for corn fo
‘ laden to be exported ; or for fo much grain as ſhall be ex-
‘ ported in any ſhip, wherein any other goods ſhall be ſhipped ;
‘ any law, ſtatute, or ufage, in any wife to the contrary not-
‘ withſtanding : And upon certificate returned, under the com-
‘ mon feal of the chief magiſtrate, in any place or places be-
‘ yond the feas ; or under the hands and feals of two known
‘ Engliſh merchants upon the place, that fuch corn was there
‘ landed ; or upon proof, by credible perfons, that fuch corn
‘ was taken by enemies, or periſhed in the feas, the examina-
‘ tion and proof thereof being left to the judgment of fuch
‘ commiſſioners, farmers, collectors, or other perfons; which
‘ proof being made, or certificate delivered, to fuch perfon or
‘ perfons, refpectively, as took bond as aforefaid ; the faid
‘ bond ſhall be delivered up to fuch exporter, or his order,
‘ to be cancelled, without any fee for the fame : And the
‘ monies, by any fuch commiſſioners, farmers, collectors, or
‘ other perfon, fo paid, in obedience to this act, ſhall be ac-
‘ cepted of in his or their accounts, as fo much paid to their
‘ Majeſties ; and he and they is, and ſhall be, difcharged
‘ therefore accordingly *.’   And when grain was at or under
the above prices, the above bounty was extended to corn ſhipped at Berwick †.

* 1 Will. & Mary, c. 12.
† Ibid. c. 24. § 18.

This policy was foon after followed in Scotland, by a law entitled, An act for encouraging the exportation of victual, in thefe words : ' His Majefty, and eftates of parliament, confi-
' dering that the grains of all forts, are the greateft product
' and commodity of this nation ; and confidering how necef-
' fary it is for the promoting of tillage, and improvement of
' trade, to the beft advantage of the kingdom, that an effec-
' tual encouragement be granted for exportation of corns and
' victual forth thereof : Therefore his Majefty, out of his royal
' bounty, with confent of the eftates of parliament, ftatutes
' and ordains, That all forts of grain, exported out of the
' kingdom, after Martinmas 1696, fhall be free of any dues
' formerly payable upon exportation : And that for encoura-
' ging export, after the faid term, there fhall be given out of
' the cuftoms, to the exporter, upon his oath of verity of the
' numbers of the bolls exported, fubfcribed with his hand,
' and attefted by the collector of the next adjacent cuftom-
' houfe, eight merks for ilk chalder of grain that fhall be ex-
' ported, by fea or land, when they fhall not exceed the prices
' following, viz. When wheat is at or under twelve pound the
' boll, (equal to L. 1 : 4s. of prefent money) ; bear, barley,
' and malt, at or under eight pound, (equal to 16s.) per boll ;
' peafe, oats, and meal, at or under fix pound, (equal to 12s.)
' per boll ; all the faid grains being of Linlithgow meafure :
' With this provifion always, that the faid exportation fhall be
' by Scotfmen, or in Scots fhips, and that the mafter and
' three-fourth parts of the feamen of the faid fhips fhall be
' Scotfmen : As alfo with this provifion, that when the grains
' exceed the forefaid rates, the Lords of his majefty's fecret

CHAP. III.
1695.

CHAP. III.   ' council may difcharge the exportation of victual of all forts,
' ay and till the grains fall to the prices forefaid *.'

But the fubfidies and duties, payable upon corn exported
from England, not having been given up by the former act,

1700.   thefe were now finally removed by the following law: ' And,
' for the greater encouragement of tillage, be it further en-
' acted, by the authority aforefaid, That from and after the
' 30th day of March 1700, the fubfidy, and all other duties
' whatfoever, payable for, or upon the exportation of wheat,
' rye, barley, malt, beans, peafe, and other forts of corn and
' grain whatfoever, ground and unground; and for, and upon
' the exportation of bread, bifcuit, and meal, or any of them,
' out of, or from the kingdom of England, dominion of
' Wales, or town of Berwick upon Tweed, as to fo much of
' the faid commodities, or any of them, as fhall be fo exported,
' after the faid 30th day of March, fhall ceafe, determine,
' and be no longer due or payable to his Majefty, his heirs,
' or fucceffors; any law, ftatute, ufage, or prefcription to the
' contrary notwithftanding †.'

Thus the great, and new fyftem of corn laws was finally
eftablifhed, both in England and Scotland; and thefe king-

1706.   doms having foon after been thoroughly incorporated, their
corn laws were in like manner united by the following fection
of the 6th article of the act of Union : ' That all the parts of
' the united kingdom for ever, from and after the Union, fhall

* William, parl. 1. c. 32.   † 11 & 12 Will. 3. c. 20. § 4.

‘ have the fame allowances, encouragements, and drawbacks,
‘ and be under the fame prohibitions, reſtrictions, and regu-
‘ lations of trade, and liable to the fame cuſtoms and duties
‘ on import and export; and that the allowances, encourage-
‘ ments, and drawbacks, prohibitions, reſtrictions, and regu-
‘ lations of trade, and the cuſtoms and duties on import and
‘ export, fettled in England, when the Union commences,
‘ ſhall, from and after the Union, take place throughout the
‘ whole united kingdom; excepting and referving the duties
‘ upon export and import of fuch particular commodities,
‘ from which any perfons, the fubjects of either kingdom,
‘ are fpecially liberated and exempted by their private rights;
‘ which after the Union are to remain fafe and entire to them,
‘ in all refpects, as before the fame : And that from and after
‘ the Union, no Scots cattle, carried into England, ſhall be
‘ liable to any other duties, either on the public or private ac-
‘ counts, than thofe duties to which the cattle of England are,
‘ or ſhall be liable, within the faid kingdom. And feeing, by
‘ the laws of England, there are rewards granted upon the ex-
‘ portation of certain kinds of grain, wherein oats, grinded or
‘ ungrinded, are not expreſſed, That from and after the Union,
‘ when oats ſhall be fold at 15s. Sterling (equal to 18s. of pre-
‘ fent money) per quarter, or under, there ſhall be paid 2s.
‘ 6d. Sterling (equal to 3s.) for every quarter of the oatmeal
‘ exported in terms of the law; whereby, and fo long as re-
‘ wards are granted for exportation of other grains, and that
‘ the beer of Scotland have the fame rewards as barley. And
‘ in refpect the importation of victual into Scotland, from any
‘ place beyond the fea, would prove a difcouragement to til-

' lage ; therefore, that the prohibition, now in force, by the
' law of Scotland, againſt importation of victual from Ire-
' land, or any other place beyond the ſea, into Scotland, do,
' after the Union, remain in the ſame force as now it is, until
' more proper and effectual ways be provided by the parlia-
' ment of Great Britain, for diſcouraging the importation of
' the ſaid victual from beyond the ſea *.'

And, by another law of the ſame year, it was enacted as
follows : 'And whereas, by the foreſaid articles of Union, it is
' provided, that from and after the Union there ſhall be certain
' allowances for all oatmeal, and grain called beer, exported
' from Scotland : Be it enacted, by the authority aforeſaid,
' that for all oatmeal, and grain called beer, *alias* bigg, which,
' from and after the ſaid firſt day of May 1707, ſhall be ex-
' ported from any port of this kingdom of England, dominion
' of Wales, and town of Berwick upon Tweed, to parts be-
' yond the ſeas, by any merchant, or other perſon or perſons
' whatſoever, there ſhall be the like premium given upon the
' exportation thereof, as is to be given upon exportation of
' oatmeal and beer from Scotland; ſuch merchant, or other
' perſon, firſt bringing a certificate, in writing, under his or
' their hands, containing the quantity of ſuch oatmeal, or
' beer, *alias* bigg, ſo ſhipped, to the collector or other perſons
' appointed, or to be appointed, for the time being, to collect
' the duties or rates ariſing by cuſtoms within any ſuch port;
' and making proof of ſuch certificate, by one or more cre-

---

* 5 Anne, c. 8. art. 6.

‘ dible perſon or perſons, upon their oaths, (which oaths the
‘ the ſaid collector or other perſon is hereby authoriſed and
‘ required to adminiſter), and giving bond in the ſum of L. 10
‘ at leaſt, for every ton of oatmeal ſo ſhipped, conſiſting of
‘ 20 hundred weight; and for every forty buſhels of beer,
‘ *alias* bigg, ſo ſhipped; and ſo proportionally for a greater or
‘ leſſer quantity; that the ſame ſhall be ſo exported to parts
‘ beyond the ſeas, and not to be relanded : which premium,
‘ every merchant or other perſon, ſo ſhipping off any ſuch
‘ oatmeal, or beer, *alias* bigg, and giving certificate and bond
‘ as aforeſaid, ſhall have and receive, from the collector or
‘ other perſon, as aforeſaid, in any port reſpectively, when
‘ the ſame ſhall be ſo ſhipped, out of her Majeſty’s revenue
‘ of the cuſtoms; and upon certificate returned, under the
‘ common ſeal of the chief magiſtrate, in any place or places .
‘ beyond the ſeas ; or under the hands and ſeals of two known
‘ Engliſh merchants upon the place, that ſuch oatmeal, or beer,
‘ *alias* bigg, was there landed; or upon proof, by credible
‘ perſons, that ſuch oatmeal, or beer, *alias* bigg, was taken by
‘ enemies, or periſhed by the ſeas : which proof being made,
‘ or certificate delivered, to the collector or other perſons, who
‘ took bond as aforeſaid, the ſaid bond ſhall be delivered up
‘ to ſuch merchant or other perſon, or his order, to be can-
‘ celled, without any fee for the ſame.

‘ And whereas, by an act of parliament, made in the firſt
‘ year of the reign of the late King William and Queen Mary,
‘ of bleſſed memory, entitled, ‘ An act for the encouraging
‘ the exportation of corn, it was, among other things, thereby

L

‘ enacted, that every such merchant, by the said act described,
‘ shipping any malt or barley, rye or wheat, and giving cer-
‘ tificate and bond, as the said act directs, shall have and re-
‘ ceive from the farmers, commissioners, collectors, or other
‘ persons appointed, or to be appointed, for the time being, to
‘ collect the duties and rates, arising by customs, within any
‘ such port where the said corn shall be shipped off, for every
‘ quarter of barley or malt, ground or unground, 2s. 6d. ;
‘ for every quarter of rye, ground or unground, 3s. 6d.; for
‘ every quarter of wheat, ground or unground, 5s. :   And
‘ whereas, since the making of the said act, there have been
‘ divers quantities of malt made of wheat, some part whereof
‘ hath been exported ; and some doubts having arisen touch-
‘ ing the bounty money to be paid upon the exportation there-
‘ of, to the discouragement of the exportation of corn ; and
‘ for clearing thereof, and for preventing future disputes
‘ touching the same, be it enacted, by the authority aforesaid,
‘ That every merchant, or other person, exporting malt made
‘ of wheat, from and after the said first day of May 1707,
‘ shall have and receive of the said farmers, commissioners, or
‘ persons aforesaid, 5s. for every quarter of malt made of
‘ wheat, or wheat malt, ground or unground, to be paid by
‘ the respective persons, in the said recited act mentioned *.’

In Scotland, some time before the Union, (anno 1703) an
act of parliament was passed, confirming the former laws of
1672 and 1686 against the importation of victual and cattle

---

* 5 Anne, c. 29. § 10. 15.

from Ireland; and to render the prohibition more effectual,
it was, befides other penalties, ftatuted and declared, ' That
' all importers of Irifh victual, as well mafters and feamen of
' the veffels wherein it is imported, as alfo the refetters, fellers,
' retailers, and buyers thereof, or any part thereof, wittingly,
' fhall not only be liable to the pains and penalties of the act
' 1672, but likewife all under the degree of heritors, fhall be
' delivered to any Scots officer, ferving her Majefty's allies
' abroad, and to be tranfported by them for recruits, when
' once difcovered and convicted, &c.   And, by the fame law,
' all importation of victual, by fea or land, from any country
' whatfoever, into Scotland; and all buying and felling, re-
' fetting and retailing, wittingly, of victual imported, is ex-
' prefsly prohibited, except that wheat, peafe, and beans, for
' feed, might be imported into England, upon payment of
' 40s. (equal to 4s. of prefent money) more than the ordinary
' cuftom, per boll; if fairly imported and entered, &c. : Pro-
' vided always, that when, by reafon of dearth, the prices of
' victual exceeds the rates aftermentioned, viz. wheat, twelve
' pound (equal to L. 1 : 4s. of prefent money) the boll; bear,
' barley, malt, and meal, eight pound (equal to 16s.) per boll;
' and oats and peafe, fix pound (equal to 12s.) per boll; the
' Lords of her Majefty's privy council fhall have power, after
' due trial by them taken, to fufpend and difcharge the
' execution of the faid prohibitory acts, for fuch fpace and
' time as the exigence of the faid dearth fhall require, and no
' longer *.'

* Anne, par. 1. c. 9.

Thefe were the laws which received the fanction of the 6th article of the Union, above ingroffed.

In all countries, laws, particularly thofe of bounty or revenue, receive an uncertain execution, where there is any material word either wanting or fupernumerary, or any claufe which can receive an equivocal explanation by perfons interefted.

The prices and duties of corn, imported, were fixed by the act 1670; but, as has been already obferved, the duties were evaded, by the act having laid down no rule for afcertaining the prices, at the times and places of importation.

This defect was fupplied by the act 1685, by which the juftices of peace of the feveral counties were enjoined and required, at their refpective quarter feffions, to inquire into and determine the prices of grain, at fixed periods; and to fend certificates thereof to the feveral cuftom-houfes, within their jurifdictions, to be hung up there, in a public place, for the direction and rule of all parties concerned.

But as, by this law, neither the trouble of the execution of it was to be compenfated, nor the neglect of it to be punifhed, it was, in many places, not attended to; and, as no method or rule had been fubftituted, in the event of this defect, importers availed themfelves of the opening; and, in the years 1728 and 1729, they introduced a great deal of foreign corn into Great Britain, without payment of the duties.

Some difficulties had also arisen, from the methods which CHAP. III.
had been practised, in ascertaining the prices and quantities of
corn exported.

A law was therefore now made, which, after narrating, in   1729.
the preamble, the two laws above noticed, proceeds thus:

‘ And whereas the justices of the peace, in some of the
‘ counties of this kingdom, have, notwithstanding the last
‘ mentioned act, omitted or neglected to settle the price of
‘ corn, at their quarter sessions, after Michaelmas last, and to
‘ return certificates thereof to the chief officer and collector of
‘ the customs, residing in the respective ports, where the
‘ said corn has been, or may be imported ; by means whereof
‘ the said officers were at a loss how to charge the custom and
‘ duty due for such corn, which *has been*, and may be a great
‘ loss to the revenue, and a detriment to the farmers and fair
‘ traders.’

The justices therefore, who had omitted their duty, were
enjoined and required, at their then next quarter sessions, or
any adjournment thereof, to inquire into and determine what
the common market prices of middling British corn, or grain,
were, at or about Michaelmas then last, in their respective
counties, by such ways as were directed by the act 1670, and
to grant certificates thereof; according to which the officers
of the customs, and all other persons concerned, were to go-
vern themselves.

And in all cases, where any corn or grain had been imported since the first day of Michaelmas quarter sessions then last past, if the importers or proprietors thereof had neglected to pay the respective duties for the same, or should neglect to pay the same upon demand, such importers or proprietors should forfeit and lose all such corn and grain, or the value thereof.

And in case the justices of peace should thereafter omit or neglect to examine and determine the prices of corn and grain, and to certify the same to the officers of the customs; then, and in such case, the collector of the customs, at the respective ports of importation, was impowered to receive the several duties, according to the lowest price of the several sorts of corn and grain, mentioned in the foresaid act 1670.

And for the better ascertaining the quantity of corn or grain, to be shipped for exportation, which, by the act 1688, is no otherwise ascertained than by the certificate to the exporter, attested upon oath, it was enacted, that the proper officers of the customs should be empowered to admeasure all corn and grain, whereon there is an allowance, payable upon the exportation thereof, by a tub, or measure, containing four Winchester bushels; and if such corn or grain, intended to be exported, should be brought to be shipped off, in sacks, they were empowered to make choice of any two of these sacks, out of twenty, and from them to compute the quantity of corn to be shipped, according to which the bounty was to be paid.

And that the like powers, certificates, and regulations, should be extended to the ascertaining the prices and quantity of beer,

alias bigg, oatmeal, and malt, made of wheat, or wheat malt,
intended for exportation *.

Still, however, the remissness of the justices, or some other
debility of the laws, had left an open door, through which
considerable quantities of foreign grain were introduced into
the kingdom, although the prices, at home, were exceedingly
low : And, to prevent that abuse, another law was made, men-
tioning that, ' Whereas by an act made in the first year of the
' reign of his late majesty King James II. entitled, *An addi-*
' *tional act for the improvement of tillage*, provision was made
' for examining and determining the common market price of
' English middling corn and grain, which nevertheless hath
' been found ineffectual :' Therefore, for the better ascertaining the same, and *for preventing the fraudulent importation of
foreign corn and grain*, it was enacted, That it should be lawful
for all and every the justices of peace, for the several and respective counties within that part of Great Britain called Eng-
gland, Wales, and the town of Berwick upon Tweed, wherein foreign corn or grain should or might be imported ; and
they were thereby enjoined and required, at every their quarter sessions, to give in charge, in open court, to the grand
jury, to make inquiry and presentment, upon their oaths, of
the common market prices of middling English corn and grain,
of the respective sorts and quantities mentioned in an act
made in the 22d year of the reign of King Charles II. entitled,
' An act for the improvement of tillage, and breed of cattle,' as

____

* 2 Geo. II. c. 18. § 1, 2, 3, 4, 5.

the fame fhould be commonly bought and fold, in every fuch county; which inquiry and prefentment, the faid grand jury were thereby impowered and required to make.

That fuch prefentment fhould be made in open court, and fhould be certified by the faid juftices, in writing, to his Majefty's chief officer and collector of the cuftoms, for the time being, refiding in every fuch port or haven, where fuch corn and grain fhould be imported; and fhould be hung up in fome public place in the cuftom-houfe, belonging to every fuch port or haven, to be reforted to by all perfons, for their information.

That the cuftom and duty of foreign corn and grain, imported into England, Wales, and Berwick, as aforefaid, appointed to be paid by the faid act of the 22d Charles II. fhould be collected and paid according to the prices contained in fuch certificates as aforefaid, and not otherwife; any thing in the faid act of King James II. to the contrary notwithftanding.

But nothing in this act to affect the authority given by the faid act of James II. to the city of London. It was alfo enacted:

That no warrant, fufferance, coaft-cocket, tranfire, or letpafs, whatfoever, fhould be granted or allowed for tranfporting, conveying, or carrying forth, to the open fea, in any fhip or veffel, from any port in England, Wales, or Berwick, to any other port or haven of the fame, any foreign corn or grain, after the importation thereof; and that no perfon, or perfons whatfoever fhould, directly or indirectly, tranfport, convey, or carry forth to the open fea; or caufe or procure to be tranfported, conveyed, or carried forth to the open fea; or from any port, haven, creek, or road, or member thereof, in England, Wales, or Berwick, in order to be landed or difcharged in any other port or place within the fame; or lade, or caufe or procure to be laden, in any fhip or veffel, in order to be landed or difcharged in any other port, haven, or place within the fame, any foreign corn or grain, mixed with Englifh corn and grain, after the importation thereof, under the fevere penalties and forfeitures therein mentioned *.

Agriculture had now recovered its ftrength, and the exertions of our farmers had become vigorous and conftant.

For feveral years preceding this period, the price of grain had been very reafonable; a great export trade of corn had been carried on from Great Britain; and proper attention had been paid to the execution of thofe laws which guarded againft fraudulent importation.

The average price of a quarter of wheat, for the 5 years from 1731 to 1735 inclufive, was only 34s.; the price of the quarter of wheat in 1736 was 40s.; in 1737 it was 38s.; and, in the prefent year 1738, it was only 35s. 6d.

* 5 Geo. 2. c. 12.

M

CHAP. III.

1738.

Yet in the midst of this plenty, the common people had been stimulated to violence from motives, or by persons, not now known. They rose in mobs in different parts of the kingdom; they seized horses and carriages on the way to the ports with corn for exportation, destroyed the horses and carriages, beat the drivers, and scattered away the corn.

In some places they pulled down granaries, and damaged or carried off the contents; they entered ships, and threw away and destroyed the cargoes of corn that had been shipped for exportation.

To repress these disorders, a law was made for the severe punishment of such offenders, and subjecting the inhabitants of the hundred, in which such offences should be committed, to the payment of the damage *.

1741.

Hitherto the prohibition to import foreign grain into Scotland, or to buy, sell, or retail such, had rested upon the act 1703, and the two preceding acts therein referred to, by which it was provided, that if, by reason of dearth, grain in Scotland should exceed certain prices, the Lords of her Majesty's privy council should have power, after due trial by them taken, to suspend and discharge the said prohibitory acts, for such space of time as the exigency of the dearth should require, and no longer. And, as is already noticed, by the 6th article of the Union, these prohibitory laws were declared to remain in force

* 11 Geo. 2. c. 22.

until more proper and effectual ways fhould be provided, by the parliament of Great Britain, for difcouraging the importation of victual from beyond fea.

Things, however, had remained in this fituation, without any fuch provifion having been made ; and, as by act of the 6th Anne, c. 6, it had been determined, that the Queen, her heirs and fucceffors, fhould have but one privy council for Great Britain ; the privy council of Scotland came thereby to be annihilated.

The prices of grain, in Scotland, having rifen in the year 1740, after a very fevere winter, fome importations of foreign grain were made, although againft law, as no power then exifted to fufpend the prohibitory acts in that part of Great Britain.

To obviate this difficulty, without entering into any new fyftem, a temporary expedient was adopted, and a law was now made, by which the powers originally committed to the privy council of Scotland, for fufpending thefe prohibitory laws, when neceffary, and removing fuch fufpenfion, when the exigence of dearth no longer required it, were vefted in the Courts of feffion, jufticiary, and exchequer, in Scotland; and rules were laid down for their procedure *.

Some difficulties having arifen with refpect to the computa-   1751.

---

* 14 Geo. 2. c. 7.

tion and admeasurement of wheat meal, and other ground corn and grain, whereon a bounty was payable upon exportation; in order to reconcile all disputes and differences that might arise thereanent, the officers of the customs, by a law now made, were impowered to allow the same bounty, and no more, upon the exportation of 224 pounds weight of wheat meal, or other ground corn or grain, whereon there was a bounty, as was allowed upon the exportation of four bushels of wheat, or other corn or grain, unground, and so in proportion for any greater or lesser quantity; and, for the greater expedition in the business, the officers were allowed to make choice of two sacks out of twenty, when the wheat meal, or other ground corn or grain, were brought in sacks; from whence they were to compute the weight of the meal, according to which the bounty was to be paid *.

These salutary laws had increased the export trade of corn to an amazing extent, while plenty remained at home, and the prices continued moderate. The average exportation for the four years, from 1748 to 1751 inclusive, amounted to 1,212,686 quarters yearly; and, the average price of wheat, for these four years, was 36s. 3d. per quarter.

The revenue applicable to the payment of the bounty upon corn exported, having been also chargeable with other payments, came to be insufficient to discharge the monies due upon these great exportations; and a law was now made, by

1753.

* 24 Geo. 2. c. 56. § 1.

which the debentures for thefe bounties were to carry intereft at the rate of 3 *per cent. per annum*, to commence fix months following the day when they fhould, or might have been produced to the commiffioners of the cuftoms at London, according to the directions of the act of the 12th and 13th of King William *.

The crop of this year having been weak, and of courfe the prices of grain having rifen, the common people, long accuftomed to plenty and cheapnefs, did not attribute the rife in the prices, to the fhortnefs of the crop, but to the arts of the farmers, dealers, millers, &c. and got into mobs, committed many outrages in different parts of the kingdom, and deftroyed mills with the grain in them, as if they had been the chief acceffories to the dearth.

The advanced prices of corn, however, brought forward laws, by which all forts of corn, meal, malt, flour, bread, bifcuit, or ftarch, were prohibited to be exported before the 25th December 1757; only malt, made for exportation, and declared to be fo before the 4th December 1756, was allowed to be exported; and veffels cleared out, before the 25th December 1756, were allowed to proceed on their voyages: But it was provided, that in cafe his Majefty fhould, at any time, before the faid 25th December 1757, judge it to be moft for the benefit and advantage of the kingdom, to permit the exportation of the corn, and the other commodities aforefaid, or

CHAP. III.

1756.

1757.

* 26 Geo. 2. c. 15.

any of them, that then it should be lawful for his Majesty, by proclamation, to be issued by and with the advice of his privy council, or by his Majesty's order in council, to be published in the London Gazette, from time to time, to permit and suffer all and every person and persons, natives and foreigners, (but not any particular person or persons) at any time or times, before the said 25th day of December 1757, to export or carry out all or any of the commodities aforesaid *.

All customs, subsidies, and duties, rates, or impositions whatsoever, upon corn or flour imported, or upon corn, grain, meal, bread, biscuit, and flour, taken from the enemy, and brought into the kingdom, were discontinued until the 24th August 1757; and the same might be also carried coastways, without duty †.

Importation of corn, duty free, was allowed in ships of other nations, in amity with Great Britain, from any port or place whatsoever ‡.

And from and after the 11th March 1757, no low wines or spirits whatever were to be extracted or distilled within the kingdom, from any wheat, barley, malt, or any other sort of grain, or from any meal or flour, for and during the space of two calendar months ‖.

---

* 30 Geo. 2. c. 1.   † Ibid. c. 7.
‡ Ibid. c. 9. § 14.   ‖ Ibid. c. 10.

And this prohibition was afterwards continued to the 11th
December 1757; but with power to his Majesty, by proclamation, to be issued with the advice of his privy council, or
by an order in council, to be published in the London Gazette, to suspend this act, and to allow the distillers to proceed *.

These laws effectually checked the exportation of corn; a-
bout 80,000 quarters had been exported, before the prohibition took place, and about 150,000 quarters of foreign corn.
were brought in.

The Exportation trade, however, was restored and recovered in the year 1759, and went on as formerly, with little or
no importation of foreign grain; but the crop 1762 having
failed a little, the importers found, that upon a very small start
in the prices, they could afford to pay the low duties, to
come in competition with the market at home; and, con-
sequently, a very confiderable importation took place for
that, and the three following years. Indeed, in the last
of these years, some panic had seized upon the kingdom,
and an embargo was laid, the 26th September, upon all
ships laded with corn for exportation, which, having been
done against law, an act of indemnity was made for it the
following year †.

There does not, at present, appear to have been any good

CHAP. III.

1766.

---

* 30 Geo. 2. c. 15.   † 7 Geo. 3. c. 7.

reafon for thofe meafures; for, in the year mentioned, there were above 300,000 quarters of grain exported, and lefs than 250,000 imported.

1767.

Laws were now made, prohibiting, for a limited time, the exportation of corn, grain, meal, malt, flour, bread, bifcuit, and ftarch; and alfo the extraction of low wines and fpirits from wheat, and wheat flour. And allowing, for a limited time, the importation of wheat and wheat flour, oats, and oat-meal, rye, and rye-meal, free of duty *.

1768.

Thefe laws were renewed this year, with fome additions; and it was enacted, that they fhould continue until twenty days after the commencement of the next feffion of parliament. The exportation of corn, grain, meal, malt, flour, bread, bifcuit, and ftarch; and alfo the extraction of low wines and fpirits, from wheat and wheat flour, was prohibited (except to fome Britifh dependencies). An importation, not only of wheat, wheat flour, barley, barley-meal, pulfe, oats, oat-meal, rye and rye-meal, from any part of Europe; but Indian corn, or maize, and rice, from North America; and wheat and wheat flour from Africa, were permitted, duty-free †.

1769.

This year the exportation of corn, grain, meal, malt, flour, bread, bifcuit, and ftarch; and alfo the extraction of

* 7 Geo. 3. c. 3. 4. 5. 8.　　　　† 8 Geo. 3. c. 1. 2. 3.

low wines and spirits, from wheat and wheat flour, was pro- CHAP. III.
hibited, until twenty days after the commencement of the
next session of parliament; and the free importation of rice
from North America was permitted.

This year the former law of last year, prohibiting the ex- 1770.
portation of corn, grain, meal, malt, flour, bread, biscuit,
and starch; and also the extraction of low wines and spirits
from wheat, and wheat flour, was continued in force, until
twenty days after the commencement of the next session of parliament; providing that the said continuation might be abridg-
ed or shortened, and this act, or any part thereof, might be
altered or varied, by any other act or acts to be made in the
present session of parliament *.

And accordingly, by another law of this session, so much
of the former acts as prohibited the exportation of malt, was
removed and repealed †.

This year also an act was made for registering the prices at
which corn is sold in the several counties of Great Britain,
and the quantity exported and imported ‡.

Laws were now made prohibiting the exportation of corn, 1771.
grain, meal, malt, flour, bread, biscuit, and starch; and also

* 10 Geo. 3. c. 1.   † Ibid. c. 10.   ‡ Ibid. c. 39.

N

the extraction of low wines and spirits from wheat, and wheat flour (except for victualling ships, and to British dependencies), until the twentieth day after the commencement of the next session of parliament *.

1772.

Upon the commencement of the session of parliament, this year, a law was made, prohibiting the exportation of corn, grain, meal, malt, flour, bread, biscuit, and starch ; and also the extraction of low wines from wheat, and wheat flour, was prohibited, until the twentieth day after the commencement of the next session of parliament. And afterwards an act was made, allowing the importation of wheat, wheat flour, rye, rye-meal, and Indian corn, free of duty, until the first day of December 1772 †.

All this would appear to have been done without any solid reason ; for the price of grain was not very high, and the quantity of grain exported, from the year 1760, to the year 1770, considerably exceeded the quantity imported.

1773.

Immediately upon the meeting of the parliament, this year, laws were made allowing the free importation, before the 1st day of January 1774, of any wheat, wheat flour, rye, rye-meal, barley, barley-meal, oats, oat-meal, pease, beans, tares, calivancies, and all other sorts of pulse, from any part of Europe, or Africa, without the payment of any subsidy, cus-

* 11 Geo. 3. c. 1.
† 12 Geo. 3. c. 1. 33.

tom, duty, or impofition whatfoever; and permitting the fame to be carried coaftways, under fuch regulations as the wheat, wheat flour, &c. of the growth of this kingdom, were allowed to be carried coaftways, provided that due entry fhould be made, as was practifed before the making of this act; and the importation of wheat, wheat flour, Indian corn, Indian meal, bifcuit, peafe, beans, tares, calivancies, and all other forts of pulfe, from North America, was alfo permitted for the fame time, duty free, upon making entry as aforefaid.

By another law, paffed at the fame time, the exportation of corn, grain, peafe, beans, meal, malt, flour, bread, bifcuit, and ftarch; and alfo the extraction of low wines and fpirits from wheat, and wheat flour, (except for victualling fhips, or to Britifh dependencies), was prohibited until the faid 1ft day of January 1774 *.

Thefe laws, however, although deftructive of our own agriculture, were only temporary, and their confequences might have been recovered, as they did not trench upon the general fyftem.

But we now come to a law of this year, by which *the venerable old code*, fo beneficial to manufactures and induftry, and fo falutary to the kingdom in general; *that code*, which had raifed the agriculture of Great Britain, from the loweft ftate

1773.

* 13 Geo. 3. c. 1. 2. 3.

of depreſſion, to the higheſt degree of proſperity; which had produced plenty, at reaſonable prices, for ſo great a number of years, at home; and had brought ſuch immenſe ſums of money for the excreſcent ſtock of corn, from abroad, was now torn up by the roots, and ſcattered in the winds *.

This ſalubrious code had not been the work of a day; it came to be reared by ſlow degrees, and was the reſult of the experience of many generations; although the multiplicity of its component parts had rendered the diſtinct knowledge of it a matter of conſiderable labour. The introduction of this new law, ſo *ſimilar in terms*, and ſo *adverſe in principle*, to the former laws, involved the corn laws in greater perplexity than ever; and it need not be matter of ſurpriſe, that perſons of the beſt underſtanding ſhould be unwilling to enter upon a ſtudy ſo dark, and ſo intricate.

The neareſt road to conviction, in ſuch caſes, is to place the objects to be compared parallel before the eye; to exhibit them in their firſt principles; to ſtudy their operations; and to determine according to their conſequences and effects.

With this view we ſhall lay before the public a comparative ſtatement of both ſyſtems, in order that we may, by contraſting them in this manner, be the better enabled to judge of the difference between the *old ſyſtem*, which had been eſta-

* 13 Geo. 3. c. 43.

blifhed, by the laws of 1670, 1688, and 1706; and the *new* *fyftem*, (for we muft confider it as fuch) which was now introduced, by the law of 1773.

CHAP. III.

AN INQUIRY INTO

CHAP. III.

Comparative Statement of the Laws for the Importation of Grain into

Table of Importation Prices and Duties, by the Old Laws.	Money of the time.						Present Money.					
	Prices.			Duties.			Prices.			Duties.		
	£.	s.	d.	£.	s.	d.	£.	s.	d.	£.	s.	d.
1670. For every quarter of wheat, when the price did not exceed	2	13	4	0	10	0	3	4	0	0	19	2
when above that price and not exceeding	4	0	0	0	8	0	4	16	0	0	9	7
when above that price	0	0	0	0	5	4	0	0	0	0	6	5
For every quarter of rye, peafe, and beans, when the price did not exceed	2	0	0	0	16	0	2	8	0	0	19	2
when above that price	0	0	0	0	4	0	0	0	0	0	4	10
For every quarter of barley, when the price did not exceed	1	12	0	0	16	0	1	18	5	0	19	2
when above that price	0	0	0	0	2	8	0	0	0	0	3	2
For every quarter of oats, when the price did not exceed	0	16	0	0	5	4	0	19	2	0	6	5
when above that price	0	0	0	0	1	4	0	0	0	0	1	6

Remarks on the fyftem e-ftablifhed by the old laws. By the old laws, particularly that of 1670, importation was not permitted until the prices, at home, were very high, and even then the duties upon importation were confiderable, fo that foreign grain could only be brought in to fupply neceffitous times, but could never ftand in competition with the home produce.

The law of 1688 did not mention importation. It was made entirely for the encouragement of our own agriculture, by providing a new market for our excrefcent corn, and thereby ftimulating the people to cultivate the wafte lands. It left importation to the preceding laws, by which it was thought to be fufficiently guarded, if not prohibited.

When thofe laws were enacted, and until the year 1714, money carried intereft at the rate of 6 *per cent. per annum*, and confequently was proportionally of more value than it is at prefent, with the intereft at 5 *per cent. per annum*.

The fpirit of the old laws did not permit the importation of flour, or manufactured grain, at any time; but only the grain at particular places where the prices fhould be very high. Nor did they give permiffion either to carry imported grain by fea, coaftways, or to tranfport it to any other place but that to which neceffity called it. And thefe reftrictions appeared fo neceffary, that they were enforced by the act of the 5th George II. under very fevere penalties.

Great Britain, according to the Old, and to the New System.

CHAP. III.

Table of Importation Prices and Duties, by the New Law.	Prices.			Duties.		
	£.	s.	d	£.	s.	d.
For every quarter of wheat, when the price was at or above ————	2	8	0	0	0	6
100 weight of wheat flour ———— ———— ———— ————	0	0	0	0	0	2
For every quarter of rye, peafe, or beans, when the price was at or above	1	12	0	0	0	3
barley, beer or bigg, when the price was at or above	1	4	0	0	0	2
oats, when the price was at or above ————' ————	0	16	0	0	0	2

1773.

The law of 1773 begins with importation, and enacts, that whenever the price of mid- Remarks on the system introduced by the new law. dling British corn and grain shall be at the prices above stated, at the ports and places where the same should be imported; then all cuftoms and duties, formerly payable upon wheat, wheat flour, rye, peafe, beans, barley, bear, big, and oats, imported into this kingdom, should ceafe, determine, and be no longer payable, during the refpective continuance of thefe prices. And that, in lieu of the former duties, there should only be paid the duties ftated in the above Table.

And it was alfo enacted, that it should be lawful to import oat-meal from Ireland, or from any other part beyond the feas, into any port or place in Scotland, where the price of oat-meal does exceed 16s. per boll, weighing 8 ftone, Troy.

By the new law importation is permitted, when the prices of grain, at home, are fo low, that foreign grain may, at all times, come in competition with our home produce, in our own markets; and this has been the cafe ever fince this law was paffed.

By this law too, wheat and other grain, imported, may be carried coaftways, and entered and landed in any other ports of the kingdom, at which the prices of middling Britifh corn, grain, or flour, are at, or above the refpective rates aforefaid, under fuch regulations as wheat, wheat flour, rye, peafe, beans, barley, beer, bigg, or oats, of the growth of this kingdom, are allowed to be carried coaftways.

And any perfon importing corn, grain, or flour, and paying the duties, if the fame shall be again exported, within fix months, the duties are to be drawn back and repaid.

CHAP. III. *Comparative Statement of the Laws for the Exportation of Grain from*

Table of Exportation Prices and Bounties, by the Old Laws.	Money of the time.		Prefent Money.	
	Prices.	Bounties.	Prices.	Bounties.
	£. s. d.	£. s. d.	£. s. d.	£. s. d.
1688. Upon every quarter of wheat, ground or unground, when the price was at or under —	2 8 6	0 5 0	2 17 7	0 6 0
Upon every quarter of rye, when the price was at or under — —	1 12 0	0 3 6	1 18 5	0 4 2
Upon every quarter of barley or malt, when the price was at or under — —	1 4 0	0 2 6	1 8 10	0 3 0
1706. Upon every quarter of oatmeal, when the quarter of oats is at or under — —	0 15 0	0 2 6	0 18 0	0 3 0

General
Remarks.

We fhall now take a view of the old laws, and of the new law, with refpect to exportation.

The laws of 1688 and 1706, have been already recited, and to which we fhall refer for any particulars that are not again ftated in the above Table.

By the new law, it was enacted, That when the price of the quarter of wheat fhould be at, or above 44s. ; rye, peafe, or beans, 28s. ; barley, beer or bigg, 22s. ; and oats, 14s. no perfon fhould tranfport, or carry out of the kingdom, any fuch corn or grain, under penalties.

That, after the 1ft day of January 1774, the bounties formerly allowed, by law, upon corn exported, were to ceafe; and inftead and in lieu thereof, when the prices of corn and grain fhould be under the rates aftermentioned, at the ports

Table of the Exportation Prices and Bounties, by the New Law.	Prices.			Bounties.		
	£.	s.	d.	£.	s.	d.
Upon every quarter of wheat, or malt of wheat, when the price is under ———— ————	2	4	0	0	5	0
rye, when the price is under	1	8	0	0	3	0
barley, beer, or bigg, or malt made thereof, when the price is under ————	1	2	0	0	2	6
oats, when the price is under ————	0	14	0	0	2	0
And for every quarter of oat-meal, confisting of 276 pounds, avoirdupois	0	0	0	0	2	6

1773.

and places in this kingdom, from whence the fame fhould be
fhipped, there fhould be allowed upon the exportation of fuch
corn or grain, either ground or unground, being the growth
of this kingdom, and put on board in Britifh fhipping, the
mafter, and at leaft two thirds of the mariners, of fuch fhips,
being his Majefty's fubjects, the following bounties, that is
to fay, when the price of middling Britifh wheat, per quarter,
fhould be under 44s. there fhould be paid a bounty, for every
quarter of wheat, or malt made of wheat, 5s. ; when the quarter of rye was under 28s. a bounty of 3s.; when the quarter
of barley, beer, or bigg, fhould be under 22s. a bounty, for
every quarter of thefe, or of malt made of them, of 2s.
6d. ; and when the quarter of oats fhould be under 14s. a
bounty of 2s. upon every quarter of oats, and 2s. 6d. upon every quarter of oat-meal, confifting of 276 pounds, avoirdupois *.

* By the act 1751, the fame bounty is allowed upon 224 pounds weight of wheat

O.

CHAP. III.

By the old laws, the method of afcertaining the prices was left to the juftices of peace, at their quarter feffions; and it was, by the prefent law, continued for England in the fame way; but, for Scotland, it was committed to the fheriffs of the feveral counties, to afcertain the prices four times in the year; and to fend certificates thereof to the refpective cuftom-houfes within their jurifdictions, to be the rule of export and import, and for the payment of the bounties and duties.

1774.

But with refpect to exportation, thefe rules were now altered; and it was enacted, that the prices of corn and grain, and oatmeal, exported, fhould be regulated and governed by the average prices, at which fuch corn and grain, and oatmeal, fhould be refpectively fold in the public market, at or neareft to the port or place from whence fuch corn or grain, or oatmeal, fhould be intended to be exported, on the laft market day preceding the fhipping of fuch corn or grain, and the bounties payable accordingly.

The different principles and operations of the old laws, and of the new law, will be readily comprehended, on a comparifon of the ftatements exhibited in the above Tables; the old laws having been clearly made for the encouragement of agriculture, at home, and prohibiting the importation of fo-

---

meal, or other ground corn or grain, as was allowed for 4 bufhels of the fame fort of grain; fo that, by the one act, 276 pounds of meal, is declared to be a quarter; and, by the other, it requires 448 pounds.

reign grain, except in cafes of neceffity; and the new law, encouraging the importation of foreign grain, whether there be neceffity or not. For inftance, while the foreign farmer is permitted to import his flour into Great Britain, without any duty but a mere trifle, the bounty upon flour, or meal made from wheat, is repealed *.

Thus have we endeavoured to give a juft idea to the Public, of the old, and of the new fyftem of Corn Laws; for the law of 1773 muft be confidered as a new fyftem. The comparifon we have made, will, we truft, be found to be both accurately, and fairly ftated. We write for no topical or partial purpofes, nor for or againft any man, or fet of men. It is for the benefit of the public, in general, that our agriculture fhould be reftored to its former efficiency; and that our children and manufacturers fhould be fed with the bread of our own lands. It is the only bread that can be eaten in plenty, and with fafety; for if we fhall be brought to depend upon the bread of foreign nations, our

* To facilitate the obfervation of the feveral laws, enumerated in this and the preceding chapter, and the duties and bounties payable in confequence, we have made up an abbreviation of them. *Vide Appendix, No 7.*

O 2

CHAP. III.

manufactures will foon be buried in the ruins of our agriculture*.

* The reader will be pleafed to recollect that this Inquiry was written, while the Corn Law of 1773 was in force; and it appears to have been a chief object in the author's view, in undertaking this Work, to fhew the impolicy of that law, and to induce Parliament to revert to the former fyftem.   Since that time, the Corn Law of 1791, by which all the former laws are repealed, has been enacted; and, on comparing it, in this manner, with the laws of 1670, 1688, and 1706, it will appear, that the legiflature have already, in fome degree, reverted to the old fyftem.   *Edit.*

CHAP. IV.

Recapitulation of the principal heads of the several Corn Laws of Great Britain, and a deduction of principles from their effects.

CHAP. IV.

LIBERTY was given to export corn, upon payment of cuf-toms and fufidies.   1393.

Which law was confirmed; referving power to the King and council to reftrain exportation, when they fhould judge that to be neceffaay.   1425.

Liberty was given to export corn, when the prices at home did not exceed certain rates.   1436.

Which law was this year continued for ten years.   1442.

And was now made perpetual.   1444.

From the grievous damage fuffered by the farmers and oc-cupiers of land, by the importation of foreign grains, all im-   1463.

CHAP. IV. portation was prohibited, until the prices at home exceeded certain rates.

Thefe form the true foundation of the corn laws. All importation of foreign grain was prohibited, until the prices were high at home; and the exportation of our own grain was allowed, when the crop was abundant, and the prices reafonable; referving power to the King and council, at any time, to put a ftop to exportation, when they fhould judge that to be neceffary for the good of the kingdom at large. And the above act of 1463, is the firft act made in England to prohibit, or regulate, the importation of foreign grain.

1552.   But the beneficial purpofes of the former laws were loft for want of execution; and the fyftem was totally overturned by a law of this year, which, in effect, prohibited all kind of trade in corn, until the prices were far below the expence of raifing it.

1554.   Which law was enforced by another act of this year.

1562.   Exportation was again allowed, when the prices were higher than thofe limited by the acts 1552 and 1554, provided the grain was carried abroad in fhips owned by Englifh born fubjects. This was the dawn of the Navigation Laws.

1570.   Exportation was allowed, without limitation of prices, out of fuch ports and creeks, where had been placed a cuftomer, or collector of the fubfidy of tonnage and poundage, to any part beyond feas, in amity with England, when not reftrained by proclamation; providing the exportation was made in fhips owned by Englifh born fubjects, and refiding in the Englifh dominions, at fuch times as the feveral prices of grain fhould be fo reafonable and moderate, where fuch exportation fhould be intended, as that no prohibition fhould be made by the Queen's proclamation, or by the prefidents of the North, or of Wales, within their feveral jurifdictions; or of the juftices of affize, at their feffions, in other fhires out of the jurifdiction of the faid two prefidents and councils; or by the major part of the juftices of peace of the county, at their quarter feffions, as follows.

Thefe feveral magiftrates were to have yearly conference with the inhabitants of the county, about the cheapnefs or dearth of the feveral forts of grain within their refpective jurifdictions; and fhould, by their difcretion, determine whether it would be meet, at any time, to prevent any grain to be carried out of the realm, by any port within their jurifdictions or limits; and fhould, by a writing under their hands and feals, make a determination, either for permiffion or prohibition, and fhould caufe the fame be publifhed by the fheriffs of the feveral counties; which was to continue in force until the fame fhould be altered by the faid prefidents and councils, or other powers refpectively; except the fame fhould, in the meantime, be countermanded by the Queen, her heirs or fucceffors; or by fome order of the juftices of peace, in the counties fituated out of the jurifdiction of the faid two councils, in their quarter feffions to be holden in the meantime, or the greateft part of them, fhould find the determination of the juftices of affize to be hurtful to the country, by means of dearth, or to be a great hindrance to tillage, by means of extreme cheapnefs; which determination was, in like manner, to be publifhed, and to continue in force until a new regulation fhould be made; except the fame fhould, in the meantime, be altered by the Queen, her heirs or fucceffors: provided always, that thefe prefidents, &c. fhould not publifh their determinations, until the fame was firft notified to, and approved by, the Queen, or her privy council, and that the cuftom or poundage fhould be paid upon exportation: provided alfo, that the Queen, her heirs and fucceffors, might, at all times, by proclamation, prohibit exportation, either generally from all parts of the realm, or from particular parts only.

1593.

The exportation prices were confiderably encreafed, but the duties payable upon grain, exported by force of the ftatute, was doubled; and an unlimited importation having been permitted, the law was thereby rendered nugatory, and the price of grain continued at an extravagant height.

1604.

The exportation prices were confiderably encreafed, provided the grain was carried abroad in fhips owned by Englifh born fubjects; and referving to the King, his heirs and fucceffors, by proclamation, to reftrain exportation from the realm generally, or from particular places; but exportation having been ftill, by this law, loaded with duties, the full operation of the act muft have been retarded.

The exportation prices were ftill farther extended, under the fame terms with the former law; but the duties upon exportation having been ftill kept up, the law could not have its proper effect; and it would appear that it had been made entirely for an extenfion of the revenue.

And it was this year renewed in the very fame terms.

This year the exportation prices were ftill extended; but the duties were raifed fo high, as to be equal to a prohibition. Importation was alfo allowed; but the duties, in like manner, amounted to a prohibition.

The exportation prices were ftill extended, but the duties were continued; and, by the infertion of the word *not* in the importation claufe, full liberty was given to import foreign grain, when the prices, at home, were at the loweft or cheapeft rate, upon payment of lower duties, than the low duties fixed by the act of tonnage and poundage.

By a law of Scotland, of this fame year, the powers of exportation were extended, referving to the King and privy council, to reftrict or to prohibit it, when they fhould judge it neceffary; but a duty of 40 *per cent. ad valorem*, was laid upon grain, imported, when the prices did not exceed the export prices; with power to the King and council to remit the duties, if the prices fhould rife.

This year the Scotch parliament removed all duties upon

P

exportation, except a mere trifle of about a penny per boll; and they authorifed the privy council to determine the prices, from time to time, according to which every perfon was to have liberty to export corn, of all kinds, unlefs prohibited by proclamation.

1670.

The prices of grain, for exportation, were ftill extended, but the duties laid on by the act of tonnage and poundage, amounted to a prohibition; and heavy duties were laid upon corn imported, when the prices did not exceed certain rates; but no rule having been laid down, by this law, for afcertaining the prices, importation was ftill carried on at the former low duties.

1685.

This defect was attempted to be remedied; and, in England, it was remitted to the juftices of peace, in the feveral counties where foreign grain might be imported, at their quarter feffions, after Michaelmas and Eafter, by the oaths of two or more fubftantial perfons, being neither merchants nor factors for the importation of corn, nor any wife concerned or interefted in the corn to be imported, and each having a free eftate of L. 20 *per annum*, or a leafehold eftate of L. 50 *per annum*, to determine the prices of the feveral kinds of grain, which they were to certify to the chief officer of the cuftoms, in the feveral counties, for his rule.

In Scotland the importation of victual from Ireland had been prohibited, under fevere penalties; referving to the Lords

of the privy council power to remove the prohibition when
the prices rofe to a certain extent.

This year, a total prohibition was made; and fuch grain as   1686.
fhould be imported from Ireland, was ordered to be deftroyed.

Exportation was permitted from England, when the prices   1688.
at home did not exceed certain rates, providing it was made
in Englifh fhipping, whereof the mafter, and at leaft two thirds
of the mariners, were Englifh fubjects; and upon the exporter
producing a certificate, under his hand, of the quantity of
corn fhipped, to the collector of the cuftoms at the port where
the corn had been fhipped, and proving the faid certificate
by the oaths of one or more credible perfons; and, upon
bond, that the faid corn fhould be exported to parts beyond
feas, and not again relanded, the exporter fhould receive a
bounty; and producing a certificate, under the common feal
of the chief magiftrate, in any places beyond feas, or under
the hands and feals of two known Englifh merchants, that
fuch corn had been actually landed; or, upon proof, by credible perfons, that fuch corn had been taken by enemies, or
perifhed in the feas, the exporter's bond was to be delivered
up; and the money, paid by the collector or commiffioner of
the cuftoms, was to pafs in his account.

This act was followed in Scotland.   All export duties were   1695.
taken off; and a bounty was granted upon corn exported,
when the prices did not exceed certain rates; provided the
exportation was made in Scotch fhips, and by Scotfmen, and

P 2

that the mafter and three-fourths of the feamen fhould be Scotfmen ; but referving power to the Lords of the fecret council, when the prices exceeded the rates fixed, to difcharge exportation.

1700.

And in England, this year, the fubfidy, and all other duties payable upon grain exported, whether ground or unground, were totally given up, and taken away.

1706.

By the articles of Union, the fame bounties granted upon grain, exported from England, by the above act 1688, were extended to grain exported from Scotland ; and bounties were alfo given for oatmeal, and for beer or bigg, exported from either kingdom.

1729.

The juftices of peace, in many places, having neglected to determine the prices of grain, whereby the duties upon corn, imported, was to be regulated, it was again recommended to them to do it, in time coming, as directed by the act 1670 ; and if they fhould omit or neglect to do fo, the collector of the cuftoms, at the refpective places of importation, were empowered to demand and receive the duties, according to the loweft price of the feveral forts of grain mentioned in the faid act 1670. And, in order to afcertain the quantity of grain fhipped, for which bounty was allowed, the officers of the cuftoms were appointed to admeafure the fame.

1732.

Still, however, neglects had been made in determining the prices of grain, according to which, the duties payable upon importation, were to be levied ; and therefore, *for better afcer-taining the fame, and preventing fraudulent importation*, it was now again recommended to the juftices of peace, at their quarter feffions, in the feveral counties where grain might be imported, to give in charge, in the open court, to the grand jury, to make inquiry and prefentment, upon their oaths, of the corn-market price of middling Englifh corn and grain ; which prefentment fhould be certified by the faid juftices, in writing, to the chief officer or collector of the cuftoms, at the port or place where importation fhould be made, and fhould be hung up in fome public place in the cuftom-houfe, for gene-ral information ; and that the duty upon foreign grain, im-ported, fhould be collected and paid according to the prices contained in fuch certificate. And, after importation, no fo-reign corn or grain was to be exported, or in any fhape laden on fhip board, or put to fea, for tranfporting it from one port of the kingdom to another, either by itfelf, or mixed with Englifh grain, under fevere penalties.

To reprefs mobbifh diforders, and lawlefs attempts, to inter-rupt the free exportation of grain, when the fame is encou-raged by law, the inhabitants of the hundred in which fuch offences were committed, were fubjected to the damages.

In Scotland, the power of fufpending the laws which pro-hibited the importation of foreign grain, having been formerly vefted in the Privy council of that kingdom, was now con-veyed to the Courts of Seffion, Exchequer, and Jufticiary ; and the judges of thefe courts were, according to the prices of grain in the county of Edinburgh, to determine whether exportation or importation should take place. By the same law the duties payable, in England, by the act of the 22d Charles II. were to be paid upon the importation of grain into Scotland; and the whole clauses and provisions of that act, and of the 2d George II. entitled, An act to ascertain the custom payable for corn imported, were extended to Scotland.

1751.

To obviate some difficulties anent the admeasurement of wheat meal, and other ground corn, whereon a bounty was payable, upon exportation, the officers of the customs were empowered to allow the same bounties upon the exportation of 224 pound weight of wheat meal, or other ground corn or grain, as was allowed for four bushels of the same sort of grain; and for the better expediting the business, they were allowed to make choice of two sacks out of twenty, and from thence to compute the weight.

1753.

Debentures for the bounty upon corn exported, when not paid within six months, were to carry interest at the rate of 3 *per cent. per annum.*

1757.

Exportation having been prohibited, by law, for a limited time, power was reserved to the King to take off the prohibition, by proclamation, and to allow all persons, natives or foreigners, (but no particular person or persons), to export grain.

1773.

The exportation prices of grain were altered and brought

down; the prices for importation were alfo brought down; CHAP. IV.
and the duties upon importation were reduced to a trifle.

The rules for afcertaining the prices of grain, in England, were left with the juftices of peace; but, in Scotland, they were taken from the fuperior courts, and committed to the fheriffs of the feveral counties.

The rules for exportation of grain were totally altered; 1774. and it was enacted, that the prices of corn, grain, and oatmeal, exported, fhould be regulated and governed by the average prices, at which fuch corn, grain, and oatmeal, fhould be refpectively fold in the public market, at or neareft to the port of fhipping, on the laft market day preceding fuch fhipping.

We have now recapitulated the principal or leading features of the feveral corn laws that have ever been enacted in England and Scotland, or in Great Britain, fince the acceffion of William I. of England, and Malcolm III. of Scotland; and upon the whole it would appear, that the chief outlines, or foundation of them, was laid down by the Englifh laws of 1393, and 1463, and the four intervening acts. Thefe indeed laid fubfidies and duties upon grain exported, which in thofe days, when commerce was in its infancy, were indifcriminately laid upon every article, whether exported or imported; and fuch is the power of habit, that the duties were continued to a very late period. The experience of 300 years at length not only detected this error, but pointed out to a diftinguifhing adminiftration, the beneficial confequences that would follow the oppofite conduct of giving bounties upon corn exported. From which it appears, that the doctrine inculcated by experience, is unqueftionably orthodox, although flow in its operation; for the duties and fubfidies, payable upon the exportation of the manufactures of Great Britain, were only removed in the year 1721 *.

No records have been preferved, refpecting the exportation and importation of corn, prior to the year 1697; or, probably the act 1688 not having removed the fubfidies and duties payable upon grain exported, little or no bufinefs of that kind had been carried on; befides, the feafons from 1690 to 1700 were, in general, very unfruitful; and agriculture not having yet become vigorous, there was probably little corn to fpare.

The average price of the quarter of wheat, from 1690 to 1700, was L. 2 : 16 : 10, equal to L. 3 : 8 : 3 of prefent money. We find, however, that during the four years from 1697 to 1700 inclufive, the exportation of the feveral kinds of grain amounted to 331,223 quarters, while the importation amounted to only 8,948 quarters †.

Upon the removal of the fubfidies and duties, payable upon the exportation of grain, in the year 1700, the feafons alfo

---

* 8 Geo. 1. c. 15. § 7.

† Vide, Appendix, No 2

having become more favourable, the face of affairs was entirely
changed; and a certain market having been opened by the
bounties, for grain in all feafons, the implements of hufbandry
were feized upon with avidity; and, from that period, the
diligence and emulation of our farmers, were rewarded by en-
creafing fuccefs.

During the ten years, from 1701 to 1710 inclufive, the average yearly exportation amounted to 248,945 quarters, while
the average importation came only to 442 quarters; and the
average price of the quarter of wheat fell to L. 2 : 3 : 2, equal
to L. 2 : 11 : 10 of prefent money. In one of thefe years (1709)
above half a million of quarters; and during thefe ten years
no lefs than 2,849,446 quarters were exported, and only 4,442
quarters imported.

The money, brought into the kingdom by this large exportation, enabled the farmers to extend their operations; and
we accordingly find that for the ten years, from 1711 to 1720
inclufive, the average yearly exportation had rifen to 449,193
quarters; the average yearly importation was only 71 quarters; and the average price of the quarter of wheat continued
comparatively low, having been only L. 2 : 4 : 10$\frac{1}{7}$ per quarter.

The exportation of thefe ten years had nearly doubled that
of the former ten years, having amounted to 4,491,933 quarters, while only 714 quarters had been imported.

It may be afferted, that we had now above 53,000 more

Q

people employed in hufbandry, than had been at any time before this period * ; and the yearly exportation of the grain had given employment for 90,000 tons of fhipping, and a proportional number of failors, for one voyage †.

Of the ten years from 1721 to 1730 inclufive, two of thefe years had carried fhorter crops than ufual ; and, upon a fmall ftart of the prices, the importers, always watchful of their intereft, however hurtful it might be to the country, introduced confiderable quantities of foreign grain to the kingdom, in the years 1728, 1729, and 1730, without payment of the duties ; upon the old pretext, that the juftices of peace had not fixed the prices of grain, according to which the duties were to be levied.

Our exportation, however, kept up nearly to that of the preceding ten years ; but the importation of foreign grain was greatly increafed, and the price of wheat continued nearly the fame it had been for twenty years paft ; the average price of it having been L. 2 : 2s. per quarter. There were in all exported, during thefe ten years, 4,479,683 quarters ; and there were imported 732,692 quarters of the feveral kinds of grain.

The act 1729 having given a check to the importation of

* Reckoning twelve people, old and young, to be employed in raifing every hundred quarters of grain. Vide chap. 1. p. 19.

† A ton of wheat, in London, commonly weighs between 2200 and 2500 lbs avoirdupois ; rye, between 2100 and 2240 ; and barley, between 1709 and 1800 lbs avoirdupois. Five quarters are commonly reckoned to a ton, in freight.

P. fllethwaite's *Dict. of Trade and Commerce,* art. *England.*

foreign grain, our agriculture again got forward, and the average yearly exportation, for the ten years from 1731 to 1740 inclufive, got up to 549,447 quarters, while the average importation amounted only to 4,690; and the average price of wheat fell to L. 1 : 17 : 6 per quarter.

There were in all exported, during thefe ten years, 5,494,471 quarters; and there were imported only 46,909 quarters of the feveral kinds of grain.

Such was the fpirit of our farmers, when they were freed from the trammels of prohibitory and improper laws, that for the ten years, from 1741 to 1750 inclufive, the average yearly amount of our exportation, rofe to the amazing quantity of 848,660 quarters; the importation amounted only to 15,193 quarters; and the average price of wheat fell to L. 1 : 13 : 8 per quarter.

At this time there muft have been above 100,000 people more employed in agriculture, in Great Britain, than there were at the time of the Union, to raife this excrefcent flock of grain, the exportation of which would employ about 170,000 tons of fhipping, for one voyage *.

Where then can be the neceflity of importing foreign grain, when, with proper laws, upon the chance of a foreign fale *only*, we have raifed, upon an average of many years, a quantity of corn, over our home confumption, equal to maintain

* Vide Notes, p. 122.

Q 2

near 450,000 people ; and, in fome particular years, quanti-ties equal to maintain near double that number ?

In the year 1748 there were exported 1,123,953 quarters ; in 1749 there were 1,250,306 quarters ; and, in 1750, the immenfe quantity of 1,667,778 quarters were exported. There were exported, in all, during thefe ten years, no lefs than 8,486,602 quarters ; and there were only imported 159,437 quarters of the feveral kinds of grain.

Is it not clear from hence, that Great Britain, under proper laws, is capable to increafe her growth of corn, to any degree for which demand can be obtained ; and that, as her quantity increafes, the prices, at home, fall, and come to be, one year with another, nearly equal ?

The direct contrary ftate may be expected from improper laws ; and, indeed, will be woefully proved from the effects of the later laws, which have checked exportation, and facili-tated importation.

During that profperous period of agriculture, a labourer or manufacturer, and every other perfon, had the bread of every one of his family at leaft 20s. in the year cheaper, than in the prefent days *.

For the ten years from 1751 to 1760 inclufive, our exporta-

* Written in the year 1786.—Vide Exp. Table, Appendix, No 8. Art. 7.

tions fell, upon an average, to 582,837 quarters; the importation was, upon an average, 37,397 quarters; and the average price of wheat rofe to L. 2 : 2 : 6 per quarter.

This was entirely owing to the failure of the crops 1756 and 1757; particularly the former, which yielded far lefs corn than any crop fince the commencement of the century. Inftead therefore of continuing an exportation of 848,660 quarters of corn, which was the average of the ten years from 1741 to 1750, or even 815,943 quarters, the average of the exportation of the five years immediately preceding, there was an importation, in the year 1757, of 167,301 quarters, and there were only 80,656 quarters, chiefly of malt, exported; fo that there was a deficiency of this crop, compared with the average of the fifteen preceding crops, of near 700,000 quarters of grain.

Here we have a frefh and a feparate proof, of the immenfe benefit arifing to a nation, in the practice of raifing more grain than it confumes; for if, in the year 1757, which depended upon the crop 1756, Great Britain had been accuftomed to be fupplied but in a fmall degree with foreign grain, this additional demand of 700,000 quarters, muft have brought on famine, or muft have raifed the prices fo high, as to have bordered upon famine; yet, by the profperous ftate of agriculture, and the accuftomed exertion of the farmers, although there was little to export, there was nearly a fufficiency to ferve the inhabitants; the importation having exceeded the exportation only about 87,000 quarters; the price of wheat in 1757 advanced only to L. 3; and, in 1758, it fell to L. 2 : 10s. per quarter.

But we have now finifhed the bright fide of the picture. In the year 1763 the great importation of foreign grain was begun, and it has been continued ever fince. The importation of 1763 and 1764 were chiefly oats; but, in 1765, there were imported 218,031 quarters of foreign grain, of different kinds, chiefly wheat, while our exportation of the feveral kinds of grain amounted to no lefs than 457,730 quarters; and it is not eafy to find out a good reafon for permitting fo large an importation of foreign grain, when we had fo much corn of our own to fpare. But the importers were, by degrees, juftling our farmers out of the market; and, in the year 1767, the immenfe quantity of 907,420 quarters of foreign grain were brought in, of which about 500,000 quarters were wheat; and upon the average of the twelve years from 1761 to 1772 inclufive, our yearly exportation had fallen to 370,703 quarters; the yearly importation had rifen to 251,279 quarters; and the average price of wheat amounted to L. 2 : 7 : 10 per quarter.

Here we muft make a paufe, to give place to the act 1773; an act entitled, ' An act for regulating the importation and ' exportation of corn.' But to carry the fpirit of this law into its title, it ought to have been called, An act to facilitate the importation of foreign corn into Great Britain, and to re-ftrain the exportation of corn the growth of that kingdom;

for fuch it certainly is, and its operations have juftified the title, which it ought to have affumed.

In the year 1774, there were imported, under the fanction of this law, no lefs than 926,174 quarters of foreign grain, about a third part of which was wheat, and wheat flour; while our exportation was no higher than 51,099 quarters. In 1775 the amazing quantity of 1,163,407 quarters of foreign grain was imported, the one half of which was wheat, and wheat flour, while our exportation amounted only to 191,007 quarters; and, upon the whole, during the twelve years from 1773 to 1784 inclufive, the average yearly importation rofe to 578,358 quarters, and our exportation fell to 267,182 quarters; and the average price of wheat continued as high as L. 2 : 5 : 1 per quarter; and for the laft four years the average price of the quarter was L. 2 : 8 : 6.

There were imported, during thefe twelve years, no lefs than 6,940,293 quarters of foreign grain; and only 3,206,184 quarters of our own grain exported: A melancholy reverfe of circumftances fince the commencement of the year 1763.

Thefe particulars will be more readily obferved, from a fcale of the yearly prices and averages of wheat, and of the general exportation and importation of grain, from the year 1697, to the year 1784 inclufive; from which it is evident, that the prices of grain fell gradually, as our exportation took place, and rofe again as our exportation decreafed; and propor-

 tionally as the importation of foreign grain came to be per‑
mitted *.

There muſt be ſomething very ſeductive, or very profitable, in the importation of foreign grain ; for all the laws, that hi‑
therto have been made to prevent it, have been evaded ; and yet, except the importer, it is clearly againſt the intereſt of every other perſon in the kingdom : for it is deſtructive of our own agriculture, and we have ſeen, from certain evidence, that it raiſes the price of grain upon the conſumer.

We have alſo learned, from the experience of paſt times, that no laws, nor any dictates of human authority, can oblige people to cultivate the lands, to build houſes of huſbandry, or to labour in that, or any other vocation, by which they can‑
not earn a reaſonable ſubſiſtence.

In many other countries, where the ſoil and climate are more favourable, and the productions of the earth more eaſily reared, but the government deſpotic, it is with indifference, that the inhabitants, in general, cultivate the lands, and even ſee the convulſions of the ſtate ; they have no ſhare in the government, and a change of maſters does not alter their con‑
dition ; but, in Great Britain, where more induſtry may be neceſſary, labour is ſweetened by freedom, and nothing but improper laws will check the ſpirit of the people.

* Vide Appendix, No 4.

While the ancient laws laid the country open to the importation of foreign grain, by injudicious duties, or reſtrictions, upon our own produce, our farmers were diſpirited; a great part of the ſoil lay without culture; the price of grain was conſequently high; and population was reſtrained.

When the reſtrictions were not only removed, but bounties given upon the exportation of our excreſcent ſtock, by the acts of 1688 and 1700, the happieſt effects were immediately experienced: theſe laws acted like magic; our agriculture immediately roſe as from the dead; population increaſed; and, inſtead of eating the bread of foreign nations, we not only maintained all our own people, at a lower rate than was ever known before, and conſiderably lower than at preſent (1786) but the kingdom received an immediate addition of riches and ſtrength, from the money brought in, from the increaſe of ſhipping, and from the people employed in raiſing and exporting the ſurplus of our produce: A ſtate of proſperity which continued, without interruption, for above half a century after the Union.

No ſooner was importation again encouraged, than our agriculture languiſhed; our exportation declined; the prices of grain roſe; and we have the mortification to receive, and poſſibly now to need, an immenſe importation of foreign grain every year.

Next to agriculture, the woollen trade may be conſidered to be the chief manufacture of Great Britain; and is protected by the moſt anxious laws, to prevent the competition of foreigners with our manufacturers at home: yet, if by some fabricated terror, or other arts of designing men, a persuasion should go forth, contrary to fact, that our own manufacturers could not clothe the people, the legislature might, for similar reasons, be induced to permit the importation of foreign cloth: Or, if by mistakes or inaccuracies in the laws, made for this purpose, or by a failure in the execution of them (all which have happened with respect to corn) foreign woollen cloth should be introduced to the kingdom, at a price below that for which our own manufacturers could afford to sell cloth of the same quality, we should soon stand in real need of foreign cloth, from the check given to our own industry, and from the number of manufacturers, that, in the mean time, would be ruined and dispersed.

This case is perfectly applicable to the Corn trade. Great Britain is certainly capable to maintain, from the produce of her own lands, an immense number of more people than have ever existed in it; but there are several nations around her, in Europe, and extensive countries in America, where neither the rent of the lands, nor the expence of raising corn, are so high as in Great Britain.

Several of the nations, in Europe, have adopted the wise laws of our King William III. by giving bounties upon the exportation of this excrescent stock of grain. And, from mistakes, or other failings of our laws, these nations have been permitted to introduce their corn into Great Britain, and to dispute the market at home with our own farmers.

By thefe means many of our fmaller farmers have been ruined, and their families difperfed; and whenever country people are driven from their ordinary employment, and habitations; to the trading or manufacturing towns, without any other means of fubfiftence than bodily labour, they foon melt away, and are loft to the community.

To vouch thefe obfervations, we have only to look around us, and obferve the immenfe increafe of the poors' rates, and the vaft quantity of landed property which has been brought to market, and fold under its former value, within thefe twelve or fourteen years paft*. And nothing but the great capitals, and the uncommon and continued exertion of many of our farmers, could have poffibly kept the agriculture of Great Britain in any fhape afloat, under the preffure of fo many difcouraging laws.

Perhaps no better laws can be made than thofe of 1688, and 1700, refpecting exportation; and thofe of 1670, and 1732, refpecting importation: although much more vigour and care, than have been hitherto exercifed, feem to be neceffary for the execution of them.

The former of thofe laws not only relinquifhed all fubfidies and duties payable upon corn exported, but granted a liberal bounty upon the exportation of wheat, when the price did not exceed 48s. the quarter, which was equal to L. 2 : 17 : 7

---

* This alludes to the period preceding the year 1786.

R 2

of prefent money, and upon other grain in proportion ; and they took no notice of foreign grain to be imported, as that was confidered to have been fufficiently guarded againft by the law of 1670, by which no importation could take place until the prices at home were confiderably higher, than thofe to which the bounties upon exportation were limited.

The bounty upon the exportation of wheat, afterwards extended to wheat flour, and malt made of wheat, was continued until the price, at home, rofe to L. 2 : 8s. equal to L. 2 : 17 : 7 of prefent money ; but, by the act 1670, if wheat was imported, when the price, at home, did not exceed L. 2 : 13 : 4, equal to L. 3 : 4s. of prefent money, it was loaded with a duty equal to a prohibition ; and this duty was only lowered as the prices rofe at home.

The bounty upon the exportation of rye was continued until the price, at home, rofe.to L. 1 : 12s. equal to L. 1 : 18 : 5 of prefent money ; and, by the above act of 1670, if rye, peafe, or beans, were imported, when the price, at home, did not exceed L. 2, equal to L. 2 : 8s. of prefent money, the duties, in like manner, were equal to a prohibition ; but were lowered as the prices rofe.

The bounty upon the exportation of barley and malt, afterwards extended to beer or bigg, was continued until the price, at home, amounted to L. 1 : 4s. equal to L. 1 : 8 : 9 of prefent money ; and, by the act 1670, if barley, malt, or buck wheat, were imported, before the price exceeded L. 1 : 12s.

equal to L. 1 : 18 : 5 of prefent money, the duties were equal to a prohibition ; but were lowered as the price at home rofe.

The bounty upon the exportation of oatmeal, was continued until the price of oats, at home, rofe to 15s. equal to 18s. of prefent money ; but, if oats were imported before the price came to 16s. equal to 19s. 2d. of prefent money, the duty was equal to a prohibition ; but was leffened when the prices rofe. Thefe and other fuch circumftances, will be readily feen from the abbreviation of the exportation and importation laws*.

Thofe laws were ftrongly inforced by the act 1732, made to prevent the fraudulent importation of foreign grain, by which corn or grain, once imported, was prohibited to be again fhipped, to be re-exported ; or to be carried coaftways, from one port to another, under fevere penalties. It would appear, from this law, that difcoveries had been made, that, under various pretences, corn imported, had been carried on fhipboard to other places, and from thence exported, and the bounty paid for it, as if fuch corn had been of Britifh growth; and, from fome late publications, it would appear that this practice has not yet fallen into difufe.

The beneficial confequences to the kingdom, which thefe wife laws brought about, have already appeared; and it is difficult, even for the imagination, to fancy any reafon for reverfing them, except the mifreprefentations of interefted and defigning men.

* Vide Appendix, No 7.

CHAP. IV.

The melancholy reverfe, occafioned by the act 1773, has however taken place, and we have feen the miferable confequences of it; a ftriking evidence that people may be wearied of the beft fituations, and even cloyed with happinefs.

It is impoffible to imagine that the legiflature had any intention to injure the beft interefts of the kingdom by this act; and, perhaps, there is not a worthier character in it, than the very man to whofe lot it fell to frame this law—*fed humanum eft errare* *.

The law, however, has had its effect; exportation has been reftrained, and agriculture of courfe repreffed; importation has been facilitated, and the trade laid open to fraud, by permitting the re-exporting, and carrying coaftways, from one port to another, grain imported.

For fifty-five years after the Union, our exportation of grain counted as 1 to 21 of our produce; and the yearly average of the importation of grain, during that period, amounted only to a 475th part of our produce †; and a great part of that importation was clandeftinely brought in upon us, without neceffity, and contrary to law. The ten years, from 1741 to 1750 inclufive, were the moft profperous. During that period our

---

* The perfon here alluded to is probably Governor Pownall, who, in 1773, laid a Memoir before the Lords Commiffioners of the Treafury, relative to the Corn Laws, and may have been employed to frame this act. Mr Arthur Young gives a copy of that Memoir, and fome able Strictures on the act of 1773, in his Political Arithmetic, publifhed in 1774. *Edit.*

† Vide Appendix, No 3. Art. 5.

yearly average exportation amounted to 848,660 quarters, and the yearly importation only to 15,943 quarters; so that our exportation was as 1 to 14, and the importation only as 1 to 742 of our produce *.

But these were our halcyon days, and we have seen the melancholy reverse.

During the twelve years from 1773 to 1784 inclusive, there were imported of foreign grain, upon an average yearly, 578,358 quarters, and our exportation amounted only to 267,182 quarters; so that the importation has encreased to the proportion of 1 to 18, while our exportation is reduced to that of 1 to 40 of the produce; and the balance of importation against us amounts yearly to 311,176 quarters †.

In the year 1775, there were imported no less than 1,163,407 quarters of foreign grain, and only 191,007 quarters of our own grain exported, which brought the importation, that year, as high as 1 to 8 of the produce, and the exportation fell as low as 1 to 53 ‡.

It is a hazardous situation, to be dependent upon the production of the lands of other nations for our bread, one day in every week; and it is a drain, which even the power and riches of Great Britain cannot long supply.

* Vide Appendix, No 4.; and No 8. Art. 5.
† Ibid.
‡ Vide Appendix, No 2.; and No 8. Art. 5.

Importation of foreign grain, acts like a mole under ground; we know nothing of its operations, but by the heaps which it raifes; and when thefe heaps come to cover an 8th, an 18th, or even a 475th part of our own foil, it is high time to turn them down.

In whatever point of view we confider this act, it has every appearance of having been furreptitioufly obtained, or having been what is commonly called a job; and certainly great muft have been the addrefs, on the part of the fuitors, and no lefs the fupinenefs on the part of adminiftration, when fuch a meafure was carried into effect.

In all cafes of commerce, and more particularly in thofe where the beft interefts of the kingdom are concerned, the trade ought to be put upon a footing as folid and permanent as poffible.

The former laws appointed the exportation and importation of grain, upon which bounties or duties were payable, to be regulated according to the prices, at the refpective places of exportation or importation; and, in England, it had been committed to the juftices of peace at their quarter feffions; and, in Scotland, to the Courts of Seffion, Jufticiary, and Exchequer, to afcertain the prices.

By the act 1773, the prices of grain, in England, were left to be fixed by the former rules; but, in Scotland, thefe powers were taken from the fuperior courts, and vefted in the fheriffs

of the feveral counties, and their fubftitutes, who were ap-
pointed to take proof of the price of grain within their feveral jurifdictions, four times in the year, which was to be the
rule both for exportation and importation from, and to, the
harbours within the feveral counties.

But there was no compulfory claufe in this act to oblige
either the juftices of the peace in England, or the fheriffs in
Scotland, to execute this part of their duty; and an incongruity
occurred, from which, indeed, the former laws were not free,
that many of the counties, upon the fea coaft, both in England and Scotland, were divided by the ftream of a river falling into the fea, the mouth of which formed a harbour for
both counties; fo that if the prices of grain in fuch adjoining
counties differed, exportation might be going on upon the one
fide of the river, and importation upon the other.

Still, however, the jobbers were not fatisfied; for the job
was not yet completed. Exportation, as well as importation,
was ftill limited from three months to three months, by which
their hands were fo far tied up.

Another law was therefore procured, in 1774, by which the
exportation of grain was appointed to be regulated, and the
bounties to be paid according to the prices at the neareft market-place to the port of exportation, on the laft market-day
preceding the time of fhipping; fo that, in the very time of
importation, a trader, who had a parcel of grain, upon hand,
which he could fell to more profit abroad than at home, could

S

eafily contrive a fale at the neareft market-place to entitle him to export his grain, and to receive the bounty ; and, confequently, exportation and importation may be going on at the fame time, and from the very fame fpot or creek. The impropriety, and inconfiftency of thefe rules, need no comment.

There is doubtlefs fome plaufibility in that part of the act of 1773, by which it would appear to mean, that if a trader imports corn to fupply the neceffities of the country, it would be hard not to allow him to re-export it, if he could not find a fale for it in the country ; and it would be ftill a greater hardfhip upon him, after having fupplied the place of importation ; and alfo unjuft to the poor of other places, where the prices were high, not to allow the remainder to be tranfported, in fhipping, coaftways, to the places where it was fo much wanted. But this illufory pretence is totally exploded, by the fpirit and ftrong fenfe of the former laws, which tell the trader : You are at liberty to fupply the wants of any part of the kingdom, where fcarcity may happen to be, and which will be known from the prices of grain, while fuch fcarcity continues, upon payment of a certain duty, which will be lowered if the prices rife at home ; but you are not to hoard up quantities of imported grain, to be a check upon the fale of the next crop of our own lands ; nor will you be allowed to re-export fuch grain, if you cannot find your own price in the country ; becaufe that would be making a free port of the whole kingdom for grain, to the utter deftruction of our own agriculture ; neither will you be permitted to fend your imported grain coaftways, from one place to another ; for befides, that fuch a meafure would be

hurtful to the fale of our own grain, it would lay the trade
open to fraud, which fhould, at all times, be avoided ; and, if
you have no fuch temptation, you will conform yourfelf to
the true fpirit of the laws, and will import no more than will
fupply the neceffities of the place to which your importation
is directed : Nor will you be allowed to import the flour or
meal of any grain ; for although we may fometimes ftand in
need of corn, we can at no time ftand in need of mills.

Thefe appear clearly to have been the fentiments of our former legiflators, with refpect to the importation of foreign
grain ; for whatever fpecious arguments may be ufed in favour
of importation, for lowering the price of grain, in times of
fcarcity, the true principle to proceed upon, is, to prevent
fcarcity, by giving every poffible protection and encouragement to our own agriculture, which we have feen, from the
experience of more than half a century, is a certain way of
procuring plenty, at reafonable prices.

It has been already clearly evinced, that the importation of
foreign grain, has invariably raifed the prices at home ; nor is
it to be imagined, that an importer will let them down, if he
can keep them up ; for he has nothing in view but his own
profit.

In an unfruitful feafon, when deficient crops oblige our farmers to raife the prices, and thereby, in fome meafure, to put
the confumer upon fhort allowance, an importer purchafes
corn in a neighbouring country, where the feafon has been

more favourable, or where corn is raifed at lefs expence than in Great Britain; or where perhaps the country gives a bounty upon corn exported; and by bringing it over, duty free, he is enabled both to drive our farmers out of the market, and ftill to keep up the prices.

To confirm this affertion, we need only have recourfe to the evidence already before us, founded upon the experience of near a century; and we fhall fee, from the Table of the yearly general exportation and importation, and the yearly price of wheat, from 1697 to 1784, that the price came down gradually, as our exportation advanced, and rofe again as it declined, and as the importation of foreign grain took place *.

It cannot therefore be doubted, but that found policy fhould direct us, to lay fuch a duty upon foreign corn, imported, as will balance the advantages which the foreign farmers have over our own; that, if there muft be a competition, both parties may ftart equally at market; and, if there muft be high prices given, it is more for the intereft of the kingdom, in general, that they be paid for the produce of our own lands, than for that of other nations.

There may be, no doubt, fuch barren feafons, as may render a fupply of foreign corn abfolutely neceffary, to prevent famine; and in fuch events, powers ought to be vefted in the King in council, to leffen, or to fufpend altogether, the duties upon corn to be imported; but, in all other cafes, refpect-

---

* Vide Appendix, No 4.

ing importation, perhaps we cannot recur to a better rule than the act 1670. But to do this with propriety, will require great circumfpection and care. We are near the brink of a precipice, at the fame time that our retreat to a place of fafety, is not without hazard.

Upon the fuppofition that there are eight millions of people in Great Britain, whereof two millions and a half are farmers and cottagers, or people entirely employed in the bufinefs of manufacturing grain, and that the other five millions and a half fill up the other departments of the community; and, reckoning that two quarters of the different kinds of grain, overhead, are neceffary for the fupport of each perfon, the amount of the annual confumption, exclufive of the maintenance of the people employed in agriculture, is eleven millions of quarters*.

If we fhall fuppofe a year, in which Great Britain can juft maintain herfelf and fow the ground, without receiving or fending out any grain, the eleven millions of quarters would be the amount both of the confumption and of the produce, being the exact quantity raifed, after fuppporting the people and cattle employed in the manufacture; and the exact quantity neceffary for the other branches of the community.

But, in years when we export more than we import, our produce muft be greater than our confumption; and in years when we import more than we export, it muft be proportionally lefs.

* Vide Chap. I. Page 21. and Appendix, No 8. Art. 4.

	Quarters.
For the ten years from 1741 to 1750 inclusive, our exportation, at an average *, amounted yearly to	848,660
And deducting our yearly average importation of	15,943
There remained of clear yearly exportation -	832,717
To which being added our yearly consumption of	11,000,000
Thefe together made up our produce, amounting to	11,832,717

	Quarters.
In the other point of view we muft firft ftate our yearly confumption of - - -	11,000,000
And our average yearly exportation from 1773 to 1784 inclufive - - - -	267,182
Amounting together to - - -	11,267,182
And from thence deducting our average yearly importation - - - -	578,358
Our produce is reduced to - -	10,688,824

	Quarters.
Now, ftating again our produce, in the times of the profperity of agriculture, amounting to	11,832,717
And our prefent produce of - -	10,688,824

The difference is 1,143,893 quarters of grain lefs, raifed in Great Britain now, than formerly, which is about 1 to 9 of our prefent produce.

* The amount of the exports and imports, in this ftatement, will be feen in the Appendix, No. 4.

This amazing difference, allowing twelve people for raiſing every hundred quarters of grain, cuts off from Great Britain, the employment of 137,256 perſons, old and young, who would have been employed in raiſing this corn, and transfers the occupation and profit of the manufacture to the lands and people of other nations.

Had Great Britain kept this branch of buſineſs to herſelf, if we compute five quarters of the different kinds of grain over-head, to make a ton weight, the exportation of the grain would have afforded employment to 228,778 tons of ſhipping for one voyage *.

And, for the ſame voyage, allowing five mariners, young and old, for the navigation of every hundred tons, it would have given employment to 11,435 ſailors, beſides labourers and boatmen, in loading, piloting, &c.

And, if we ſhall ſuppoſe this voyage to take up only one eighth part of the year, this navigation would have been equal to the conſtant ſupport of above 1400 ſeamen, or to the manning of two ſhips of the line; all which, with many other beneficial conſequences, which would attend ſuch an extenſive branch of commerce, have been totally loſt to Great Britain.

It appears, by an extract from the Corn Regiſter, that, for

* Vide Note, p. 121.

CHAP. IV.

the fourteen years from 1771 to 1784 inclufive, the average prices of the quarter of the different kinds of grain, were as follows, viz.

		L.	s.	d.
The quarter of wheat	-	2	8	0
barley	-	1	3	8
oats	-	0	16	0
rye	-	1	10	3
beans	-	1	8	4

which makes the average price of the quarter of thefe different kinds of grain, over-head, to be   -   L. 1 9 3.

If Great Britain had continued, as formerly, to raife and export at the rate of 832,717 quarters of grain, fhe would have received, befides the advantages already ftated, for the price of the grain yearly   -   L. 1,217,848 12   8
But inftead of that receipt fhe has yearly
to pay for 311,176 quarters of foreign
grain imported, over the amount of all
her exportation, which comes to   -   455,094 18   0

Which makes a yearly balance againft Great
Britain of   -   -   L. 1,672,943 10   8

Thefe facts merit the moft ferious confideration *.

* In the fupplies for the year 1796, no lefs than a million Sterling is voted, to pay bounties on the importation of foreign grain. This fum, at the rate of feventeen

Having feen our average yearly produce brought to nearly twelve millions of quarters, when Great Britain enjoyed the export trade; and again reduced to little more than ten millions and a half, when that trade was loft; there can be nothing more clear than that the quantity of corn fown, will, at all times, be proportioned to the demand; and that, as our agriculture fhall be extended, the number of our people will be increafed.

It is, however, to be confidered, that we have now, for a confiderable period, been accuftomed to' receive a yearly importation of near 600,000 quarters of grain, or about an eighteenth part of our own provifion, from foreign countries; and if we fhall cut off or lofe that fupply, before our agriculture fhall be fo far extended, as to be fufficient to fupport the kingdom, at reafonable prices, without it, the fhock might be ruinous.

The great increafe of population in Great Britain, during the prefent century, would appear to have taken place chiefly from the year 1708 to 1763, when agriculture flourifhed, and when the great trade, of raifing and exporting corn, felt the

---

fhillings per quarter, being the average of the different rates of bounty for wheat, may produce an importation of 1,177,064 quarters; which, if reckoned to fell at L. 4 per quarter, would, together with the million for bounties, amount to L. 5,708,256; and although it may not be poffible to procure even half that quantity of wheat, yet, from the vigorous meafures taken to prevent dearth, the reft of the fum may be applied to the purchafe of other grain. Allowing that the odd feven hundred thoufand pounds may remain with our own merchants, as their profit; the drain of money, from Great Britain, for foreign grain may, and probably will, amount to *five* millions Sterling in one year! *Edit.*

T

fame protection and enjoyed a like fuccefs with our other manufactures. For, fince that time to the year 1784, emigration, colonization, and war, have drawn fo largely from the number of our inhabitants, that the alarming increafe of importation, in fo fhort a period as thefe twenty years, cannot be afcribed to an additional confumption, from advancing population; nor does it appear, that it can be entirely accounted for in a fatisfactory manner, by any other caufe, than the difcouragement occafioned by the change of fyftem in the Corn Laws, which has turned the induftry of the people, from the raifing of corn, to objects of lefs importance to the profperity of the kingdom.

From the refult of experience, during a period of feven hundred years, we have found, that the principles of the Corn Laws ought to be calculated to encourage the people to improve their lands, and to raife as much corn as the foil and climate will admit: An object which can only be attained, by fecuring a certain and fteady market to the farmer for his produce; not only by preventing importation, but alfo, whenever it fhall appear, from the moderate price of grain at home, that a greater quantity has been raifed, than is required for the annual fupply of the inhabitants, by giving fuch a bounty on exportation, as fhall enfure a ready vent for our excrefcent ftock in foreign countries. It is not enough that a nation raifes, in general, a fufficiency of corn for the confumption of its inhabitants: It muft be accuftomed to raife confiderably more, in order to afford plenty in bad feafons; and its annals ought be diftinguifhed by a greater or lesser *exportation* ; but, on no occasion, ought it be reduced to the necessity of *importation*, and having recourse to foreign countries, for an expensive and precarious relief.

In the course of this Inquiry, it has appeared, that those happy effects have been best promoted by the laws of 1670, 1688, 1706, and 1732 ; and, in order that the principles of those laws may be clearly understood, we shall exhibit a Table, shewing the prices, bounties, and duties, by which the Corn Trade was regulated, under the old system *.

* To enable the reader to compare these with the prices, bounties, and duties, by which the Corn Trade is *now* regulated, under the law of 1791, a similar Table of them is given along with that referred to by the Author.   *Edit.*

T 2

TABLE of the Prices, Bounties, and Duties, upon the Exportation and Importation of Grain, according to the Laws of 1670, 1688, and 1706.

Bounties per Quarter. Money of the time. £ s. d.	Present Money. £ s. d.	EXPORTATION.	Price of Grain per Quarter. Money of the time. £ s. d.	Present Money. £ s. d.	IMPORTATION.	Duties per Quarter. Money of the time. £ s. d.	Present Money. £ s. d.
		1. Wheat, Wheat Flour,	-	-	or Malt made of Wheat.		
0 5 0	0 6 0	Bounty, when the price did not exceed -	2 8 0	2 17 7			
		when the price was not above -	2 13 4	3 4 0	there was payable upon importation -	0 16 0	0 19 2
		when above that price, and not above	4 0 0	4 16 0	there was payable - - -	0 8 0	0 9 7
		and when above that price -	-	-	there was payable - - -	0 5 4	0 6 5
		2. Rye, Peafe, - .	-	-	Beans, Buck Wheat.		
0 3 6	0 4 2½	Bounty, when the price did not exceed -	1 12 0	1 18 5			
		when the price was not above -	2 0 0	2 8 0	there was payable upon importation -	0 16 0	0 19 2
		and when above that price - -	-	-	there was payable - - -	0 4 0	0 4 9½
		3. Barley, Beer, -	-	-	Bigg, Malt.		
0 2 6	0 3 0	Bounty, when the price did not exceed -	1 4 0	1 8 9			
		when the price was not above -	1 12 0	1 18 5	there was payable upon importation -	0 16 0	0 19 2
		and when above that price -	-	-	there was payable - - -	0 2 8	0 3 2½
		4. Oats, - -	-	-	Oatmeal.		
0 2 - 6	0 3 0	For the quarter of oatmeal, when the price of oats did not exceed - - -	0 15 0	0 18 0			
		when the price was not above -	0 16 0	0 19 2	there was payable upon the importation of oats	0 5 4	0 6 5
		and when above that price - -	-	-	there was payable - - -	0 1 4	0 1 7

TABLE of the Prices, Bounties, and Duties, upon the Exportation and Importation of Grain, according to the Law of 1791.

Bounties per Qr. £ s. d			EXPORTATION.	Prices of Gr. per Qr. £ s. d			IMPORTATION.	Duties per Qr. £ s. d		
			1. Wheat.				Wheat.			
0	5	0	Bounty, when under - - -	2	4	0				
			Exportation prohibited, when at or above -	2	6	0				
			when under - -	2	10	0	there is payable upon importation - - -	1	4	3
			when at or above -	2	10	0	ditto ditto - - - -	0	2	6
			but under - - -	2	14	0				
			when at or above -	2	14	0	ditto ditto - - - -	0	0	6
			2. Rye, - -			-	Peafe and Beans.			
0	3	0	Bounty, when under * - - -	1	8	0				
			Exportation prohibited, when at or above -	1	10	0				
			when under -	1	14	0	there is payable upon importation - -	1	2	0
			when at or above -	1	14	0	ditto ditto - -	0	1	6
			but under -	1	17	0				
			when at or above -	1	17	0	ditto ditto - - - -	0	0	3
			3. Barley, - -			-	Beer, or Bigg.			
0	2	6	Bounty, when under - - -	1	2	0				
			Exportation prohibited, when at or above -	1	3	0				
			when under - -	1	5	0	there is payable upon importation - -	1	2	0
			when at or above -	1	5	0	ditto ditto - - -	0	1	3
			but under - - -	1	7	0				
			when at or above -	1	7	0	ditto ditto - - -	0	0	3
			4. Oats.				Oats.			
0	2	0	Bounty, when under - - -	0	14	0				
			Exportation prohibited, when at or above -	0	15	0				
			when under - -	0	17	0	there is payable upon importation - -	0	6	7
			when at or above -	0	17	0	ditto ditto - - -	0	1	0
			but under - - -	0	18	0				
			when at or above -	0	18	0	ditto ditto - - -	0	0	2

N. B. Flour, Meal, and Malt, are regulated in proportion to the feveral forts of grain. The importation of Malt is at all times prohibited.

* The Bounty, by the Tables in the Act of Parliament, appears to be given only upon Rye, and not alfo upon the exportation of Peafe and Beans.

REMARKS ON THE FOREGOING TABLES.

From this comparifon, it will appear, that although the legiflature have raifed the import prices and duties higher, in a fmall degree, than the low ftate to which they were reduced by the law of 1773, and have, in fo far, reverted to the old fyftem, ftill the encouragement given to agriculture, by the law of 1791, is far inferior to what it enjoyed under the old laws.

Without including the difference between the value of money, in the prefent and in former times, it is fufficient to remark, that the bounty of 5s. upon wheat, is now withdrawn, when it rifes to 44s.; and exportation is ftopped, when it rifes to 46s. per quarter; whereas, by the old laws, exportation, with the bounty, was continued till the price rofe to 48s.

With refpect to importation, it is now permitted, on low duties, when the price of wheat rifes to L. 2 : 10s.; whereas, the duties, by the old laws, were equal to a prohibition, till the price rofe to L. 4; and even then, the duty was confiderable, inftead of being reduced to a trifle, as it now is, before wheat reaches a price that can repay the farmer in a bad feafon.

In fhort, the law of 1791, appears to be liable to all the material objections that have been ftated by the author of this work, againft the law of 1773; and the continuance of our agriculture, in any degree of profperity, feems to arife rather from the impoffibility of obtaining adequate fupplies from foreign countries (our farmers thereby retaining, in a great meafure, the monopoly of our own markets) than from any protection, or encouragement, it has received from our late laws.   *Edit.*

If we fhall return to the fyftem eftablifhed by the old laws, CHAP IV
it is to be hoped that we may foon recover the happy fituation
in which our agriculture flourifhed for more than half a century after the Union; and, taking thofe laws for our bafis,
we may thence deduce the following *theorems:*

1*ft*, That, whenever the prices of grain, at home, are fuch
as indicate plenty, a bounty ought to be given upon exportation; and that bounty ought to be continued, until the prices
rife to a certain height.

2*d*, That, when the prices rife to the *firft degree*, the bounty
ought to ceafe; but exportation fhould ftill be permitted, until the prices rife to a fecond degree.

3*d*, That, when the prices rife to the *fecond degree*, exportation ought to be prohibited.

4*th*, That, when the prices rife to a *third degree*, importation ought to be permitted, upon payment of duties; and
thofe duties fhould be leffened, if the prices increafe.

5*th*, That, no flour, or ground-grain, ought to be allowed
to be imported.

6*th*, That, corn, once imported, ought not to be again exported; nor carried coaftways, from one port to another.

7*th*, That, as either exportation or importation may be

CHAP. IV. carried to excefs, powers ought to be vefted in the King in Council, to reftrain or prohibit exportation, or importation ; and that either generally, or in particular places, as may appear to be moft beneficial to the kingdom at large *.

---

* The power here propofed to be vefted in the King in Council, for fufpending the operation of the laws, might render them too uncertain to be fully depended upon by the Public; efpecially by that part of the community, who are engaged in raifing corn : a bufinefs of itfelf fo precarious, as to require both a fixed and permanent fyftem for its encouragement. This objection is obviated in the following Chapter, where it is propofed that the fufpending power, vefted in the King in Council, fhould be exercifed upon the recommendation of an Executive Board, by which the ftate of the grain in the country would be conftantly afcertained ; and, by whofe reports, exportation and importation would be regulated. *Edit.*

CHAP. V.

*Arrangements propofed for carrying into execution, and giving effect
to the Corn Laws.—Conclufion of the Work.*

ALTHOUGH the true fpirit and conftruction of the Corn
Laws have already been conveyed to us, by our fore-
fathers, they have not been equally fuccefsful in the rules laid
down for the execution of thofe laws.

A national object of this importance would require to be
put under the direction of perfons of the firft confideration;
and the laws, for its encouragement and protection, ought
to be executed with the utmoft precifion. We have feen
the agriculture of Great Britain flourifhing under the benign
influence of the former falutary laws; and we have feen it
blafted by the hafty application of contrary rules.

If we fhall fuppofe the principles, ftated in the feven theorems, which concluded the foregoing chapter, to be the foundation of our Corn Laws, we may confider how far the exe-

U

cution of them may not be rendered more prompt and certain than heretofore, and fraud more effectually prevented.

Although England and Scotland be politically incorporated, and that, in the present case, the same prices, bounties, and duties, and the same rules, will answer for both countries; yet, from their being under a separate jurisdiction, as well as from a diversity of climate and crops, it appears necessary that each should have a separate institution for the execution of the laws.

Let us suppose the three junior Judges of the courts of King's Bench, Common Pleas, and Exchequer, with a secretary or clerk, with suitable appointments, to be formed into a Court for the *Conservation* of the *Agriculture* of *England;* and two of the Judges to be a quorum *. And the three junior Judges of the courts of Session, Justiciary, and Exchequer, in Scotland, with a secretary or clerk, and suitable appointments, to be formed into a Court for the *Conservation* of the *Agriculture* of *Scotland;* and two of these Judges to be a quorum.

Let us suppose England to be divided into ten districts, and Scotland into five; and, to avoid the confusion and irregularity arising from exportation and importation going on at the same time, in the same harbour or creek, let the divisions be made, as much as possible, from headland to headland, or places

---

* The three junior judges are mentioned, as they are supposed to be at a more vigorous time of life than their seniors, and of course more capable of bearing the additional fatigue of this office.

where there are no harbours or creeks; and let the neighbouring counties form the diftrict, as follows*:

ENGLAND.

From Berwick to Redcar, comprehending the fea coafts of the counties of Northumberland and Durham; and thefe counties to form the diftrict.

From Redcar to Spurn-head, comprehending the fea coaft of Yorkfhire; and that county to form the diftrict.

From Spurn-head to Orfordnefs, comprehending the fea coafts of the counties of Lincoln, Norfolk, and Suffolk, and the navigation of the Humber; and thefe, with the counties of Cambridge, Huntington, Northampton, Warwick, Leicef-ter, Rutland, Derby, and Nottingham, to form the diftrict.

From Orfordnefs to Dungenefs, comprehending the fea coaft of Effex and Kent, with the navigation of the river Thames; and thefe, with the counties of Surry, Berks, Ox-ford, Buckingham, Middlefex, Hertford, and Bedford, to form the diftrict.

From Dungenefs to the Eafter limit of Dorfetfhire, compre-hending the fea coaft of Suffex and Hampfhire; and thefe, with Wiltfhire, and the Ifle of Wight, to form the diftrict.

CHAP. V.

1ft Diftrict.

2d Diftrict.

3d Diftrict.

4th Diftrict.

5th Diftrict.

* The divifion of the diftricts, in the act 1791, not being made from headland to headland, appears to be liable to the objections, which the author has endeavoured to obviate in his arrangement. *Edit.*

U 2

From the Eastern limit of Dorsetshire to Minehead, comprehending the sea coast of Dorsetshire, and that of Devonshire and Cornwall; and these counties to form the district.

7th District.

From Minehead to Pen Kenny's Point, comprehending the sea coast of Somersetshire, Monmouthshire, Glamorganshire, Caermarthenshire, and Pembrokeshire, with the navigation of the Severn; and these, with the counties of Gloucester, Hereford, and Brecknock, to form the district.

8th District.

From Pen Kenny's Point to Great Orm's Head, comprehending the sea coasts of Cardiganshire, Merionethshire, Carnarvonshire, with the Isle of Anglesea; and these, with Montgomeryshire, Radnorshire, and Shropshire, to form the district.

9th District.

From Great Orm's Head to Rossal Point, comprehending the sea coast of Denbighshire, Flintshire, Cheshire, and Lancashire; and these, with Staffordshire, to form the district.

10th District.

From Rossal Point to the bottom of the Solway Firth, comprehending the sea coast of Westmoreland and Cumberland; and these counties, with the Isle of Man, to form the district.

SCOTLAND.

1st District.

From the bottom of the Solway Firth, to the bottom of Loch Long, comprehending the sea coast of the counties of Dumfries, Kirkcudbright, Wigtoun, Air, Renfrew, and Dumbarton, with the navigation of the eaft fide of Loch Long, and the navigation of the Clyde; and thefe, with the county of Lanark, to form the diftrict.

From the bottom of Loch Long to Arderfeer, comprehending the fea coaft of the counties of Bute, Argyle, Invernefs, Rofs, Cromarty, Sutherland, and Caithnefs, Shetland, and Orkney, with the whole iflands that belong to thefe counties, and the navigation of the Murray Frith, upon the north fide as far as Arderfeer, and upon both fides, above Arderfeer; and the above counties to form the diftrict.

From Arderfeer to Mather Point, fouthward of John's Haven, comprehending the fea coafts of the counties of Nairn, Moray, Banff, Aberdeen, and Mearns; and thefe counties to form the diftrict.

From Mather Point, fouth of John's Haven, to the Bridge of Stirling, comprehending the fea coaft of the counties of Angus and Fife, with the navigation of the Tay to the Bridge of Perth, and of the north fide of the Forth; and the above counties, with thofe of Clackmannan, Kinrofs, and Perth, to form the diftrict.

From the Bridge of Stirling to Berwick, comprehending the fea coaft of the counties of Stirling, Linlithgow, Edinburgh, Haddington, and Berwick; and thefe counties, with Peebles, Selkirk, and Roxburgh, to form the diftrict.

These are the divisions which occur to us to be the most convenient and proper, according to the best of our information and judgment; but we are far from laying them down as unexceptionable. In a work of this nature, it is sufficient that a reasonable plan be proposed, leaving it to be canvassed at the county meetings in the several districts, and the particulars to be afterwards arranged and fixed by the legislature.

Now, supposing these courts to be constituted, and the districts to be fixed.

At Michaelmas, yearly, when the harvest will be generally over in England, let the sheriffs call a jury of twenty-four grave substantial people, such as are ordinarily called upon grand juries, in every county; and, in Yorkshire, in every Riding; and let this jury declare, upon oath, from their own knowledge, or from such evidence as they shall think proper to call before them, their opinion of the state of the crop, and of the prices which the several kinds of grain may be worth for the ensuing season, within their respective counties.

Let these verdicts be immediately sent to the Secretary of the Court of Conservation, who, from thence, is to make out an average account of the several prices of grain within the respective districts; which is to be laid before the Court, and, by their authority, published in the Gazette, and to stand as the rule for exportation and importation within the several districts, until another general report shall be published, unless

the fame fhall, in the mean time, be altered by the King's proclamation.

At Ladyday, when the feed, in England, will be moftly in
the ground, let juries again be impannelled in every fhire, and
in every Riding of Yorkfhire ; and let them declare, upon
oath, from their own knowledge, or from fuch evidence as
they may think proper to call before them, their opinion of
the value or prices which the feveral forts of grain, within
their feveral counties, may be worth until harveft; which verdicts are to be immediately reported to the Secretary of the
Court of Confervation, from whence he is to make out an
average account of the prices of the different kinds of grain,
within the feveral diftricts, which is to be laid before the Court,
and, by their authority, publifhed in the Gazette ; and to
ftand as the rule for exportation and importation within the
feveral diftricts, until another general report fhall be publifhed,
unlefs the fame fhall, in the mean time, be altered by the
King's proclamation.

Let a weekly account be kept in one or more towns in each
county, and in each Riding of Yorkfhire, where corn or meal
markets are ufually held, and if more than one, at leaft twenty
miles diftant from each other, of the prices of the feveral
kinds of corn, grain, or meal, per quarter, allowing
pounds avoirdupois, for the quarter of meal in thofe markets ;
which accounts are, immediately after the markets, to be fent
to the Secretary of the Court of Confervation, from whence
he is to make up an average account of the prices of the dif-

ferent kinds of grain, within the feveral diftricts, to be laid before the Court once every week *.

Thus the Court of Confervation, being in poffeffion of the general ftate of the crop, and of the value of the different kinds of grain, in the feveral diftricts, twice every year, and of the weekly ftate of the markets, in the event of any fudden rife of the prices of grain, either from known or unknown caufes, or from the appearance of a late or a bad harveft, or in the cafe of any confiderable fall in the prices, the judges have it in their power to lay the cafe before the King in Council, in order to procure fuch an alteration in the exportation or importation, as they fhall judge moft for the good of the kingdom at large.

In executing this part of their duty, it is not to be doubted that the judges will act with fufficient caution and circumfpection, to fruftrate any artifices for raifing or falling of markets.

And here it may be proper to obferve, that the weftern coaft, both of England and Scotland, from the difference of climate, is not fo well adapted to the production of corn, as the eaftern coaft, and confequently that the prices of grain muft, in general, be higher in the one fide of the ifland than the other; befides, there are other populous grafing and manufacturing counties, which never raife corn fufficient for their own con-

---

* The act 12 Geo. 3. cap. 39. with fome amendment might anfwer this purpofe.

fumption ; and, upon the eaftern coaft, fome of the diftricts may enjoy a plentiful harveft, while others, from a lefs favourable feafon, have reaped but a fcanty one.

In fuch cafes it is well worthy of the attention of the legiflature to confider, how far it would not be proper to give fome bounty equal to the freight, for tranfporting grain from one diftrict to another, or even from the one fide of the ifland to the other, rather than to import foreign grain ; for it fhould be never out of view, that for every hundred quarters of foreign grain, which we bring into the kingdom, we cut off the bread and employment of twelve of our own people, old and young ; or, more properly fpeaking, we prevent the exiftence of fuch a number of additional people, with the proportional production of cattle, horfes, &c. by employing the lands and labour of other nations *. At any rate it would appear to be neceffary to give every cafe poffible to the tranfmiffion of our own corn from one part of the kingdom to another, by permitting it to be fhipped and carried coaftways, or by inland navigation, without any cuftom-houfe difpatch, or any other detention whatever. And to prevent frauds, by carrying fuch corn abroad, it may be declared, by a law, to be highly penal to load any corn for exportation, without entry at the cuftomhoufe : And all reftraints upon buying and felling of corn, except thofe upon foreftalling and regrating the particular markets, ought to be removed.

The fame rules for carrying on the bufinefs of the Court of

* *Vide* Appendix N° 8. Art. 9.

X

Confervation in England, will apply to that of Scotland, and they need not therefore be repeated.

We fhall now proceed to mention what occurs to us, with refpect to the particular bufinefs of exportation and importation ; what the probable expence may be attending the execution of the laws ; and in what manner the funds may be raifed for that purpofe.

The bufinefs of importation will be much circumfcribed, by the general plan for afcertaining the prices ; but ftill this branch of the trade, ought, for reafons already enumerated, to be attended to with the utmoft precifion.

It is not to be doubted, that the reports of the juries, at Ladyday and Michaelmas, will eftablifh the general ftate of the prices of the feveral kinds of grain throughout the kingdom ; and thefe being the index of the trade, will guard it againft improper importation ; and, if any fraud fhall be attempted, by the artificial raifing or falling of particular markets, the general, as well as the particular, ftate of the prices, over all the kingdom, being conftantly in the view of the Courts of Confervation, the judges will thereby be enabled completely to prevent fuch attempts from having any effect ; at the fame time that the community at large, may fafely repofe fuch confidence in thefe courts, as to believe that the judges, upon due confideration, will, from time to time, when they fhall fee it proper, by their reprefentations to the King in Council, foften the neceffary rigour of the laws to be

made againſt importation, until the agriculture of the kingdom ſhall furniſh grain ſufficient for its conſumption.

With reſpect to exportation, the law gives the bounty to the
farmer, for enabling him to ſend his crop abroad, and to diſ-
poſe of it in another country, when he cannot find a market
for it at home; and by that means to continue his trade of
raiſing corn, preferably to other productions of the ſoil, which
are not ſo neceſſary nor ſo profitable to the kingdom.

It no doubt anſwers the ſame purpoſe to give the bounty to
the merchant who exports the grain, becauſe he is thereby
enabled to pay a proportionally higher price to the farmer;
and, from his knowledge and correſpondence in the trade, he
may find a market for it, when the farmer cannot.

But to guard againſt fraud has been always the chief difficulty in the execution of the Corn Laws; for where profit
is to be obtained, there will be people ready to break through,
or to evade the ſtricteſt laws, even thoſe moſt beneficial to
the kingdom.

On the plan recommended, it will be the object of the laws
to provide, that the corn and meal to be exported, upon which
a bounty is to be paid, is really and truly of Britiſh growth;
that it is neither corn of foreign growth, nor mixed with foreign corn; that it is not corn ground, or malt made from
corn of foreign growth, nor mixed with foreign grain; and

that it is not corn of Britiſh growth which had been formerly exported, and afterwards relanded.

To obviate theſe difficulties, as far as poſſible, it may be propoſed, that the exporter ſhall make oath, that the corn intended to be ſhipped by him, for exportation, was purchaſed by him, or by perſons immediately employed by him, from Britiſh farmers, or raiſers of corn; and that, to the beſt of his knowledge and belief, it is not of foreign growth, nor mixed with corn of foreign growth; and that it is not corn of Britiſh growth, which had formerly been exported, and afterwards relanded, nor mixed with ſuch corn.

It may be objected, that ſuch niceties would be a reſtraint upon the trade, and a bar to the transference of property; but where bounties are to be given for the general good, upon as eaſy terms as is conſiſtent with a proper guard againſt fraud, the receivers are not entitled to ſcrutiniſe, or to find fault with the rules preſcribed by the generous benefactor.

Fair dealers will find no fault with proper reſtrictions, nor can theſe rules in the ſmalleſt degree obſtruct exportation. In all countries there are people who tread upon the heels of the fair trader; and, in caſes of this kind, where penalties muſt be affixed to tranſgreſſions, ſuch people might name perſons as exporters, to qualify their cargoes, as had neither character nor property to loſe.

Exportation of corn, according to the former laws, ought

to be made in fhips owned by Britifh born fubjects, refiding in the Britifh dominions, and whereof the mafter, and at leaft two thirds of the mariners, are alfo Britifh fubjects; and the exporter ought to give bond, under the penalty of L. 10 per ton, that the corn fhipped, fhall be carried abroad, and not relanded in Britain; but the bounty fhould be payable, although the grain fhould perifh at fea, or be taken by enemies; and the bond ought to be given up, upon producing proper certificates that the corn was really landed in a foreign country, or that it had perifhed at fea, or had been taken by enemies.

The difpatch of bufinefs is of great confequence; and the laws have allowed the officers of the cuftoms to make choice of two facks out of twenty, and from the quantity of corn contained in thefe, to compute the quantity fhipped.

If we could expect the long wifhed for equalifation of the weights and meafures of Great Britain, we would propofe, that the bounties fhould be made payable according to the weight of the quarter of well dreffed middling Britifh grain. This rule, while it deals out juftice to the public, would tend greatly, in a fhort time, to ftamp a fuperior value upon Britifh grain, at foreign markets. But, if this cannot be the cafe, the farmer is much fafer to fell his grain to the merchant by meafure, than by weight; becaufe his own meafures will be fome fort of check, and there is probably lefs opportunity of deceit, in the diverfity of the meafures, than in that of the weights, which at prefent are to be found in every part of Great Britain.

By the act of the 24th George II. when ground corn is fhipped, the fame bounty is to be allowed upon 244 pounds weight of wheat meal, or other ground corn or grain, whereon there is a bounty, as was allowed upon the exportation of four bufhels of wheat, or other grain or corn unground; and, for the difpatch of bufinefs, when fuch ground corn fhould be brought in facks to be fhipped, the officers of the cuftoms were authorifed to make choice of two facks out of twenty, and from thence to compute the weight of the meal to be fhipped, for which the bounty is to be paid.

By the act 1773 the bounties payable upon corn ground (except oatmeal *) are taken off, while the foreign farmer is permitted to import his flour, upon payment of a mere trifle of duties.

It is not eafy to difcover a reafon for this part of that law; for if our farmers are to be allowed a bounty upon the ex-

---

* By the act 1773, the quarter of oatmeal is fixed at 276 pounds avoirdupois, upon which a bounty of 2s. 6d. is payable. By the former laws, the bounty upon 244 pounds of meal, made from wheat or other grain, upon which a bounty was payable, was the fame as was allowed for four bufhels of the grain from whence the meal was made; which brings the weight of the quarter to 448 pounds. The weight of the quarter of all kinds of meal, ought to be the fame; and a bounty of 4s. upon 448 pounds of oatmeal, will be equal to 2s. 6d. upon 276 pounds.

portation of wheat in body, they are much better entitled to
it, in found policy, when, by the manufacture of it into flour,
they add 10 *per cent.* of the value of it, to the common flock
of the induſtry of the kingdom; and 10 *per cent.* more, for
the cloth uſed in facks for it. It is therefore to be hoped, that
this bounty, and the clauſe for difpatch in the buſineſs of exportation, will be replaced.

The bounties upon exportation ſhould be paid according to
the certificates of the officers of the cuſtoms, at the port of
ſhipping, within ſix months after the certificate ſhall be pre-
ſented to the commiſſioners of the cuſtoms at London or Edinburgh reſpectively; and, failing ſuch payments, the money to
bear intereſt at the rate of 3 *per cent. per annum*, until paid,
agreeable to the act of the 26th George II.

Having mentioned what occurs to us reſpecting this propoſed law, and the execution of its different branches, we
ſhall now take under conſideration the expence and funds neceſſary for carrying on the external and internal buſineſs of
the propoſed Court.

It may be preſumed, that the jurymen will attend the feveral meetings upon their own expences, for the public good;
but to call them together, to ingroſs the feveral fteps of their
procedure, and make the reports to the Court of Conſervation,
muſt be attended with ſome expence, and this being an additional piece of duty to be fixed upon the ſheriffs, they

ought to have a reafonable allowance for their trouble and expences *.

By the act of the 10th George III. for regiftering the prices
of corn, the perfons to be appointed to take up the prices of
corn, at the feveral markets, and to tranfmit the fame, were
to be rewarded according to the determination of the juftices
of the peace, and to be paid quarterly out of the county rates;
but, in counties where there were no county rates, this part of
the law could not be executed †. Befides, this law extends
only to the prices of wheat, rye, barley, oats, and beans, in
England, and only to beer or bigg, in Scotland: And, to anfwer the prefent purpofes, the prices of all kinds of grain in
ufe for the food of mankind, and the prices of meal, made
from fuch grain, muft be returned.

Reafonable falaries muft be made to the judges, and to
their fecretaries or clerks, and a proper allowance for the contingent expences of the courts.

As every plan, fuggefted to the public confideration, ought
to be made as complete as poffible, we fhall here fpecify cer-

---

* Hitherto, when fuch duty was committed to the juftices of the peace, in
many places it was not executed; and, as a law of the propofed kind, cannot have
the wifhed-for effect, without prompt and diftinct execution, it would appear to be neceffary to convey the power to the fheriffs, as an indifpenfable part of their office.

† Although provifion may be made for the payment of the perfon who takes up
and tranfmits the market prices, ftill it would appear neceffary to have a penal claufe
inferted to infure the execution of his duty.

tain articles, which it appears to us may form the principal heads of the expence of executing this law.

In England there are 51 counties, beside Yorkſhire, in which there are 3 Ridings, each of them larger than many counties; and as we have propoſed a jury in each county, and in each of theſe ridings, there would be in all 54 juries in England.

In Scotland there are 34 counties, but as 6 of theſe are very ſmall, and are, at preſent, ſeverally conjoined with other counties, under the juriſdiction of one ſheriff; 28 juries will ſerve for Scotland.

The number of market towns, from whence the weekly return of the prices are to be made, ought to be regulated according to the numbers of people, and extent of the counties or ridings. We ſhall propoſe theſe to be arranged as follows:

IN ENGLAND.

No	COUNTIES.	MARKET TOWNS.	No
1	Cornwall		
2	Devonſhire		
3	Dorſetſhire		
4	Somerſetſhire		
5	Wiltſhire		
6	Hampſhire		
7	Suſſex		
8	Surry		
9	Kent		
10	Glamorganſhire		
11	Monmouthſhire		
12	Glouceſterſhire		
13	Berkſhire		
14	Oxfordſhire		
15	Buckinghamſhire		
16	Middleſex		

No	COUNTIES.	MARKET TOWNS.	No
17	Hertfordshire		
18	Essex		
19	Pembrokeshire		
20	Caermarthenshire		
21	Brecknockshire		
22	Cardiganshire		
23	Radnorshire		
24	Herefordshire		
25	Worcestershire		
26	Warwickshire		
27	Northamptonshire		
28	Bedfordshire		
29	Huntingdonshire		
30	Cambridgeshire		
31	Suffolk		
32	Montgomeryshire		
33	Merionethshire		
34	Shropshire		
35	Staffordshire		
36	Leicestershire		
37	Rutlandshire		
38	Norfolk		
39	Carnarvonshire		
40	Anglesea		
41	Denbighshire		
42	Flintshire		
43	Cheshire		
44	Derbyshire		
45	Nottinghamshire		
46	Lincolnshire		
47	Lancashire		
48	Westmoreland		
49	Cumberland		
50	Durham		
51	Northumberland		
52	Yorkshire, E. Riding		
53	Ditto, North Riding		
54	Ditto, West Riding		

SCOTLAND.

No	COUNTIES.	MARKET TOWNS.	No
1	Edinburghſhire		
2	Haddingtonſhire		
3	Berwickſhire		
4	Roxburghſhire		
5	Perthſhire		
6	Mearns		
7	Aberdeenſhire		
8	Inverneſsſhire		
9	Selkirkſhire		
10	Peebles		
11	Lanark		
12	Dumfriesſhire		
13	Wigtonſhire		
14	Ayrſhire		
15	Dumbartonſhire		
16	Renfrewſhire		
17	Stirling and Clackmanan		
18	Linlithgow		
19	Argyleſhire		
20	Bute		
21	Fife and Kinroſs		
22	Forfarſhire		
23	Banffſhire		
24	Caithneſs and Sutherland		
25	Elgin and Nairn		
26	Orkney and Shetland		
27	Roſs and Cromarty		
28	Kircudbright		

Let us suppose the salary of the three Judges in
    England to be L. 300 each   -   -   L. 900 0 0
To their secretary or clerk   -   -   250 0 0
Contingent expences   -   -   -   60 0 0
                —————————
                L. 1210 0 0
Salary of the three Judges in Scotland, suppo-
    sed to be L. 200 each   L. 600 0 0
To their secretary or clerk   -   200 0 0
Contingent expences   -   40 0 0
            ———————— 840 0 0
Expence of calling 108 juries in England yearly,
    and of engrossing their procedure, and ma-
    king their reports, at L. 10 each jury   -   1080 0 0
Expence of calling 56 juries in Scotland yearly,
    and of ingrossing their minutes of procedure,
    and making their reports, at L. 10 each jury   560 0 0
Expence of the weekly returns from
market-towns in England, and   in
Scotland, in all   , at L. 5 yearly each
                ——————————
            Total ·L.

The above being the probable amount of the expences attending the establishment of the proposed Court of Conservation, we shall proceed to state the probable means by which
these expences may be defrayed.

For the forty-four years, from the 1741 to 1784 inclusive,
there have been, upon an average, imported and exported

yearly, to and from Great Britain, 737,697 quarters of grain,
of which more than one third has been wheat, or wheat flour,
or malt made from wheat, and the remainder of other grain.

It may be presumed, that the amount of importation and
exportation together, will rather exceed than fall short of this
quantity in future, as we have seen, that for many years,
when the exportation trade was entirely in the possession of
Great Britain, the quantity yearly exported, upon an average,
amounted to 848,660 quarters.

Taking, therefore, the average of the importation and exportation, as above, and fixing an executive premium of only 2d. upon the quarter of all wheat, wheat flour, or malt
made of wheat, imported and exported; and 1½d. upon the
quarter of every other kind of grain: this premium, upon
245,899 quarters of wheat, &c. at 2d. per quarter,

   will amount to - L. 2049 3 2
    And upon
491,798 quarters of other grain, at 1½d. per
   quarter - - 3073 14 9

737,697   In all L. 5,122 17 11

Having, for many years, bestowed great attention upon the
subject which gave rise to this Work; and, feeling it the duty
of every member of the community, to suggest such ideas as
may in any way contribute to the public good; we have, with
the utmost deference, stated the measures that have occurred
to us, by which the Agriculture of Great Britain may be pro-

CHAP. V.

moted, with the moſt certain proſpect of ſucceſs ; and by which, the export trade in corn may, in a reaſonable time, be revived in this country : a branch of commerce, the extenſion of which is the ſureſt index of national proſperity, and of an encreaſing population, ſuch as adds effectually to the ſtrength and power of the ſtate *.

It were to be wiſhed, that the community at large would view Agriculture, as the firſt object of national importance ; becauſe, unleſs it proſper, all other purſuits are viſionary : Yet, ſuch is the fluctuation in the minds of men, that ſometimes it has been treated as of the firſt conſequence .to the ſtate, and, at other times, caſt off as unworthy of conſideration.

Perhaps the time may be yet to come, when, amidſt the multiplicity of other ſuitors, Agriculture ſhall be enabled to preſs

---

* So great is the difference between the population produced by the extenſion of Agriculture, and that ariſing from a premature encouragement of Manufactures and Commerce, that it is remarked by Mr Arthur Young, in his Tour through France, that ſuch was the wretched ſtate of the lower claſſes of the people, in that country, in conſequence of the depreſſed ſtate of Agriculture, and the ſcarcity of proviſions, that the nation would at that time, in 1789, have been in a far more flouriſhing ſtate with four or five millions leſs of inhabitants. See vol. 1. chap. 17. page 469, on Population, and chap. 20. page 510, on Manufactures.

In the whole of this able Work, particularly in theſe two chapters, the important deductions, drawn from facts of great magnitude, ſhew, in the cleareſt and moſt convincing manner, the preference due to Agriculture in every country.

Edit.

through the crowd, and claim the attention of the Public. To become its patrons would do honour to the higheſt characters in the ſtate; and, in any eſſential effort made for its advancement, we might look up with confidence to the protection of our Sovereign, the beneficent promoter of whatever can tend to increaſe the happineſs of his people, and the proſperity of his kingdom.

CHAP. V.

THE END,

SUPPLEMENT.

LETTER I.

From Mr Mackie, Farmer in Ormiston, to the Editor, containing a Review of the Corn Laws, and an Account of the Corn Trade, from the periods to which they are brought down in the preceding Inquiry to the year 1793; with farther Suggestions for the Improvement of the Corn Laws.

Ormiston, in East Lothian,
10th December 1795.

DEAR SIR,

IN consequence of your desire, I have perused, with attention, your late Father's Inquiry into the Corn Laws of this country, and agree with him in opinion, that a judicious system of regulation, restricting the *free* importation of foreign corn, and affording a bounty on the exportation of our own produce, when low priced in the home market, is absolutely necessary for preserving the agriculture, prosperity, and independence of Great Britain; and for securing that decided superiority of internal resource, which at present she so happily enjoys, even in times of necessity, over the surrounding nations.

Previously to assigning my reasons in support of the principles laid down in the preceding Inquiry, it may be necessary

Z

to remark, that they ſtand in oppoſition to the theory of one of the firſt political writers in this or any country, (Dr Adam Smith on the Wealth of Nations) who aſſerts, that the re-ſtraining laws are hurtful, and that a free importation and exportation of Corn would at all times be beneficial to the ſtate. I ſhall therefore, firſt, take a view of your Father's ſentiments, contraſted with thoſe of Doctor Smith, on the Corn Laws ; and afterwards, by way of Supplement, bring down his account of the Import and Export trade in Corn to the preſent time ; giving, at the ſame time, a ſhort ac-count of the particular ſtatutes which have been enacted by the Legiſlature of this country, for regulating this eſſential branch of national policy, ſince he finiſhed his Treatiſe on that ſubject.

The intention of your late Father's Work is to eſtabliſh this principle—That a judicious ſyſtem of laws, prohibiting the importation of foreign corn, except in caſes of abſolute neceſſity, and giving a bounty on the exportation of our own produce, when low-priced in the home market, gives a per-manent impulſe to the exertions of the huſbandman, ſo as re-gularly to promote agriculture, and afford uniformly a more plentiful ſupply of grain in the home market, and at more moderate prices, than if no ſuch laws were in force ; by which means the neceſſaries of life being more eaſily procured, po-pulation and active induſtry are greatly promoted, on which the power of a ſtate chiefly depends.

In ſupport of this opinion, he brings forward the well au-thenticated fact, that ſince the 1670, when the national policy

of prohibiting the importation of foreign corn affumed a
more fettled form, and particularly fince 1688, when the
bounty on our own produce was eftablifhed by a permanent
law, for near a century after thefe periods, the average prices
of corn, in the home market, were not only confiderably
cheaper than in the one immediately preceding, but alfo an
immenfe fum was brought into the country, for the furplus
quantity of corn exported, after liberally fupplying the inhabitants.

The author of the Inquiry into the Nature and Caufes of
the Wealth of Nations, admits that the average prices of grain
were higher in the laft than in the early part of this century,
after the bounty took effect; but he denies that it proceeded
from this caufe. ' The bounty (he fays) was granted for the
' exprefs purpofe of raifing the price of corn in the home
' market;' and he attributes the fall which afterwards took
place, to the demand for money, now neceffary for repre-
fenting the accumulating capitals, arifing from the increafing
induftry of the different European ftates, in almoft every
country, even where no bounties were eftablifhed, particularly
in France, where, fo far from any bounties being allowed,
corn of all kinds was then totally reftricted from being fent
out of the kingdom, to find a foreign market, exportation
being rigoroufly reftricted by the laws of that defpotic government. Allowing, however, that the fall in the price of corn
proceeded from the caufe which Dr Smith has here affigned,
I fhall afterwards endeavour to fhow the danger that would
refult to Great Britain, in her prefent fituation, from relaxing

the force of thofe falutary laws that have hitherto fupported the agriculture of this country; but which, from the accumulating burdens that now reprefs the induftry of the farmer, will in future, it may be feared, be unable to keep pace with the growing confumption arifing from the increafing population, the opulence, and luxury of the inhabitants; unlefs the wifdom of the legiflature remove thofe obftructions which prevent the improvement of the wafte lands, and the adoption of a more perfect mode of cultivation on the fields already under the management of the hufbandman.

The inhabitants of this country may be divided into two claffes, known by the appellation of the landed and mercantile intereft, viz. thofe who draw their immediate fupport from the produce of the foil, and the manufacturers and merchants, who are confumers of the produce. Although the welfare of thefe two claffes depends, in a great meafure, on each other's profperity, yet, at firft fight, their intereft appears diametrically oppofite. The manufacturers, and thofe who live in towns, being daily fupplied from the country, with provifions for themfelves and thofe employed in their manufactures, are greatly alarmed at the fmalleft advance in the price; being regularly informed from the newfpapers, and other vague authorities, of the moft abundant crops, which they pretend every year cover the face of the country. If, notwithftanding this regular prediction, a bad crop enfues, and the prices of corn get up in confequence of a real fcarcity, it is attributed only to a manœuvre of the farmers, and corn dealers; they are liberally branded with the epithets of foreftallers and regraters, and loud complaints are raifed, that by keeping up the corn from market, the high price of provifions will put a ftop to manufactures, and involve the country in ruin. Open the ports, is the general cry ; allow us to bring in corn from the Baltic, where we can purchafe it for half the money it cofts us at home, and then our drooping manufactures will revive, and our country reaffume its wonted profperity. To fuch language, the government of this country has always lent a willing ear, when ftrengthened with the united importunities of the manufacturing and mercantile intereft ; men whofe fole occupation, is to feize every favourable opportunity to improve their fortunes ; and who, living in towns, know the force of combination, and of acting in concert. Whilft, on the other hand, gentlemen of landed property, whofe revenue, arifing from the productions of the earth, without any particular efforts of their own, cannot perceive with the fame acutenefs, when their general intereft is attacked, nor be brought to act with unanimity and fpirit in warding off the blow. Let me add, alfo, that this apathy or indolence of the landed intereft, on every fubject refpecting agriculture which is brought before the legiflature, has of late become more confpicuous, fince rents were wholly paid in money, which prevents them from feeling the immediate bad effects of thofe regulations on the agriculture of this country, which proceed from the repeated complaints of the mercantile intereft. Accordingly we find government, on many occafions, interfering in favour of that intereft, and abrogating the laws refpecting the export and import of corn ; but it was not till the year 1773, that a new law was framed, repeal-

    ing a number of ancient ſtatutes, made at and prior to the Re-
volution, and putting the corn trade under an entire new code
of regulations.

When we review the growing proſperity of Great Britain, in
the period above mentioned, and the immenſe wealth and capital *acquired* by this country in 1773, when compared with that
in 1688, and the conſequent fall in the value of money, we
ſhould imagine, that if any alteration in the Corn Laws had
been neceſſary, it would have been to raiſe the rates at which
foreign corn was allowed to be imported, in order to protect
the agriculture of Great Britain, by removing every impediment which might obſtruct the value of home produce from
keeping pace with the advance in the price of labour, and of
every manufactured commodity. But there was no occaſion
for ſuch an alteration ; the ancient laws had been framed with
ſufficient wiſdom to protect and cheriſh agriculture, for a
great length of time, (one error excepted, which I ſhall afterwards take notice of) and they would have continued to
have done ſo, if they had not been altered by the new code,
framed for the evident purpoſe of lowering the price of corn
in the home market, thereby ſinking the revenue of the landed intereſt, and repreſſing the induſtry of the huſbandman.

Although it was the expreſs intention of the original inſti-
gators of this law (1773) to reduce the prices of corn in the
home market, to a par with what they had been at, in the
period of forty years immediately preceding; it, however,
produced no ſuch effect. The large addition to the national

capital now in circulation, arifing from the increafe of the
public debt, from the revenue and internal trade of India,
and the rapid advances which the country had made in manufactures and commerce, fince the peace of 1763, counter-
racted the intended effect of the law. It, neverthelefs, repreffed agriculture, by encouraging the importation of foreign
corn, and funk the profit on the ftock employed in the cultivation of the foil, below that which was embarked, during
the fame period, in trade and manufactures ; thereby preventing the additional capital neceffary for producing a return, to
fupply the growing confumption of the country, from being
invefted in agriculture, and even endangering the drawing
out of part of that already engaged in this moft productive
branch of human induftry.   The impolicy of fuch a fyftem is
evident ; and accordingly it is to this law that your Father af-
cribes the lofs of the export trade of corn to Great Britain.   I,
however, do not go this length ; I admit its evil tendency,
but am of opinion, it was only one of the caufes that have
produced this effect ; the others, I fhall endeavour afterwards
to explain.   Previoufly to the paffing of this act, the export
trade of grain was rapidly declining, and verging towards
that period, when the balance began to appear on the
other fide of the account, and to ftand againft this country.
We muft not therefore be furprized, after the legiflature
had thus given way to the folicitations of the mercantile intereft, in lowering the import rates of foreign corn, to
find, that a regular fyftem of importation was immediately
formed by the corn merchants, under the fanction of this eftablifhed law, which could not before be carried into execu-

tion, the bringing in of foreign corn being almoſt prohibited, on account of the high importation rates and duties then in force, and being only allowed by the authority of partial and temporary ſtatutes.

I muſt here obſerve, that in years of plenty, the farmer is in general beſt paid for his corn; the low price, which follows from the abundance of the crop, naturally occaſions want of attention, and conſequently prodigality and waſte in the conſumers; and the increaſed conſumption, ariſing from this cauſe, has the effect to raiſe its money price above its real value. On the other hand, when the price gets high in conſequence of a deficient crop, every purchaſer becomes of neceſſity an œconomiſt, the conſumer is ſtinted to a bare ſufficiency, and the diminiſhed conſumption, of courſe, ſinks the price below its real value, that is, its prime coſt, or expence beſtowed in rearing and bringing it to market*. In this ſituation, how diſtreſſing muſt it be to the huſbandmen of Great Britain, to have the prices of grain ſtill lowered by the importation of foreign corn; which, when once brought into the country, being lodged in the warehouſes of opulent

---

* I know the contrary is alledged, viz. That a certain deficiency in the crop produces an advance in price in favour of the farmer. I cannot, however, admit the fact; in the natural courſe of things, the price of every commodity is regulated by the demand and quantity at market. We muſt, however, except any interference of government, which impedes the regular courſe of circulation, whereby an alarm is excited in a country; witneſs the maximum and paper money in France, and the effect of the laws and regulations, propoſed by the legiſlature of this country, for lowering the price of corn.

merchants, in the populous towns, where the grain is chiefly confumed, they are therefore always at hand to pufh a fale, and fupply every demand, in which they are aided by bank accounts, and difcount of bills, to give long credits to pur-chafers. From thefe caufes, the corn merchants have a de-cided fuperiority in the market over the farmers; and they ac-tually difpofe of their foreign corn from 10 to 15 *per cent.* dearer than the farmer can procure for grain of the fame qua-lity, and the produce of our own foil.

I have obferved above, that the act of 1773, by lowering fo confiderably the import rates and duties on the introduction of foreign corn, gave rife to an eftablifhed fyftem of impor-tation, and opened the door to fpeculation, of which the corn merchants wifhed at all times to keep the key, i. e.—The prices of corn in the foreign markets being generally much lower than in Britain, they were therefore always ready, by artifice, to open the ports, before the price of Britifh corn in the home market, rofe to the rate at which the law allowed the importation of foreign grain: It was therefore found neceffary, from time to time, to pafs acts for counteracting thefe infidious defigns, in order to render the general law more effectual. Of thefe particular ftatutes, the following were enacted, after your Father finifhed his Treatife on the corn laws:

By the act, 21 Geo. 3. cha. 50, fo much of the acts of 1ft Jas. 2.; 5 Geo. 2.; 6 Geo. 3.; and 14 of Geo. 3. as refpects the determining the prices of middling Englifh wheat and other

.A .a

grain, in the port of London, and counties of Kent and Effex, are repealed ; and in lieu thereof, by this act, an infpector is appointed, to afcertain the weekly average prices, made
out from the actual fales in the port of London, which are to
regulate exportation, and the bounties paid thereon. An average price is alfo directed to be made up from three months
weekly returns, on the firft day of the feffions in London,
held in January, April, July, and September, to regulate importation, and the duty paid thereon, for three months, in the.
port of London, and counties above mentioned.

1783.

The Corn Law was fufpended, importation at low duties was
allowed, and exportation prohibited, till 25th Auguft 1783, in
England, and 25th September in Scotland*.

1789.

The act 29 Geo. 3. chap. 58. improved and extended the act
21 Geo. 3. chap. 50. Every corn factor in London and fu-
burbs, was obliged to give in weekly returns of his fales to the
infpectors. Importation was allowed into London, Kent, and.
Effex, when the prices of middling Britifh grain rofe to the
rates prefcribed in act 1773, as taken by the fix laft weekly returns in the port of London, immediately preceding the quarterly feffions, oats excepted, which continued to be regulated.
by twelve weekly returns, as formerly. The act was extended
to the maritime counties of England, which are divided into
eleven diftricts. Infpectors of corn returns are to be appointed
by the juftices of the peace in each county, to make weekly
returns of the prices of corn, from not more than twelve, nor

23 Geo. 3. chap. 1.   23 Geo. 3. chap. 53.   23 Geo. 3. chap. 81.

fewer than eight market-towns in each county; the average prices arifing from the weekly returns, are to be fent to the collectors of the ports in the diftrict for regulating exportation; and the average prices for the whole diftrict, made up from the fix weekly returns, immediately preceding the 1ft day of February, May, Auguft, and November, are to regulate the importation of foreign corn, and duties paid thereon.

30 Geo. 3. chap. 1. is an act of indemnity, for abrogating the Corn Laws, in purfuance of orders from the Privy Council, dated 11th and 18th November, 23d December 1786, 2d and 8th January 1790. By this act, the above orders are confirmed, and the Corn Laws fufpended; no kind of Britifh grain being allowed to be exported, except the particular quantities fpecified for the ufe of the fugar colonies; and all forts of foreign grain freely allowed to be brought into every port in Great Britain at the low duties; the act to continue in full force till 29th September 1790.

30 Geo. 3. chap. 43. The execution of the corn laws further fufpended, till 28th February 1791; but full powers given to the Privy Council, to permit the exportation of all forts of Britifh grain, or ftop the importation of foreign grain, whenever the Privy Council judged it neceffary.

31 Geo. 3. chap. 4. The above two acts amended, and by a claufe in the general Corn Law, which paffed this feffion, they are continued in force till its commencement on the 15th November 1791.

A a 2

It will be obferved, that none of thefe acts for rendering the law of 1773 more effectual were extended to Scotland ; the confequence of this was, that owing to the average prices not being afcertained by the actual fales, whenever the ports were opened for the importation of foreign grain into Scotland, it always took place, when the current price of our produce was confiderably below the reduced rates, at which even the law of 1773 allowed the bringing in of foreign grain, viz. wheat at 48s. the Winchefter quarter, &c.   And, on the other hand, when the furplus quantity of grain was fo abundant, as to admit of exportation, the ports in Scotland were always fhut, before the price of home produce got up to the limit at which exportation ends; both cafes militating againft the Agriculture of this country.

1791.

I fhall now proceed to give an account of the new general Corn Law, viz. 31 Geo. 3. ch. 30. which commenced on the 15th November 1791. It repeals 1 Jas 2. ch. 19 ; 1 Gul. and M. ch. 12 ; 5 Geo. 2. ch. 12 ; 10 Geo. 3. ch. 39 ; 13 Geo. 3. ch. 43 ; 21 Geo. 3. ch. 50 ; 29 Geo. 3. ch. 58 ; and fo much of the 15 Cha. 2. ch. 7th as prohibits the buying of corn to fell again, and laying it up in granaries, when above certain prices.

As you have already had occafion to give a Table fhewing the prices, bounties, and duties, by which the Corn trade is regulated, under this act[*], I fhall refer to it, and proceed to give an account of the general regulations, contained in the act.

[*] Vide p. 149.

The maritime counties of England are divided into 12 dif-
ricts, and Scotland into 4 diftricts, in all 16 diftricts. The prices
of grain at the Corn exchange in London, are made to regulate
export and import in the firft diftrict, containing the port of London, and the counties of Kent, Effex, and Suffex. In the other
diftricts, the act mentions the particular market towns, at which
the prices and quantities of grain actually fold are collected.
All dealers in grain are to give in, upon oath, weekly accounts of their actual fales made during the week, to an officer
called the infpector of returns; who, from thefe returns,
makes out an account of the general weekly average price of
the whole diftrict, and tranfmits the fame to the collectors of
the cuftoms at the different ports within the diftrict; which
regulates the bounties to be paid on exportation.

Four times in the year, viz. within feven days after the 15th
of February, 15th May, 15th Auguft, and 15th November, the
receivers of corn returns, in each diftrict, make up the average
prices of corn within the fame, taken from the laft fix weekly
returns; (excepting that of oats which is made up from twelve
weekly return) this quarterly average is tranfmitted to the
collectors of the cuftoms at the different ports within the diftrict, at the periods above mentioned, which regulates importation, and the duties payable thereon, for the enfuing quarter.

In Scotland, the average prices of grain are not afcertained
by the actual fales. Once in the month, the fheriffs of the different counties convene juries to determine the average price
at which it is generally felling; but the witneffes examined,

produce no account of their actual purchafes, or fales; they
only depone, to what they believe from their own experience,
and the opinion of others, to be the current prices; and there
is great reafon to think, that either from carelefsnefs or de-
fign, this is often done in an erroneous manner*. The fheriffs
of the different counties in Scotland make up monthly accounts of the average prices of grain within each county, (afcertained in the inaccurate manner above mentioned) which
they fend up to the receiver of corn returns in the port of London; from thefe, the receiver makes up an average account for
each diftrict, and tranfmits it to the collectors of the ports within
the fame, which regulate the bounties upon exportation; and,
at the quarterly terms above mentioned, he makes up average
prices, from the two laft monthly returns; which regulate the
duties upon importation for the enfuing quarter.

Foreign corn may be imported and landed at any time,
without payment of duties, provided it is warehoufed under
certain regulations; but it cannot be taken out of the ware-
houfe for home confumption, before firft paying the low duties, and any other duty payable at the time, in the diftrict in
which it is intended to be confumed; nor corn of any kind,
either foreign or of home produce, can be carried coaftways,

* Upon enquiring at a confiderable corn dealer, who is frequently adduced as a
witnefs, he acknowledged that the corn dealers gave themfelves very little trouble
about the matter; and added, tha the laft time he was examined, he and other dealers
whom he mentioned made up their minds, by copying off the prices from the newfpapers immediately before going into Court.   Let me add, that thefe prices are not
inferted in the newfpapers by any authority.

from the port of any diſtrict, when exportation is not allowed
at the time of ſhipping to the ports in any diſtrict where exportation is allowed.

When the general average of the whole kingdom, exceeds
the rates of import at the low duties*, in that caſe, the parliament not being ſitting, his Majeſty, with the conſent of the
Privy Council, can ſuſpend the execution of the corn law, ſo ſar
as to prohibit all exportation, and allow importation at the low
duties, which permiſſion muſt continue in force for three
months ; but the power does not extend to the prohibiting the
exportation of foreign grain formerly warehouſed.

The above contains a ſhort abſtract of the general regulations of the Corn law of 1791.   The following laws have been
enacted for further regulating the trade in corn :

33 Geo. 3. ch. 3.   Act of indemnity for ſtopping the execu-
tion of the general Corn Law, by an order of Council dated 9th
November 1792, prohibiting the exportation of home produce,
and granting liberty to import foreign corn, until 1ſt March
1793 ; and further ſuſpending the ſaid law, by granting power
to his Majeſty and Council, at any time during the ſitting of
parliament, to allow importation and prohibit exportation.

33 Geo. 3. ch. 65.   General Corn Law of 1791 altered, by
repealing the clauſes for aſcertaining the average prices of

---

* Vide, p. 149.

grain in England, and adopting others of the fame tendency, with certain variations in their place. Further altered, by granting liberty to his Majefty and Council, when parliament is not fitting, to allow the importation of grain, and prohibit the exportation of home produce, when the general average of the whole kingdom exceeds the prices at which grain can be imported at the low duties from Ireland, and the colonies of North America, viz. wheat 48s. rye 32s. barley 24s. oats 16s. Further altered, when oat-meal is under 13s. per boll, exportation to be allowed, with a bounty of 1s. 6d : When a-bove 14s. per boll, exportation to foreign countries prohibited.

1795.

35 Geo. 3. ch. 4. 13th February 1795. Sufpends the general Corn Law of 1791, by empowering his Majefty, with confent of the Privy Council, to prohibit exportation, and allow the importation of all kinds of foreign grain, without payment of any duties whatever. The act to continue in force till fix weeks after the next meeting of parliament.

Having thus gone through the whole of the laws relating to corn which appear on the ftatute book, up to the prefent meeting of parliament, I muft obferve, that the leading features of the act 1791, bear a ftriking refemblance to the amendments on the Corn Laws propofed by your Father in his Treatife, infomuch, that it would appear his fentiments, on this important fubject, had been communicated to the framers of the bill*. The plan

---

* The Author of the preceding Inquiry correfponded with feveral Members of Parliament, and with other perfons converfant in this fubject, for fome time before his death ; and it is very poffible that fome of his fuggeftions may have been found deferving of notice. *Edit.*

of fending up the average prices of corn in Scotland to London, before the ports in this country can be opened or fhut, is certainly an idea of his ; if not that of dividing the whole kingdom into large diftricts, which in a great meafure prevents the miftakes in fhutting and opening the ports in the different counties for the importation of foreign grain, when there was no abfolute neceffity for it, and thereby allows the produce of the contiguous counties, united in the diftrict, to find a more general and certain demand. It is fomewhat furprifing, that none of thefe falutary regulations, for afcertaining the average price of corn, from accounts of the actual fales, were ever extended to Scotland. Mr Chalmers in his excellent eftimate of the ftrength of Great Britain, fays, ' had thefe laws produced ' no other benefit to the country, than eftablifhing an effectual ' mode for afcertaining the average price of corn, and there- ' by preventing caufelefs alarm, they had merited the praife of ' moft ufeful regulations.' It is true, Scotland is alfo divided into diftricts, but in no part of this country, is there a clerk to the market, or any officer appointed to afcertain the prices of corn, by an average of the actual fales. By the act of 1791, the fheriffs of the different counties, once a month, appoint a jury, who examine dealers in corn as to the current prices ; but thefe dealers, as mentioned before, do not produce, or depone to the quantity and prices of the refpective purchafes, from which alone, a juft average can be formed ; they only fwear to what they judge to be the current prices of corn within the county. The intereft of the corn dealers leads them to make the prices of corn appear as high as poffible, firft by con-

LETT. I.

B b

cealing the profits on their fales, which every perfon wifhes to
·keep, or be fecret; and fecondly, with a view to bring up the
prices to the rates at which exportation ceafes, or importation begins, thereby to check the brifk demand for corn from the farmer, and occafion dull fales, on which the profits of the corn dealers trade very much depend. Let me add to this, that in many
counties of Scotland, there are no public markets for corn e-
ftablifhed. In the county of Mid-Lothian, and city of Edinburgh, the metropolis of the kingdom, in particular, there is
no public market for either wheat or barley, nor officer appointed to form a fair average from the account of actual fales. It
is partly owing to thefe caufes, that in the city of Edinburgh,
where the grinding of wheat is performed at from 1s. to 1s. 8d.
per quarter, where fuel is cheap, and the price of labour in ba-
king is moderate, the price of bread to the inhabitants, is often
confiderably dearer than in London, where the grinding of
wheat cofts from 4s. to 6s. per quarter, where the prices of
fuel and labour, and the public burdens, are confiderably
higher than in Scotland. It therefore appears, that in Scotland, unlefs this important branch of the corn law is executed in the fame manner as in England, particularly in the
city of London, and the average prices of grain fairly calculated
from the price of actual fales, the average prices will always
be returned higher than they ought to be; of courfe the public
will be impofed upon, in fixing the affize and price of bread,
and the ports will always be fhut againft the exportation of
home produce, and opened for the importation of foreign grain,
before the average prices of Britifh corn, in the home market,

get up to the rates prefcribed by the ftatute, as happened under
the law of 1773. The evidence produced of the current prices
of corn in Scotland is now equally defective as under that
law, when many errors were committed ; for what greater ac-
curacy can accrue from the average prices being fixed by a jury
in place of the fheriff, when the evidence of the facts, on which,
they found their verdict, is equally defective.

It appears, by the ancient laws and practice, both of England and Scotland, that the Crown could fufpend the execution of the Corn laws, without the confent of parliament, a
privilege which it frequently exercifed. This was a dange-
rous power, as it rendered the laws in fome degree nugatory,
and counteracted their good effects. In every free country,
agriculture, an object certainly of the greateft national confequence, ought at all times to be under the facred protection
of ftanding laws ; for if thefe are to be fet afide occafionally,
it may be feared that the cultivators of the foil will not
have fufficient protection for encouraging their induftry. In
ancient times, the relative fituation of Britain, as to agriculture, commerce, wealth, and population, was nearly upon
a par with the other countries in Europe, and the expence of
raifing corn would be nearly equal every where ; the Britifh
hufbandmen of courfe could not be underfold in the home
market, and foreign corn would only be imported in cafes of
abfolute neceffity. At prefent, when the expence of cultivation is fo much increafed in Britain ; when a nation of merchants, (if I may ufe the expreffion,) with overflowing capi--

tals, are always on the watch to open the ports and fpeculate in bringing in foreign grain, importation ought never to be allowed, but with the greateft caution, nor exportation prohibited, contrary to the eftablifhed laws, unlefs in cafes of abfolute neceffity, fuch as would be fanctioned by all the branches of the legiflature. If the executive power judge it expedient, at any time to act otherwife, let the minifters ftand accountable to their country; and if it is found that they have acted wifely, they will be acquited by an act of indemnity.

By the law of 1773, all power was taken from the Crown, of abrogating the Corn laws; but that of 1791 gives liberty, to his Majefty, with the advice of the Privy Council, when parliament is not fitting, to fufpend the execution of the law, by ftoping exportation, whenever the general average price of the whole kingdom exceeds the rate at which grain is allowed to be carried to a foreign market; although, in any particular diftrict, the price is fo low as to admit of it: A power which as already mentioned is further extended by the 33 Geo. 3. When the Privy Council prohibits the exportation of home produce, or allows the bringing in of foreign corn, in the particular inftances above mentioned, or in any other, which would require an act of indemnity, the witneffes they fummon before them, on the fpur of the occafion, are generally merchants or meal men, members of the mercan ile intereft, who are ever anxious for importation on the pretext of lowering the price of corn; an expedient on which they are always ready loudly to affert, that the welfare of the ftate depends. As a balance to the influence of this clafs, your Father

propofes in his Treatife, that a court of confervation fhall be
formed, compofed of the chief Judges of England and Scotland,
who, when it appears neceffary to them, fhould recommend
to his Majefty, to fufpend the Corn laws, or apply to the legiflature for alterations or amendments. Some inftitution of
this kind feems abfolutely neceffary, to watch over the agriculture of this country, and combine the landed intereft in its
fupport ; and the Board of Agriculture, lately eftablifhed, appears
of all others the beft fuited to accomplifh this end, becaufe of
its poffeffing ample information on every branch of agriculture,
from an extended corefpondence throughout the whole kingdom. Every diviation from the eftablifhed fyftem of Corn
laws might either originate with this Board, or be fubmitted
to their confideration, before the Privy Council gave orders
for putting it in execution.

LETT. I.

The barriers, which the wifdom of our anceftors had fo
judicioufly erected to prevent the importation of foreign grain,
being thus broke through, by repealing the ancient laws, and
lowering the import rates, an alteration in the Corn laws,
which was firft eftablifhed by the ftatute of 1773, has certainly
been the principal caufe of Great Britain not being able to fupply herfelf with corn of the growth of her own foil. In
proportion as the country advanced in profperity, the furplus quantity, after fupplying the inhabitants, which ufed
formerly to be exported, was gradually abforbed by the increafing population and luxury of the nation ; and the law in queftion, amongft other caufes, giving a check to the further extenfion of agriculture, neceffary to counterbalance the addi-

tional confumption, the tide at laft turned againft the country, and a regular influx of foreign grain became expedient to fup-ply the growing wants of the inhabitants.

After the year 1784, the period to which your Father has brought down an account of the Corn trade, Great Britain has exported, and imported, from foreign countries, in nine years from 1785 to 1793 inclufive, the following quantities of grain.

An Account of the Corn of all kinds Exported from, and Imported into, Great Britain from 5th January 1785 to 5th January 1793.

Great Britain. Dr. — Cr.

Year		Quarters.	Price s.	Price d.	Amount	Year		Quarters.	Price s.	Price d.	Amount
1785	To foreign Wheat imported —	110,863	41	10		1785	By Wheat exported	132,685	41	10	
1786	——	51,463	38	10		1786	——	205,466	38	10	
1787	——	59,339	41	2		1787	——	120,536	41	2	
1788	——	148,710	45	0		1788	——	82,971	45	0	
1789	——	107,324	51	2		1789	——	67,868	51	2	
1790	——	216,374	53	2		1790	——	229,754	53	2	
1791	——	459,490	47	0		1791	——	71,546	47	0	
1792	——	22,131	42	2		1792	——	310,684	42	2	
1793	——	459,611	48	4		1793	——	81,755	48	4	
	Average price of the above 9 years 45s. 9d.	1,635,305	45	9	L.3,740,760 3 9			1,303,265	45	9	L.2,980,831 1 3
							Balance paid, in nine years, by Great Britain for foreign Wheat,	332,040			759,929 2 6
		1,635,305			L.3,740,760 3 9		Or, per annum, 36,893 1-3d quarters—L. 84,436 11 5d.	1,635,305			L.3,740,760 3 9

Great Britain. Dr. — Cr.

Year		Quarters.	Price s.	Price d.	Amount	Year		Quarters.	Price s.	Price d.	Amount
1785	To foreign Barley imported —	67,212	24	0		1785	By Barley exported	166,4 8	24	0	
1786	——	62,374	24	4		1786	——	111,598	24	4	
1787	——	43,244	22	8		1787	——	135,089	22	8	
1788	——	11,479	22	0		1788	——	212,811	22	0	
1789	——	12,295	22	10		1789	——	344,631	22	10	
1790	——	30,117	25	6		1790	——	51,163	15	6	
1791	——	61,135	25	10		1791	——	41,590	25	10	
1792	——	118,527	26	8		1792	——	47,555	26	8	
1793	——	147,169	31	8		1793	——	4,463	31	8	
	Average price of the above 9 years 25s.	553,552	25	0	L. 691,940 0 0			1,115,348	25	0	L. 1,394,185 0 0
	Balance received by Great Britain in the above 9 years for Barley exported	561,796			702,245 0 0						
	Or, per annum, 80,199 7-9th quarters—L. 78,027 4 5 1/7.										
		1,115,348			L. 1,394,185 0 0			1,115,348			L. 1,394,185 0 0

Great Britain.   **Dr.**

		Quarters.	Price s.	Price d.		
1785	To Foreign Rye imported	28,761	28	0		
1786	——	3,643	27	2		
1787	——	7,054	27	8		
1788	——	—	27	8		
1789	——	14,844	29	10		
1790	——	21,683	34	0		
1791	——	56,378	31	4		
1792	——	13,027	30	10		
1793	——	5,124	34	10		
Average price o the above 9 years, 30s. 1¼d.		150,514	30	1¼	L. 226,868	9 11
		150,514			L. 226,868	9 11

Cr.

		Quarters.	Price s.	Price d.		
1785	By Rye exported	13,163	28	0		
1786	——	6,736	27	2		
1787	——	12,683	27	8		
1788	——	31,220	27	8		
1789	——	39,946	29	10		
1790	——	47	34	0		
1791	——	3,528	31	4		
1792	——	16,151	30	10		
1793	——	512	34	10		
		123,986	30	1¼	L. 186,495	12 2
Balance paid by Great Britain in the above 9 years for Rye imported		26,523			40,372	17 9
Being per annum, for 2947 5-9th qrs.—L.4485 17 6		150,514			L. 226,868	9 11

Great Britain.   **Dr.**

		Quarters.	Price s.	Price d.		
1785	To Foreign Pease and Beans imported	16,813	30	8		
1786	——	35,709	33	2		
1787	——	42,884	31	10		
1788	——	10,902	27	2		
1789	——	391	27	2		
1790	——	43,168	31	0		
1791	——	14,726	30	6		
1792	——	43,259	31	4		
1793	——	48,274	37	4		
Average price of the above 9 years, 31s. 1d.		256,126	31	1	L. 398,061	6 9
		256,126			L. 398,062	6 9

Cr.

		Quarters.	Price s.	Price d.		
1785	By Pease and Beans exported	15,904	30	8		
1786	——	16,309	33	2		
1787	——	18,260	31	10		
1788	——	15,135	27	2		
1789	——	27,891	27	2		
1790	——	17,577	31	0		
1791	——	13,721	30	6		
1792	——	17,291	31	4		
1793	——	13,483	37	4		
		155,571	31	1	L. 241,783	5 3
Balance paid by Great Britain in the above 9 years for Pease and Beans imported		100,555			156,279	1 6
Being per annum, for 11,172 7-9th qrs.—L.17,364 6 10		256,126			L. 398,062	6 9

Great Britain.   *Dr.*   *Cr.*

		Quarters.	Price. s.	d.	£.	s.	d.			Quarters.	Price. s.	d.	£.	s.	d.
1785	To Foreign Oats Imported	274,089	17	2	235,259	5	6	1785	By Oats Exported	25,273	17	2	22,097	13	2
1786	———	478,473	18	0	430,625	14	0	1786	———	19,293	18	0	17,308	10	0
1787	———	512,004	16	8	426,670	0	0	1787	———	17,098	16	8	13,535	18	1
1788	———	413,827	15	8	313,814	12	10	1788	———	14,418	15	8	11,294	2	0
1789	———	429,722	16	0	343,777	12	0	1789	———	32,683	16	0	26,146	8	0
1790	———	735,173	18	10	692,282	18	2	1790	———	14,275	18	10	13,422	5	10
1791	———	788,709	18	2	716,410	13	6	1791	———	16,358	18	2	14,853	10	4
1792	———	1,008,401	18	2	915,964	4	10	1792	———	25,709	18	2	23,352	6	10
1793	———	722,523	21	10	788,754	5	6	1793	———	17,473	21	10	19,074	13	0
Average price of the above 9 years, 17: 10d.		5,362,921	17	10	4,863,559	6	4			182,580	17	10	161,090	14	1
								Balance paid by Great Britain in the above 9 years for oats imported being per annum for 575,593 9-4ths quarters, L. 522,496 10 3.		5,180,341			4,702,468	12	3
		5,362,921			4,863,559	6	4			5,362,921			4,863,559	6	4

General Abſtract Account of the Grain Exported from, and imported into, Great Britain, for 9 years, from 1785 to 1793 incluſive.

Great Britain.   *Dr.*   *Cr.*

	Quarters.	£.	s.	d.		Quarters.	£.	s.	d.
To Foreign Wheat imported from 1785 to 1793	1,635,305	3,740,760	3	9	By Wheat Exported from 1785 to 1793	1,303,265	2,980,831	1	3
To Barley ditto	553,552	691,940	0	0	By Barley ditto	1,115,348	1,394,185	0	0
To Rye ditto	150,514	226,868	9	7	By Rye ditto	123,986	186,495	12	2
To Peaſe and Beans ditto	256,126	398,062	6	9	By Peaſe and Beans ditto	155,571	241,783	5	3
To Oats ditto	5,362,921	4,863,559	6	4	By Oats ditto	182,580	161,090	14	1
					By ſurplus quantity of grain imported by Great Britain in the 9 years above mentioned, after deducting the quantity exported, being at the rate of 564,185 qrs. 9-3ds. value, L. 550,756 2-9ths per annum	5,077,668	4,956,804	13	8
	7,958,418	9,921,190	6	5		7,958,418	9,921,190	6	5

I have noticed before, that the greateſt miſtake which government appears to have committed, in paſſing the act 1773, was in
attempting, by lowering the import rates of foreign grain, to
ſink unduly low the money price of corn, which had only advanced with the price of labour, and with the growing wealth
and proſperity of the country ; and which cannot be reduced by
any act of the legiſlature, without ſhackling the induſtry of the
huſbandman, and diminiſhing the annual produce of the ſoil.
Your Father has juſtly cenſured this policy, as a deviation
from the wiſdom of our anceſtors ; and he recommends the
returning to the ancient rates eſtabliſhed in 1670 and 1688,
for regulating exportation and importation, as the means of
encouraging agriculture, ſecuring abundance in the home
market, and recovering to the country the advantage of a favourable balance, on the export and import of corn. Agree-
ably to this idea, indeed, the legiſlature, in 1791, has ſome-
what heightened the importation rates, and ſo far diſcouraged
the bringing in of foreign corn. This ſtatute, however, is
ſtill far from being perfect: A material error had found its
way into the formation of the Corn Laws, at their inſtitution
in 1670, which has never yet been rectified: It is obvious,
that the rates, which regulate the exportation and importation of the different ſorts of grain, ought to have been relatively fixed, in proportion to their real values, the labour and
expence they coſt the farmer in rearing and bringing them to
market ; and that in particular, if the import rate of any of
the grains was fixed under the prime coſt, or its relative value,
the Britiſh farmer would be obliged to abandon, in a great
meaſure, the cultivation of that grain ; for the corn merchant
would, in conſequence of the low import rate, obtain an al-

moſt complete command of the home market, as he could ſupply it cheaper from foreign countries, than the article could
be raiſed for in Britain; our farmers would, of courſe, turn
their ſkill and attention to the raiſing crops of the other
grains, which, being higher rated in the table of importation, would thereby give them a better chance of profit.

That this is now the caſe in England, with reſpect to
oats, I ſhall endeavour to prove from the following ſtatement. It muſt be allowed, that the great accumulation of
wealth, and the immenſe quantity of money in circulation
in this country, when compared with what was the caſe in
any former period, have raiſed the price of labour, and
augmented, in an aſtoniſhing manner, the rents of land, and
the expences of cultivation in Britain, whilſt, at the ſame
time, theſe have not much advanced in the countries that
ſupply us with corn. It is therefore obvious, that the Engliſh
farmer, muſt now in a particular manner be underſold, when
he attempts to raiſe and bring to market, any kind of grain, to
the culture of which, the ſoil and climate of the northern
countries in Europe are peculiarly adapted; and he will at laſt
be obliged to abandon the cultivation of that grain, if the im-
portation-rate continue ſo low as not to allow the price in the
home market to get up, ſo as to indemnify him for the expence
of raiſing it, and leave a ſufficient profit on the capital employed; or even if it does not afford him an equal profit with the
other grain of the moſt general conſumption. That this is
the caſe at preſent, with the cultivation of oats in England,
is obvious from the following ſtate of facts: By the ancient
law, eſtabliſhed in 1670, for regulating the import and export
of corn, foreign wheat could not be imported at the low duty,

till the price got up to L. 4 per quarter; and even then, a duty of 5s. 4d. per quarter was impofed on importation. Mr King who wrote about the fame period, and who is celebrated by Davenant as a good political arithmetician, whofe calculations, he fays, cannot be controverted, computes the average price of Englifh wheat at 28s. and oats at 12s. per quarter. By a medium of the average prices of grain upon record, in the county of Edinburgh, for 84 years, from 1628 to 1712, the price of wheat, reducing the meafure to the Englifh quarter, amounts to 28s. 8d. and of oats to 12s. 5d. which correfponds with furprifing exactnefs with Mr King's calculations. If the import rate of oats had therefore been originally regulated, in proportion to their current values, in 1670 and 1688, when the prefent fyftem of corn laws was firft enacted, it ought to have been fixed by law in the following proportion: As 28s. the average price of wheat is to 85s. 4d. the import rate of wheat, including the duty, fo is 12s. the average price of oats to 36s. 6d. being the relative import rate at which oats ought to have been imported, including the duty: whereas this law allowed foreign oats to be imported at 17s. 4d. including the duty.

Upon turning up Mr Young's Annals of Agriculture, vol. 18. page 431, wherein he gives an account of the agriculture of a diftrict in Effex, we find he mentions that the courfe of crops there is, turnips, oats, clover, wheat; and that the wheat produces 2½ quarters, and the oats 4½ quarters per acre. Upon putting the following queftion to an intelligent farmer in this parifh; If from fields, which after being fummer fallowed, manured, and fown with wheat, 10 bolls per acre is produced, what quantity of oats might have been expected, if they had been fown with that grain? his anfwer was, 12 bolls per acre. This produce, allowing for the difference of the meafure, is nearly in the fame proportion to the quantities mentioned by Mr Young, viz. as 5 is to 9. I fhall however admit, that in any fituation, where wheat is fown, double the quantity of oats would be produced. The real value of oats therefore, being the labour and expence incurred by the farmer in raifing and bringing them to market, may at the loweft be eftimated at one half of the value of wheat.

The rate at which foreign wheat could be imported at the low duty by the act of 1773 was 48s. per quarter: and the equivalent rate to infure the farmer an equal chance of profit, when he fows oats, fhould of courfe have been 24s. per quarter; whereas the law allowed the importation of foreign oats when the price in the home market got up to 16s. per quarter, a price at which the Englifh farmer is at prefent by no means indemnified for the expence of cultivation: It is therefore obvious, that the prefent fyftem of Corn laws, from their original eftablifhment in 1670, has always been defective, in allowing the importation of oats at too low a rate, when compared with that of the other grains; and that the legiflature, when it paffed the act 1791, in place of amending the error, made matters worfe, by increafing the import rates of the other grains, more than they have done that of oats, and thereby finking the relative value and money price of that grain. Its price was, in fact, much too low before the law was altered, and had occafioned the Englifh farmer fo far to abandon the culture of that grain, as to require a large annual importation of foreign oats, to fupply the great number of horfes now uſed in luxury, and in tranſporting the extended manufactures of this country. By the law of 1791, the import rate of wheat, at the low duty, is now fixed at 54s. per quarter. · As it has been ſhown, that the real value of oats, is at preſent, to the real value of wheat, as 5 is to 9, the import rate of oats in proportion to that of wheat ought to have been fixed, by law, at 30s. per quarter, in order to give the farmer an equal chance of profit, and to encourage him to go on with the cultivation of this grain ; but the law of 1791 allows foreign oats to be imported, when the price in the home market gets up to 18s. per quarter. The effect of theſe low rates has been, that in the 9 years from 1785 to 1793, of which I have given an account of the corn trade, the average price of wheat was 45s. 9d, while the average price of oats was only 17s. 10d ; whereas, in proportion to the price of wheat, and the expence they coſt the farmer, it ought to have been 25s. 5d. The price of oats being thus reduced, by the low import rate, no leſs than 7s. 7d. per quarter below their relative value, the natural conſequence has been, that the cultivation of this grain has been neglected, and Great Britain, in the 9 years above mentioned, has been obliged to import oats from foreign countries to the amazing amount of 5,362,921 quarters, value L. 4,863,599 : 6 : 4.

The oats which are imported from abroad, growing chiefly in the northern countries of Europe, are of a very inferior quality to the growth of Great Britain; but being imported into England, and chiefly given to horſes, their imperfection is never properly aſcertained. In Scotland, however, where the value of oats is immediately known by the meal they produce, the inferior quality of the foreign oats is readily detected, and confequently none are brought into this country, except in cafes of abfolute neceffity. Upon making inquiry into the quality of the oats imported from the Baltic, in confequence of the very defective crop in 1782, at a reputable meal_maker, he informed me, that upon infpecting his books, he found thofe oats were about 22s. per cent. worfe in quality, than the oats of the growth of the Lothians, and Northumberland, of the fame defective crop; a circumftance the more deferving of notice, as the feafon of that year was even more unfavourable in this ifland than in the north of Europe.

It is in vain perhaps to look for our recovering foon a favourable balance to any confiderable extent from the exportation of corn, till the expences of the hufbandmen, in the different countries in Europe approach nearer to a par, as was the cafe in the early part of this century, unlefs that object be attained by an adequate bounty. But Great Britain may, and ought undoubtedly to cancel the unfavourable balance paid to foreigners, and fupply herfelf with corn, the produce of her own foil. This fupply, however, muft become deficient, whenever foreign corn is allowed to be imported at cheaper rates than it can be raifed at home. From like caufes, Rome, when miftrefs of the world, by purfuing an impolitic fyftem, deftroyed the cultivation of Italy, and was at laft reduced to tremble for her exiftance, at every blaft of adverfe wind; on the other hand, check the importation of foreign corn, and the more that wealth and luxury abound, fo much the more will an additional capital be invefted in agriculture, for carrying on rural improvements, to fupply the increafing confumption. Let it therefore be the care of the legiflature, by wife laws, to reftrain the importation of corn, except in cafes of abfolute neceffity ; cafes which then indeed would but feldom occur. If Great Britain is to continue to fupport the confpicuous character fhe at prefent difplays in the eyes of Europe, fhe muft not ftoop to depend for fuftenance upon any nation. It is alfo to be confidered, that Poland, which formerly at all times opened its granaries, to fupply the deficient crops of every country in Europe, cannot now be depended on; its government being deftroyed, and the kingdom difmembered by afpiring nations, who formerly united in a formidable combination to diftrefs us, when involved in a tedious and expenfive war; and who, although fome of them are at prefent in amity with this country, are neverthelefs jealous of our naval power. Were Great Britain to depend on the ports in the Baltick, or on America, for a regular fupply of corn, they might tell us with impunity; you fhall not have a bufhel, till you alter your navigation laws, and allow our fhips to participate in your trade. The decided part, which the different nations of Europe took in the conteft with our colonies, clearly proves, what we are to expect from them in the time of diftrefs : if Great Britain had ftood in need of a confiderable fupply of foreign corn at that period, fhe muft have made peace on the moft humiliating terms.

It ufed to be the boaft of the mercantile intereft, that whilft we preferved our navy and commerce, corn would flow in

from other countries, at a cheaper rate, than it could be purchafed at home; the danger, however, of trufting to this fupply, is at prefent obvious; for we are informed from high*
authority, that the different countries in Europe are now
raifing no more corn than what is barely fufficient to fupply
themfelves.

Seeing therefore our dependence on foreign nations for corn
is every day becoming more critical, let us hope that the Britifh legiflature will, by wife laws and judicious regulations, take
every meafure in its power to encourage agriculture at home.
The requiring an annual fupply of foreign oats, or indeed of
any other grain, is the more to be lamented, whilft fuch large
tracts of wafte land, to the extent of many millions of acres,
remain uncultivated in Great Britain. Oats being the crop,
which at firft can be raifed to the greateft advantage on
thefe wafte lands, it would be neceffary that the legiflature
fhould give fuch encouragement as might enfure the cultivators
a fuitable price for their produce, fo as to indemnify them for
the expence of cultivation, and leave a profit on the capital
employed, in fome degree adequate to that which is invefted
in trade and manufactures. And for fecuring this, in carrying on improvements on the wafte lands, the raifing the import rate of oats to a par with that of other grain, in proportion to their real value, appears to be one of the moft effential
regulations.

* See the Reprefentation on the Corn Trade, by the Privy Council, in 1789.

D d

It may be objected, that this measure would be pernicious, as it might tend, by increasing the cultivation of oats, to diminish the quantity of wheat or barley: on the contrary, it would encourage the British farmer, gradually to extend cultivation over three or four millions of acres of waste land, and to pursue a more perfect system of husbandry, on a more extensive field. Nature delights in variety; the seldomer a crop of any particular sort of grain is sown upon a field, the more bountiful is her return for the seed and labour; repeat it often, and at last, in general, you will not reap a produce equal in quantity to the seed. Any regulation, therefore, that renders the rotation of crops more various, increases the productive powers of the soil. Less wheat would be sown on the land at present under culture, but more might be brought to market: and when we take into the account the cultivation which would be extended over the immense tracts which at present lie waste, there is not a doubt, but that the supply of wheat would be much more abundant, and fully adequate to answer the consumption of the inhabitants. The decided preference given, for many years past, to the raising of wheat in Britain, owing to the high price it brings in the market, in proportion to other grain, stimulates the husbandmen to sow too much, and repeat that crop too often on the soil; the consequence is, that the plants, not receiving a sufficient supply of nourishment necessary for perfecting their seeds, which nature digests and stores up in the soil, by a slower process, than the rapid succession of the crop admits of, they of course become weak and sickly, and in adverse seasons, blight, smut, mildew, and disease, attack the crop. I have not a doubt, but that the deficiency of

the wheat crops in England, has, of late years, in part proceeded from this cause; and that in the end, repeating it
seldomer on the land, from a more various and judicious syf-
tem of cultivation being adopted, would not diminish the
quantity brought to market. That raising considerably the
import rate of oats would produce the falutary effects above-
mentioned, cannot be denied : It would also increase the confumption of beans, as provender for horses; which, containing three times more meal than oats, is a much heartier food
for that useful animal; and as a crop of beans is an excellent
preparation for a crop of wheat, increasing the confumption
of the one would promote the cultivation of the other. In
this point of view, it seems no small defect in the Corn
Laws, that a bounty is not given on the exportation of peafe and
beans; an encouragement that ought to be equally extended
to all forts of grain, in proportion to their real value. Thefe
kinds of pulfe are a nourishing food for the negroes in our
colonies; and by a simple and cheap procefs, they can be strip-
ped of their skin or hull, and split, when they become a pa-
latable dish, even on the tables of the opulent.

The frequency with which the Corn Laws have been set aside,
with refpect to fending grain to our colonies, plainly evinces,
that the present fystem is erroneous, and that a free exportation, at all times, should be allowed from the mother country; more efpecially, as our ships go out without a full loading, and the produce they bring back has an almost complete
monopoly of the British market. The old government of
France adopted the policy of a free export to their colonies in

the Weſt Indies; and before the preſent diſturbances broke out, its colonies were certainly the moſt flouriſhing, and its colonial trade the moſt extenſive of any nation in Europe.

All the writers on the national policy of regulating the export and import of corn, whom I have read, ſeem to think, that a permanent law is neceſſary for perfecting the ſyſtem. Such an idea appears to me extremely erroneous, eſpecially during the very unequal diviſion of wealth, population, and national expenditure, that ſubſiſts amongſt the different nations, at preſent connected by the extended commerce of Europe, which gives ſuch a decided ſuperiority in point of expence, to one country over another, in the raiſing of corn. Although the agriculture of Great Britain was never carried on with ſo great a capital, ſkill, and induſtry, as at preſent, it has, nevertheleſs, relatively ſunk. Formerly a large ſurplus quantity of grain was annually exported, now corn is not raiſed to ſupport the increaſing conſumption of the inhabitants, and a large ſupply of foreign grain is annually imported to make good the deficiency. This appears to ariſe from our agriculture being depreſſed by various burdens, which ſhackle the induſtry of the huſbandman, and particularly by Corn Laws, injudiciouſly framed, which allow the importation of foreign grain, at prices below what the farmer can at preſent afford to raiſe it; occaſioned by the immenſe capital in circulation, and the increaſing demand for our manufactures, which have raiſed the price of labour, the expence of cultivation, and of every article of conſumption in the kingdom.

Seeing the wealth of nations varies conſiderably at different

periods, fo ought the rates which regulate the export and import of foreign corn; if thefe affect the money price of our
own produce in the home market, and tend to fink its relative value below the current price of labour, with which
it muft always bear a juft and neceffary proportion, the rates
muft confequently be raifed in order to preferve agriculture, the only folid bafis on which the real wealth and
lafting profperity of a ftate can be founded. Should the induftry and capital of Great Britain continue to increafe for
30 years, in the fame proportion it has done fince the peace
of 1783, money in circulation, the price of labour, and expence of cultivation, may be double what it is at prefent; the
price of corn will naturally rife in the fame proportion : And
if the rates, at which the importation of foreign corn is then
allowed to be imported, tend to obftruct this rife, they muft
either be heightened, or Great Britain will lofe her agriculture ; a ftriking inftance of which has already taken place in
the article of oats. On the other hand, was the profperity of
this country to decline, fo as to diminifh the demand for labour, or the floating capital one half, the price of corn ought
to fall in proportion to the reduced price of labour, and the
importation rates be lowered, if they were the means of preventing the neceffary reduction.

Should thefe principles be found juft, a permanent law
to regulate the export and import of corn, is incongruous
with found policy; it ought therefore to expire regularly at
ftated periods, fuppofe at the end of every twenty or thirty years, when the wifdom of Parliament, taking the then
fituation of the country under its ferious confideration.

should regulate the Corn Law, in conformity with the price of labour; the moft certain index of the growing profperity, ftationary fituation, or declining ftate of the nation.

From what I have ftated, I hope it will be allowed, that the reafon why Britain does not now fupply her confumption of oats, with the growth of her own fields, (from which caufe, the permanent balance, that now ftands againft this country in the foreign trade of corn, moft generally arifes,) is the low rate at which the importation of foreign oats is allowed; thereby preventing the Englifh farmer from receiving an adequate price to indemnify him for the expence of raifing them, efpecially of late years, fince the charges on cultivation, from a variety of caufes, have been fo much increafed.

This circumftance alone may convince every friend to his country, of the neceffity of a well regulated fyftem of Corn Laws. If, from the importation price of foreign oats being too low rated, we are yearly lofing the cultivation of that grain, what could we expect from the total abolition of thefe laws, which a celebrated author fo warmly contends for: moft affuredly the confequences would be, that Great Britain, like ancient Italy, would gradually lofe her agriculture, and depend at laft on foreign countries for every fpecies of corn; of courfe, the immenfe confumption of manufactures ufed by three or four millions of inhabitants, who derive their fupport from the immediate labour of the fields, would be loft to this country, and a moft complete check be given to that bufy circulation of wealth and induftry, on which the ftrength and energy of this nation chiefly depend.　As fhe could not, like the empire of Rome, be fupplied with the fpoils of conquered provinces, and the plunder of the induftrious hufbandman; a rapid current would therefore perpetually be carrying out the riches of the country, till gradually falling from the exalted ftation fhe at prefent occupies in Europe, her wealth and refources would at laft fail, and finking below the level of the furrounding nations, fhe would be reduced to the prefent feeble and abject fituation of Spain, and exhibit to the world, another melancholy picture, of the downfal of a great nation, by withdrawing her capital and induftry from the cultivation of her own fields, and embarking it in the improvement of diftant colonies and foreign commerce.

I fhall be happy, if thefe obfervations ferve to elucidate your late Father's Treatife on the Corn Laws of this country, and am,

Dear Sir,

Your moft Obedient

Humble Servant,

Wm Mackie.

To Lieutenant-Colonel Dirom of
　Mount Annan, Edinburgh.

LETTER II.

*Containing an Examination of Dr Adam Smith's Theory on the Corn
Trade: An Inquiry into the Cause of the present Scarcity of Grain,
in Great Britain; with Suggestions for promoting Agriculture,
and particularly the Cultivation of the Waste Lands; and for rendering the produce equal to the increasing consumption of the Kingdom.*

Ormiston, 13*th February*
1796.

DEAR SIR,

IN my former Letter, my endeavours were used to in-
force the arguments contained in your late Father's
Inquiry into the Corn Laws, and to shew, that to preserve the
agriculure of Great Britain, whilst she possesses such a decided
superiority in point of wealth and circulating capital over
the surrounding nations, it becomes absolutely necessary to
restrain the importation of foreign corn, by laws judiciously
framed, so as to secure to the cultivators of our own soil a
sufficient value for their produce, corresponding with the current wealth and prosperous situation of the country; a principle, in political œconomy, which appears to be fully exemplified at present by the deficiency in the culture of oats, as
stated in my former Letter; and to which perhaps the cultiva-

tion of wheat is alfo faſt approaching in ſome parts ,of England.

This being an objeƈt of the firſt national conſequence, it
certainly merits the fulleſt diſcuſſion, particularly at a period
when this country, labouring **under an** alarming ſcarcity, is
even threatened with an abſolute famine. I ſhall therefore
proceed to inveſtigate the cauſes that now render our corn
crops ‚inadequate to ſupply the demand, and point out the
means which, in my humble opinion, will remedy the evil.

As my ſentiments coincide with the general tendency of your
late Father's Treatiſe, that a well regulated ſyſtem of Corn
Laws is abſolutely neceſſary for encouraging agriculture at
home,˙on which every nation that wiſhes to preſerve its
wealth and independence ought only to rely; I find my-
ſelf under the neceſſity of examining and combating the
opinions of a juſtly celebrated political writer Dr Adam
Smith, in his Inquiry into the Nature and Cauſes of the
Wealth of Nations. The arguments of this author tend
to prove, that the free importation of foreign grain ſhould
at all times be allowed, in order to lower or keep down
the money price of corn in the home market, which he
ſays will encourage agriculture, promote the intereſt of
the proprietors of land and cultivators, and finally prove of
the greateſt advantage to the ſtate. His own words are: ' If'
' importation was at all times free, our farmers and country
' gentlemen would probably, one year with another, get leſs

E e.

' money for their corn than they do at prefent when importa-
' tion is at moft times in effect prohibited; but the money
' which they got would be of more value, would buy more
' goods of all other kinds, and would employ more labour :
' Their real wealth, their real revenue, therefore, would be
' the fame as at prefent, though it might be expreffed by a
' fmaller quantity of filver; and they would neither be dif-
' abled nor difcouraged from cultivating corn, as much as
' they are at prefent*.' In another part of his work, where
he argues in favour of the monopoly of the home market,
and bounties granted on the exportation of manufactures,
which raife their price in the home market, he fays, ' You
' thereby increafe, not only the nominal, but the real profit,
' the real wealth, and revenue of thofe manufacturers, and you
' enable them either to live better themfelves, or to employ a
' greater quantity of labour in thofe particular manufactures.
' You really encourage thofe manufactures, and direct towards
' them a greater quantity of the induftry of the country,
' than what would probably go to them of its own accord.
' But when, by the like inftitutions, you raife the nominal or
' money price of corn, you do not raife its real value; you
' do not increafe the real wealth, the real revenue, either of
' our farmers or country gentlemen; you do not encourage
' the growth of corn, becaufe you do not enable them to
' maintain and employ more labourers in raifing it†.' The
truth of thefe affertions is founded on the pofition which he
lays down, that the money price of corn regulates the money

---

* Book 4. chap. 5. p. 311. 7th edit.   † Ibid. p. 277.

price of all things: he says, ' By regulating the money price
' of labour, it regulates that of manufacturing art and induf-
' try; and by regulating both, it regulates that of the com-
' plete manufacture. The money price of labour, and of
' every thing that is the produce either of land or labour,
' muft neceffarily either rife or fall in proportion to the mo-
' ney price of corn*.'

I readily agree, that the money price of corn may produce
this effect in a nation where the ftate of fociety is ftationary,
or declining, fuch as China or Hindoftan; but when applied
to Britain, or any country advancing in wealth and population, the argument appears to me to be unfounded. In
China, where wealth and population are ftationary, the production and confumption of the country are fo exactly balanced, that it is with the utmoft difficulty the great mafs of the
people can drag on a wretched exiftence; Dr Smith himfelf
draws a melancholy picture of their miferable fituation in the
8th chap. of his 1ft book, to which I refer. It is obvious, that
in this ftate of fociety, the money price of corn muft regulate
the money price of labour, and every other commodity whatever. The wretched labourer, or mechanic, whofe confumption correfponds fo exactly with his gains, is frequently
under the neceffity of deftroying his offspring, in order to
narrow his expences, as he can fee no profpect of relief
from any additional demand for his labour, to increafe his
wages and add to his gains. Thus, from dire neceffity, is one

* Page 159.

E e 2

of the univerſal laws of nature diſſolved, the moſt engaging tie with which ſhe binds the whole animal creation broken, and the moſt neceſſary duty impoſed upon a government diſregarded. If therefore at any time the neceſſaries of life advance in price, in conſequence of bad crops, numbers of the miſerable inhabitants are ſtarved to death, till the price of corn is again reduced, and arrives at its former ſtationary equilibrium with the price of labour and every other neceſſary commodity. Even in China, were the government to interfere, and reduce the price of corn below this ſtandard rate, either, if poſſible, by promoting the importation of foreign corn, or by fixing a maximum, it would afford no relief to the great maſs of inhabitants ; for the price of labour would ſtill fall in proportion, till it ſunk to the loweſt rate at which the labourers could afford to work ; on the contrary, it would make their ſituation worſe, by depreſſing agriculture, part of the capital employed in cultivation would be diſſipated, and the cultivators which it had kept in employ being thrown idle, would regorge upon the reſt of the inhabitants and add to the general diſtreſs. In this ſtate of ſociety, therefore, it appears to be extremely impolitic in a government to eſtabliſh a ſyſtem of policy which favours the importation of foreign grain, in order to ſink the price of corn in the home market below the natural rate ariſing from the wealth and ſituation of the country. But as Dr Smith has recommended this ſyſtem as proper to be introduced into the political œconomy of the preſent European ſtates, and particularly into that of Great Britain, a country where the ſituation of the inhabitants is diametrically oppoſite to what I have deſcribed, and where

the population, and particularly the wealth, induſtry, and
capital of the ſtate are increaſing with a rapidity unknown
in any age or country; it will therefore be neceſſary particularly to enquire if the principles are juſt, on which
this celebrated œconomiſt has formed his theory, of allowing the free importation of foreign grain, for the purpoſe
of keeping down the price of home produce, by which he
maintains the agriculture of this country would be encouraged. Upon peruſing his chapter on bounties, and digreſſion
on the corn laws, it will be found, as I mentioned before,
that he grounds his arguments on the ſuppoſition that the
money price of corn regulates the money price of labour,
and every other commodity. I have ſhown, that in China,
where ſociety is ſtationary, and directly the reverſe of every
thing in this kingdom, the price of corn produces this effect:
But in countries where induſtry, population, and wealth, going on in a progreſſive ſtate of improvement, are conſtantly
increaſing the national capital, and continually adding to the
general conſumption, theſe cauſes alone operate to raiſe the
money price of labour, and every other commodity, without being, in the ſmalleſt degree, affected by the money
price of corn. ' For inſtance a demand comes to Manchcſter,
Leeds, and Glaſgow, which raiſes the price of goods 4d. per
yard, and the profits on ſtock 10 per *cent.* Every manufacturer anxious to ſhare an additional profit, in order to procure an additional number of workmen to ſupply the increaſing demand, offers them one penny per yard advance on
their work: they, in their turn, finding three or four ſhillings per week added to their earnings, increaſe their con-

fumption; in place of brown bread, they can now buy wheaten, and in place of dining upon bread and beer, they can now afford to add a few pounds of beef, or a quarter of mutton: thefe articles rife in their price with the demand, and the farmers, finding more profit in fattening beef and mutton, turn their attention from the raifing of corn till its price is alfo advanced in proportion. On the other hand, a gentleman returning from abroad, or retiring from trade or public employments, with a large fortune, purchafes an e- ftate in the country, and to adorn and improve it is to be the future objeft of his life; the labourer is bribed by higher wages to quit the plough, and the mechanic his former maf- ter: The hufbandman now finds difficulty in procuring hands to cultivate the earth, and, in his turn, muft raife the price of labour before he can get ploughmen to engage in his em- ploy: Every article, either of rude material or manufaftured commodity, which he has occafion for, he finds alfo encreafed in price, and the expence of raifing corn, advancing with a rapidity which threatens to wreft from him his capital em- ployed in the cultivation of the fields; but, on the other hand, the natural effeft of the fame caufe, univerfally diffuf- ing itfelf through every rank of fociety, operates in favour of the hufbandman. When he goes to market with his corn, and other rude produce of the foil, he finds a competition amongft the purchafers, who offer him higher prices in confequence of the increafing confumption. The landlord, in his turn, requires an additional rent, this is again expended in manu- faftures, and other articles of luxury, and an additional capital is thus put in circulation, for encouraging population, and the induſtrious exertions of every member of the ſtate.

It is obvious that in this natural courſe of events, whenever the wealth of Great Britain is ſo much accumulated as to increaſe the expences of cultivation, and advance the real value of Britiſh grain above what it can be raiſd and brought to market from foreign countries, the bringing in of foreign corn, for the purpoſe of reducing the money price of home produce, or even rendering it ſtationary, would neither ſink nor render ſtationary the money price in this country. As long as it continued to advance in proſperity, every addition to the capital and conſumption of the nation would infallibly increaſe the money price of labour, and every manufactured commodity, even although the importation rate of corn from foreign countries ſhould not allow the money price of that article to riſe in the ſame proportion. The conſequence of this would be, that the capital employed in agriculture would be gradually diſſipated, the revenue and conſumption of the landed intereſt and cultivators much diminiſhed, and of courſe, a check would be given to the internal circulation of induſtry, and the proſperity of the country; although perhaps its bad effects might not be immediately felt on the power and reſources of the ſtate, if the gradual extenſion of foreign commerce made good the deficiency. Nevertheleſs, as foreign commerce is the moſt precarious ſource of wealth and proſperity, if at any time, it happened to be cramped by war, or any other cauſe whatever, enervated by the conſtant drain for foreign corn, and the languid circulation of internal induſtry, the ftate would become feeble, like a foldier fainting with the lofs of blood after a fevere conflict with the enemy. Dif-aftrous in the extreme, would it prove to this country, if, by any combination amongft the naval powers, we loft our fu-periority at fea; being then cut off from our fupply of bread corn, famine and peftilence would follow in the train of our misfortunes.

In order to try Dr Smith's theory by the teft of experience, and to prove that the money price of corn does not regulate the money price of labour, and other commodities in coun-tries, that are in a progreffive ftate of improvement, but which rife in price folely from the quantity at market not being fufficient fully to fupply the increafing demand, it is only neceffary to compare the money price of corn, with the price of labour in different countries, and at different periods. I fhall begin with the American States: There the demand for labour is fo great, that, although corn and other kinds of rude produce, fell in general for half the money they do in Britain; neverthelefs, the price of labour, from the excef-five demand, is three times higher than in England. In the accurate account which Mr Young has given us of the agri-culture and commerce of France, in his Tour through that kingdom, immediately before the breaking out of the revolu-tion, he informs us that provifions are as dear in France as in England, that labour is 76 *per cent.* cheaper, and the price of manufactured commodities dearer than in England. Here are effects produced totally different from what Mr Smith's theory points at, that the money price of corn regulates the money price of all things, on which he founds his arguments for a free importation of foreign corn, whilst, at the same time, he argues for prohibiting foreign manufactures.

It must, however, be observed, that the account, which Mr Young has given us of the average price of provisions and labour in France, seems to contradict the idea I have thrown out, that the money price of labour, in a country advancing in improvement, regulates the money price of corn. The discerning eye, however, which runs over Mr Young's work, will soon discover that the kindgom of France, even under the old government, appears not to have been advancing in prosperity, and if not declining, was at least stationary, having followed, for upwards of a century, the destructive policy of foreign conquest, and diverting the capital which ought to have been invested in agriculture, into the cultivation of distant colonies, and encouragment of foreign commerce. We must not therefore be surprised, that although of late years, the commerce of France had advanced with greater rapidity, than even that of England, neverthelefs, her power and resources have declined, with her agriculture and internal industry. This cannot be doubted by any person, who considers the erroneous system of husbandry, carried on in France, where two white crops, following a fallow in constant rotation, must destroy the productive powers of any soil. Were the lands in Great Britain to be cultivated in the same manner, for a series of years, I have not a doubt, but that the annual produce of the soil would be diminished one half

F f

of what it is at prefent. The wretched policy of France has
hitherto prevented her manufactures and commerce from
affording aid to her agriculture, whilft the luxury introduced
into the cities has raifed the price of corn without advancing
in proportion the price of labour, and the confumption of the
cultivators. Hence the torpor and languid ftate of internal
commerce and intercourfe in France, for want of the rapid interchange of the productions of labour fo confpicuous
in England, which, like the circulation of the blood, gives
ftrength and vigour to the whole fyftem.

Were Great Britain to adopt Mr Smith's fyftem of a free
importation of foreign grain, fhe would certainly be reduced
to the political fituation of France, immediately before the revolution as defcribed by Mr Young. But the prices of corn
and labour in France, during the laft and prefent century,
demonftrate, in the cleareft manner, the fallacy of Mr Smith's
arguments in favour of his theory. Of this we have accurate
information, in the excellent fpeech of M. de Carraduce, de
la Chalotois, Procureur General to the Parliament of Britta-
ny, made before that Court, on the 20th Auguft 1764, when
the edict for allowing the free commerce of grain was regif-
tred, when he gave the following account of the then fituation of the agriculture of France. ' It is manifeft, that for
' about an age paft, the price of labour and merchandife
' is confiderably raifed in France, there are none that for
' fifty years paft hath not experienced this. The price of
' corn, which is the meafure of the whole, fhould then have
' rifen in proportion. In the mean time, it hath not only
' not increafed ; but it is a certain fact, that it hath fallen

' considerably, and that it would, an age ago, require a
' greater weight of silver to pay for a setier, than it doth at
' present. In 1649, the deputy of M——, Procureur General at
' the Chatilet, said in his requisition of the 6th March to the
' police, as a known fact, that wheat was at 15 livres the setier,
' a moderate price, (these are his words) but the same setier,
' hath, this present year, 1764, been at Paris at 14 livers,
' and 14 livers 10 s. It was of less value in the neighbouring
' cantons, and of necessity in the country. What shall we
' think, Gentlemen, of so great a difference, when we reflect
' that the mark of silver was, in 1649, at 28 livers 13 s. 8
' deniers, that is to say, at almost one half less than at this
' present day*.' Here is complete evidence, that the price of
corn has no effect on the price of labour, but that it is regulated like every other commodity, by the demand and quantity at market. For 50 years, previous to 1764, the price of
labour and manufactured commodities in France, had risen
considerably, when, at the same time, wheat had fallen one
half; and at no period, within these hundred years, does
that country discover any strong marks of general prosperity,
which no great nation can attain, unless agriculture is encouraged by prices for the produce of the soil, proportioned to
the price of labour, and of every manufactured commodity.
The bad effects of the low price of corn in France, M. de C.
describes in the following manner: ' If the farmer does not
' gain all his expences, and wherewith to satisfy all charges,
' the earth will remain untilled, as more than the moiety of
' this province doth. The starving proprietor will be forced

* Vide Corn Tracts, page 216.

' to fuftain bankruptcies and loffes ; the farmer ruined, badly
' clothed, and badly fed, will fell his little property ; he will
' take up, with his indigent family, the art of begging, too
' common, and which is a difgrace to the nation : The ftate itfelf
' will fuffer, the taxes will not be collected, but with extreme
' difficulty, and with the greateft rigour. And it muft be
' acknowledged, that this hath been the ftate of the kingdom
' of France, for more than an age. In every province, the
' earth fhews, in an infinity of places, the marks and veftiges
' of a deferted cultivation ; houfes unroofed proclaim a de-
' fertion and depopulation ; the cities, and even the capital,
' are peopled with poor, whilft thofe who have ruined fo many
' families, and enriched themfelves with their fpoils, make
' a parade of luxury, which is an infult on public mifery*.'
I muft here remark, that, in the laft century, France exported
confiderable quantities of corn, and fome of the old Englifh
writers complained that what was brought into England, funk
the value of home produce, and cramped the agriculture of
this kingdom.

I fhall next proceed to give an account of the effect of
the money price of corn, on that of labour and manufactured
commodities in Britain. Dr Smith informs us, in the 11th
chapter of his 1ft book, that the average price of wheat in the
Windfor market (which Mr Young has proved to be nearly
the average price of wheat in England) for fixty years, end-
ing in 1790, amounted to L. 2 : 11 per quarter, that the a-
verage price of the firft 64 years of this century amounted to
L. 2 : 6d. and during a feries of the cheapeft years from 1731
to 1750 (in which one year of fcarcity intervened) to only

* Vide Corn Tracts, p. 215.

L. 1 : 13 : 9 per quarter; but it is well known, that the low price of corn in the early part of the century, and particularly in the period of remarkable cheapnefs, produced no effect in lowering the price of labour, or of any manufactured commodity.: On the contrary, they were gradually on the rife. The profperity of Britain had been advancing from the Revolution, when the furplus produce of her land and labour only amounted to 4 millions, till at the latter period of 1750, when it had reached to 12 millions*. This advance however had not much increafed the price of country labour and expence of cultivation, and the f arm os, by puring a more judicious mode of cultivation, and probably by extending it over lands that had lain uncultivated during the civil wars in England, increafed the annual produce of the foil fo as not only to counterbalance the growing confumption of the country, but alfo to afford a confiderable quantity of corn for exportation.

The hufbandry of this country continued much in the fame fituation till the peace of 1763, which may be looked upon as a new epoch in the annals of agriculture, and every fpecies of Britifh induftry. After that period, the number of hands which had been diverted from the channel of productive induftry, to fupply the army and navy during the war, the increafing demand for our manufactures, our extended commerce to every quarter of the globe; the large fortunes that had been made by individuals during a profperous war; the increafe of the public debts and taxes; all confpired to raife the price of labour and cultivation; and had

* Vide Chalmer's Eftimate of the comparative ftrength of Great Britain. Table fronting page 234; new edition in 1794.

not the rapid circulation of induſtry pervaded all ranks, and by an increaſing conſumption raiſed the money price of corn, and other articles of the rude produce of the ſoil, in proportion to the growing wealth and proſperity of the country ; the agriculture of Great Britain muſt have declined, like that of France, where land of a better ſoil, and ſituated in a better climate, is far leſs productive than in England.

The wealth and capital of Great Britain having increaſed with an amazing rapidity of late years, ſo has the demand and money price of labour. In the year 1792, when the ſurplus produce of the land and labour of Great Britain, exported, amounted to near 25 millions*, in the ſame year did the farmers find the greateſt difficulty in procuring hands to carray on the cultivation of the fields ; the wages of labour and price of every manufactured commodity rapidly advanced, and agriculture, as well as manufactures, was encouraged by an additional conſumption increaſing the money price of corn. Dr Smith himſelf bears teſtimony to this material progreſs of induſtry in a country advancing in improvement like Britain. The whole tenor of his firſt book tends to prove it, where, amongſt other arguments, he ſays ' the demand for thoſe who ' live by wages therefore neceſſarily increaſes with the in- ' creaſe of the revenue and ſtock of every country, and cannot ' poſſibly increaſe without it. The increaſe of revenue and ' ſtock is the increaſe of national wealth, the demand for ' thoſe who live by wages, therefore naturally increaſes with ' the increaſe of national wealth, and cannot poſſibly increaſe ' without it†. And finally, ' The money price of labour in

* Vide Chalmers' Eſtimate of Great Britain, ibid.
† Book 1. chap. 8. p. 104.

‘ Great Britain has indeed rifen during the courfe of the pre-
‘ fent century. This, however, feems to be the effect not fo
‘ much of any diminution in the value of filver in the Euro-
‘ pean market, as of an increafe in the demand for labour in
‘ Great Britain, arifing from the great and almoft univerfal
‘ profperity of the country*.’

It is fomewhat furprifing, that Dr Smith fhould afterwards abandon his own arguments, founded in truth, and the experience of this country, and endeavour to eftablifh a theory, framed on the fuppofition, that the money price of corn regulates the money price of all things; principles totally different from what he himfelf had laid down, as mentioned above, and incompatible with the political fituation of this country, for the purpofe of overturning the eftablifhed national policy refpecting corn, by allowing the free importation of foreign grain, which, as it would have the effect of lowering the price of corn, and every article of produce, would thereby, in his opinion, encourage agriculture, and promote the intereft of the proprietors and farmers. In fupport of this theory, he advances fome extraordinary arguments; for inftance, he fays, in Book 1. ch. 8. ‘ In years of plenty, fervants frequently leave their maf-
‘ ters, and truft their fubfiftence to what they can make by
‘ their own labour: But the fame cheapnefs of provifions,
‘ by increafing the fund which is deftined for the main-
‘ tenance of fervants, encourages mafters, *farmers efpecially, to*
‘ *employ a great number. Farmers, upon fuch occafions, expect*

* Chap. 11. p. 313.

‘ *more profit from their corn, by maintaining a few more labouring*
‘ *servants, than by selling it at a low price in the market.* The
‘ demand for servants increases, while the number of those
‘ who offer to supply the demand diminishes; the price of
‘ labour, therefore, frequently rises in cheap years.’ The
first observation is certainly just; but that agriculture will be
encouraged, and carried on with greater spirit from cheapness of price, owing to farmers expecting greater profits by
employing more servants, and consuming their corn at home,
rather than selling it at a low price in the market, will not
be admitted by any farmer of common sense. The assertion
is founded on *two* positions: *1st*, That the money price of
corn regulates the money price of every commodity, which I
have proved does not apply to the present state of society in
this country; and *2dly*, that in agriculture, as in manufactures, the produce of a farm is increased in proportion to the
number of hands employed, which is by no means the case;
nothing, therefore, will give encouragement to farmers hiring
a greater number of servants, and extending cultivation, but actually receiving a high price for their corn, in the same manner
as a manufacturer is encouraged to hire more hands, and extend
his operations, in consequence of receiving high prices for his
fabrics. As a farther proof that Dr Smith's ideas, on the state
of agriculture in Britain are erroneous, it may be observed, that
he does not allow that the high prices of corn, which followed
the peace of 1763, proceeded from an influx of wealth, occasion-
ing an increase of luxury and consumption, but ascribes it entirely to bad crops; and whilst he views the high price of corn
as a public calamity, he looks upon the high price of butcher

meat, cheefe, butter, wool, hides, tallow, *and every fort of rude produce, corn excepted, as the forerunner and attendant on the greateft of all public advantages,* imagining that the high price of thofe articles will be followed by the low price of corn, potatoes, and every vegetable production ; a conclufion which he draws from erroneous principles, and in which it is now evident he has been miftaken.

When we recur to firft principles, and the immutable laws of nature, in judging of Dr Smith's opinion on the free importation of foreign corn into Britain, and the propofed monopoly in favour of manufactures, we fhall find fufficient caufe for drawing oppofite conclufions, and that whilft agriculture requires to be protected by a monopoly, manufactures may be left free. In order to fhew this in a clear point of view, I fhall point out the different principles on which the productive powers of agriculture and manufactures are founded. And fhall firft begin with manufactures.

It is obvious that the Supreme Difpofer of all things has given to the general mafs of mankind, in every country, nearly an equal fhare of bodily ftrength, and faculties of mind fufceptible of cultivation and improvement. This being the cafe, as manufactures are performed by the labour of the body, facilitated by the inventions of art, in this point of view all nations are nearly on a par for carrying on manufactures ; if, however, one nation advances confiderably in population beyond the other, their wants increafe in proportion, and a fpur is given to their ingenuity, in order to fupply them. In

G g

  the boundlefs progrefs of improvement, new wants multiply
with every refinement of art, and manufactures are carried on
to a degree of perfection, to which it is impoffible for a fociety more rude and with fewer wants to attain; and though
from the wealth accumulated by the induftrious nation, in
this ftate of refinement, the price of labour fhould be raifed
fo high, as to allow another nation, lefs advanced in wealth,
to bring manufactured articles to market at a cheaper rate,
yet the rich nation will ftill maintain its fuperiority, by avail-
ing itfelf of the fuperior capital it poffeffes, and of its fuperior fkill in the divifion of labour, of which manufactures
are fufceptible. If, again, the divifion of labour is not found
adequate to anfwer the end, renewed exertions of fkill and
capital, by calling in the aid of machinery, fo far reduces the
effect of the high price of manual labour on the articles manufactured, as to give a decided fuperiority to the rich and
ingenious nation, over all others lefs advanced in wealth and
refinement. Hence the manufactures of Britain are found
fuperior to thofe of every country in Europe, and are even
rivalling the fabricks of Bengal, where the money price of labour is about only a tenth part of what it is in England *. It
being therefore obvious, that the induftrious country, whilft it
preferves its fuperiority in wealth and ingenuity over other nations, has an evident advantage in carrying on its manufactures;
there feems to be no neceffity for the manufacturers of Great
Britain obtaining a monopoly againft thofe of other nations,
lefs advanced in wealth, ingenuity, and refinement; and the
decided fuperiority which the manufacturers of this country

---

* The wages of a weaver in Bengal are only two and a half rupees, equal to 5s.
7½d. a month.

maintain over thofe of every country in Europe, in the free
American market, is a proof of the fact.

Having thus finifhed the propofed fketch of the progrefs
of manufactures, I fhall proceed to defcribe the principles
on which the productive powers of agriculture are founded.

Although the Author of Nature has given to man, in the
different countries of the world, an equal fhare of ftrength
of body, and faculties of mind, fo as to enable him to per-
form nearly equal portions of productive labour, when thefe
powers are alone employed; yet, for wife purpofes, He has
formed the foils and climates of the different countries of the
earth, with that aftonifhing diverfity which univerfally per-
vades the face of nature, from the fertile fields of Sicily, Flan-
ders, and England, to the frozen regions of Norway, Lap-
land, and Kamfchatca. As the fuccefs of agriculture, depends,
in a great meafure, on the productive powers of foil and climate, it is obvious that an equal portion of fkill and capital,
may produce a much greater quantity of corn in one country
than it can do in another. This being the cafe, let us fuppofe
that the foil and climate of Poland, for inftance, is fo much fuperior to that of Britain, that the exertion of an equal portion of
labour and fkill, will produce double the quantity of corn, or
of other fuftenance in Poland, that it will do in Britain. As
nothing could counteract this phyfical difference, corn in Britain would fell at double the price it did in Poland, as it would
require double labour and capital to produce an equal quantity. Thus, it is obvious, if Poland could fupply Britain with

a confiderably quantity of grain, at one half or two thirds of the price it could be raifed at home, the agriculture of Britain muft either be protected, by granting to the cultivators a monopoly of the home market, or if left free, agriculture would decline in the laft mentioned country. On the other hand, let us fuppofe that the foil and climate of Poland and Britain are equally good and fertile, and that two hundred years ago, the wealth, population, and induftry of the two countries were exactly fimilar, and that only one fourth of the lands in each country, being kept under the plough, was fufficient to fupport their refpective inhabitants. In this fitnation, both countries would be upon a par for raifing corn, and a free intercourfe in grain could not hurt the agriculture of either country. If, however, from the blefling of a free government, or any other caufe, Great Britain fhould, in the courfe of two or three hundred years, by extending every branch of national induftry, quadruple her population and wealth, fo as now to require feven-eighths of the land to be kept in conftant cultivation, for fupplying food for the inhabitants; the improvement of the productive powers of agriculture, not depending entirely on capital and ingenuity, as in manufactures, but being in a great meafure influenced by the good or bad qualities of the foil and climate, no fkill or capital poffeffed by the cultivators could prevent the money price of corn in Britain from rifing very confiderably above the money price of corn in Poland: for two reafons, *firft*, the fall in the value of money; and *fecondly*, the additional labour and expence that muft now be beftowed in raifing and bringing it to market. To prove the laft pofition, I muft revert to the œconomy of nature, and its effect upon agriculture. Nothing is more certain, than that the fertility of the soil is exhausted by too constant a succession of crops of corn, and restored by allowing it to remain for a certain time in pasture. It is therefore obvious, that in a country only so far advanced in population, as to require but one fourth of the land being kept in cultivation for supporting the inhabitants, the other three fourths remaining in pasture, more abundant crops of corn will be then raised, with lefs labour and expence than can afterwards be produced on the same soil, by any exertion of skill and capital, when a more extensive population requires perhaps seven eighths of the lands being kept constantly under the plough. This progrefs in the œconomy of nature is fully exemplified in this country, by the rich crops raised on the ploughing up of old pastures. The luxuriant crops that grow on new soils are also found to decline and to be rendered lefs certain, being more affected by the influence of bad seasons in proportion to the length of time the land has been kept under the plough. Hence in England, and in other countries advanced in wealth and population, corn is raised at a greater expence of manure and cultivation, and the crops are more precarious, than in countries thinly peopled, such as America or Poland, where a simple plowing, or rather scratching and throwing in the feed, are frequently sufficient to secure a good crop.

As a testimony of the above mentioned progrefs in agriculture, and the effect of wealth and population in advancing the price of corn, I shall add that Mr Young, in his 13th volume of the

Annals of Agriculture has given us the expence to the farmer of raising a crop of wheat in some of the counties in England at this present day, the prime cost amounting to from 5s. 10d. to 7s. 10d. *per* Winchester bushel. In vol. 15th he has also given the selling price of grain in the Bannat on the river Tybuscus, viz. wheat at 1s. 4¾d. rye at 1s. barley at 7½d. per bushel, and hay at 3s. per tun. No skill nor industry could enable the farmers in England to raise corn at as cheap rates; but notwithstanding the amazing low price of corn, which Dr Smith says regulates the price of all things, allow the free importation of British manufactures into the Bannat, and they would not only rival but annihilate every manufacture in that country.

From every view of the subject, in the preceding discussion, it plainly appears, that agriculture and manufactures are established on very different principles, and that whilst wealth and population raise considerably the money price of corn, and other rude produce of the soil, they have not an equal effect in advancing the price of manufactures. Thence, although contrary to Dr Smith's opinion, we may fairly deduce the following political maxim: That agriculture, in rich and populous countries, stands more in need of a monopoly for its support than manufactures; and that the farther a nation advances in prosperity, it becomes the more necessary to secure its agriculture, not only by restraining the importation of foreign corn, but also by removing every impediment which may prevent, and by giving every encouragement, which may promote

the extenfion of cultivation and improvement over the whole
face of the country.

From a review of the arguments of this juftly celebrated
author, I can fee nothing that overturns the principle laid
down in my former Letter, that if Great Britain wifhes to
preferve her prefent fuperiority in wealth and refources over
the furrounding nations, agriculture muft be protected by allowing to the hufbandmen prices for their produce proportioned to the internal wealth and profperity of the country;
and that if, at any time, the bringing in of foreign corn tends
to fink the money price of Britifh grain below the corref-
ponding value of labour and other commodities, the importation muft be checked by judicious laws, altered from time to
time, at different periods, to correfpond with the profperous or declining ftate of the country. In the inveftigation
of Dr Smith's opinions, I have no other intention than, by
fair difcuffion, to fearch out the truth; and to his theory of
free importation, founded as I think on erroneous principles,
I have laftly to oppofe the favourable effects of a contrary
fyftem, on the agriculture and profperity of this country,
as cleary fhown in the preceding Inquiry into the Corn Laws,
and fully afcertained from the profitable experience of more
than one hundred years.

It no doubt will prove a matter of furprife, and a juft caufe
for alarm to find, that, at prefent, in the moft flourifhing æra of Britifh induftry, when agriculture is carried on
with a larger capital than at any former period, and
when the fkill and induftry of the hufbandmen were never

fo confpicuous, the quantity of corn raifed in this country is gradually becoming more and more inadequate to
the confumption and maintenance of the inhabitants, and that
in place of having a large annual furplus quantity of grain
to fpare, we are now every year becoming more and more
dependant on foreign nations, for fubfiftence; a fact which
is inconteftibly proved by the accounts of the exports and
imports of grain. In purfuing the inquiry into the caufe of
this deficiency, it will be found to proceed, 1*st*, From the accumulating wealth and luxury of the country, which will tend
to elucidate the principles which I have laid down, when
examining Dr Smith's theory; and, 2*dly*, From our agriculture being cramped by fuch reftraints as prevent the opening
up a more extenfive field for cultivation, and which might
render the fupply equal to the increafed confumption of the
kingdom.

It has been fhown, in the former part of this Letter, that it is
generally from countries thinly peopled, and having a confiderable portion of their good land in pafture, that confiderable
quantities of corn can be exported at a low price. But
this furplus quantity alfo arifes from the ftate of fociety in
thofe countries at the time; the inhabitants being cultivators
with few wants, and living with fimplicity, chiefly on vegetable food and the produce of their herds, a larger furplus remains after fupplying their frugal neceffaries. If, however,
the population of the country increafes, and the inhabitants
ftill retain their fimple manners, and continue to live on vegetable food, it is aftonifhing how great a number of inhabitants the foil will maintain, if it poffeffes a moderate degree of

fertility. The population of Hindoſtan when under an effici-
ent government, and the preſent ſtate of China, are a ſtriking
proof of the obſervation. It is obvious, however, that if
theſe nations were to alter their manner of life, and ſubſiſt
in a great meaſure on animal food, like the people in England,
the countries could not afford proviſion for their numerous
inhabitants; and that if they could not procure an additional quantity from other countries, their population would
ſoon be conſiderably diminiſhed.

In order to ſhow the effect which living on vegetable or
on animal food will produce on population, or the abundance
or ſcarcity of ſubſiſtence which it may occaſion to the inhabitants of a country, their numbers remaining ſtationary, I
ſhall calculate the population, which a farm of 504 acres of
fertile land will maintain, when under a judicious mode of
cultivation, the inhabitants living entirely on vegetable food;
and the numbers which can be ſupported on animal food by
the produce of a like farm when in paſture.

With a view to aſcertain this point with as much preciſion as
the nature of the calculation will admit of, I called at the families of ſeveral labourers and mechanics in this place, who live entirely on vegetable food, to learn if poſſible the exact amount of
their conſumption, which I knew, that, out of policy, they
are always at pains to exaggerate. In the firſt houſe I entered,
I luckily found the kettle full of potatoes, juſt ready to be put
upon the fire, to be boiled for dinner; the family conſiſted of
one man, his wife, and one child, a remarkable ſtout boy

H h

of eleven years of age. I was informed, they regulary dined
and fupped upon them every day, and that the quantity
in the kettle ferved them for both the meals. I immediately weighed the potatoes in the kettle, and found that they a-
mounted to nine pounds Avoirdupois, and was informed that
eight pounds of oat-meal ferved them for breakfaft, in pottage,
a week. The fecond family I entered was compofed of three
men, one woman, and fix healthy children, three of whom
were born at one birth: this family alfo dined and fupped upon
potatoes ; the quantity they had prepared to drefs for dinner
weighed thirteen pounds, and I was informed it required
near four pounds oat-meal each day for their breakfaft. After examining the confumption of feveral families that had
two meals of potatoes per day, I found, to my aftonifhment,
that about $2\frac{3}{7}$ libs. Avoirdupois raw potatoes, and $5\frac{1}{7}$ ozs.
good oat-meal, when made into pottage, did actually maintain,
for one day, in good health and condition for labour, on an
average, each individual of a family, compofed of two parents
and three children, as long as their ftock of potatoes lafted.
Having thus afcertained the length which potatoes and oatmeal will go as food, when a vegetable diet only is ufed, I
fhall proceed to calculate the *quantum* of population that the
farm of 504 Englifh ftatute acres, fertile land, well cultivated,
will maintain, under the following mode of cropping.

Produce after deducting Seed.

No		*lbs. Meal.*	*lbs. Potatoes.*
I.	84 acres of potatoes, average produce of Lancashire 250 bushels per acre, at 90 lbs. deducting 18 bushels for seed - -		1,753,920
II.	84 acres wheat, at 30 bushels per acre, at 58 lbs. per bushel, deducting 3 lbs. per bushel rough bran, product 2520 bushels of meal, at 55 lbs.* per bushel	138,600	
III.	84 acres pease and beans, at 24 bushels, 2016 bushels, one half eaten by the horses on the farm; one half 1008 bushels, at 40 lbs. meal per bushel - -	40,320	
IV.	84 acres barley, at 36 bushels, 3024, at 46 lbs. meal per bushel - - - - -	139,104	*lbs. Bread.*
	Pounds meal	318,024	or 397,530
V.	84 acres clover consumed by cattle.		
VI.	84 acres oats, at 60 bushels, 5040 bushels, 13,440 pecks of oat meal, at 8 lbs. per peck.		

		Meals.
504 acres	1,753,920 lbs. potatoes, at 1½ lbs. per meal to each individual - -	1,312,940
	397,530 lbs. bread, at ¾ lb. per meal to ditto	530,040
26* Garden ground.	13,440 pecks oat-meal, at 24 meals per peck to ditto - -	322,560
530 acres.	365 days, at 3 meals per day,	1095)2,165,540(1977

In this manner, 504 acres of fertile land, the garden ground not included, will maintain, when well cultivated, 1977 people old and young; and if the population of Great Britain amounts to nine millions, it would require only 2,412,746 fertile acres, well cultivated to maintain them when living on the same portions of vegetable food as the common people do in Scotland.

* This is the quality of the flour, of which the bread presently used in my own family is made. Upon comparing it with Sir George Young's experiments, *vide* page 259, I find it to correspond pretty accurately, only coarser, principally from being made of wheat of an inferior quality.

I shall next proceed to inquire into the number of people which the same farm of 504 acres in pasture would maintain when living entirely on animal food.

This branch of rural œconomy, of determining the quantity of animal food which land will produce, although of considerable importance, has never been properly attended to. Mr Young, indeed, has begun the investigation; but as yet it has been confined to ascertain the fattening quality of different animals and vegetables. Upon consulting several intelligent farmers, it seemed to be their opinion, that an acre of good grass might, in the season, increase the weight of the animals fed upon it twelve stone, at 14 lbs to the stone; which at 5s. per stone, would afford a good rent, and leave a handsome allowance for management and profit on the capital employed. Fixing therefore upon 12 stone as the *quantum* of animal food, which an acre of our farm will produce; upon this data, the 504 acres will give 6048 stones, or 84,672 lbs. I have not been able to learn what proportion of weight the bones in the carcase of an ox bears to the flesh; but allowing three quarters of a lb. of bones and flesh on an average to a meal for each individual, at 3 meals per day, 84,672 lbs. will support an individual 37,632 days; or, in other words, the produce of the farm will support a population of 103 individuals throughout the year; dividing these into 20 families, and allowing one fourth of an acre of garden ground to each family, it amounts in all to 509 acres. Upon calculating from these data, it will be found-that it would require 44,475,728 fertile acres, to maintain the population of Great Britain, each individual, upon an average, confuming 2¼ lbs. of butcher meat per day ; but the fame number of acres would fupport a population of 165,921,725 individuals of all ages, if the inhabitants lived on the fame portions of vegetable food, which at prefent fubfift the common labourers in Scotland.

I have calculated thefe two extremes of the produce of land under the plough, or in pafture merely for fatrening cattle, without including a dairy in either cafe, in order to place this object in a ftrong point of veiw, and to fhow the different effects which living on vegetable or animal food will have, in fupporting an increafed population, or in rendering fuftenance plentiful or fcarce in a country. Hence it may be inferred, that it was to encourage or preferve the immenfe population of the eaftern nations, the original lawgivers of India difcharged the eating of animal food, and ingrafted this political maxim upon the ancient ftock of fuperftition in the country. The abftaining from animal food, however, feems beft fuited to thefe countries, fituated under a burning fun, where water alone renders the foil perpetually fertile, in producing vegetable food for fupporting the inhabitants. In more temperate climates, the foil cannot be kept in a conftant ftate of producing bread for man, without materially injuring its fertility. The beafts of the field are alfo the children of nature ; fhe wills to fupport them, and the land muft be allowed to afford grafs for their fuftenance, which reftores, at the fame time, its fertility for raifing corn ; and man being formed to live on a mixture of animal and vegetable food, avails himfelf of this œconomy of nature, to add to his enjoyment.

From this caufe agriculture, in temperate climates, will be carried to the greateft perfection in thofe countries where the inhabitants add a certain portion of animal to their vegetable food.
But there is a certain proportion from which, if, in the progrefs of luxury, they deviate, by increafing the quantity of
their animal food, they will certainly feel the want of bread
corn, which appears to be one of the principal caufes that,
of late years, there is an evident deficiency in the growth of
corn in Britain, or rather in England, to fupply the inhabitants ; and that we are every year becoming more and more
dependent on foreign nations for our daily fupport, in place
of being able, as formerly, to fpare a large furplus quantity
annually for exportation.

In order ftill farther to elucidate this important object, and
to fhow, in the cleareft manner, the effect of an increafed confumption of animal food, in diminifhing the quantity of corn
raifed in Britain, I fhall fketch out a fcheme of cultivation
fuited more nearly to the average confumption and population
of the country.

LETT. II.

*Produce of a Farm of 504 acres, very fertile land, and in a high state
of cultivation.*

Nos.

I.   72 acres pasture, to be ploughed up in rotation, reckoned to produce 12 stones
        beef or mutton per acre,   *Pounds.*   *Meals.*
                    Being in all   12,096 at ¼lb. per meal   16,128

II.   4 ⎧ Potatoes, 250 bushels per acre,
         ⎪   90lb. per bushel   -   90,000 at 1¼lb. ——   67,500
     68 ⎨ Turnip, at 24 stones beef or
         ⎩   mutton per acre   -   22,848 at ¾lb. ——   30,464

III. 72 acres barley, consumed in ale and
        spirits.

IV.   72 acres clover and hay, consumed by
        the horses.

V.   72 acres wheat, at 32 bushels, at 60lb.
        bread per bushel   -   148,240 at ¼lb. ——   197,653

VI.   72 acres pease and beans, consumed
        by horses.

VII. 72 ⎧ acres oats, at 60 bushels,   4,320
         ⎪ of which one half consumed
         ⎪   by horses   -   -   2.160
         ⎨ one third in pottage   -   1,440   3,840 pecks oat-meal
         ⎪   at 24 meals   92,160
         ⎩ one sixth in bread   -   720 bushels, or 19,200 lbs.
                                           bread at ¾ per meal   25,600

    ——
    504
    10

    ——
    514 acres.   Meals in the year   1,095)429,505(392¹⁴⁄₁₀₉₅

In this manner, a farm of 504 acres of very fertile land, in
a high state of cultivation, could maintain 392 people, old
and young, living on a mixture of animal and vegetable food,

of which the above quantities would afford to each individual for daily confumption

Of animal food   -   -   -   -   * $\frac{1}{4}$ oz.

Of vegetable food $\left\{\begin{array}{l}\text{Bread Wheaten } 1 \text{ lb.} \quad \frac{1}{2} \text{ oz.} \\ \text{Ditto Oaten} \qquad\qquad 2\frac{1}{4} \\ \text{Oat-meal in Pottage} \quad 3\frac{1}{2} \\ \text{Potatoes} \qquad\qquad\quad 10 \end{array}\right\}$ 2 lb. $\frac{1}{4}$ oz.

And to maintain the inhabitants of Great Britain, computing the number at nine millions, and each individual to confume daily, on an average, the quantity of animal and vegetable food mentioned above, there would be occafion for 11,793,799 acres of very fertile land, in a high ftate of cultivation; of which it would require

3,212,318   acres   for   fattening   animal   food,   producing nearly 18 ftones per acre.

91,780   —   for potatoes.

1,652,050   —   for barley.

1,652,050   —   for clover hay.

1,652,050   —   for wheat.

1,652,050   —   for peafe and beans.

1,652,050   —   for oats.

229,451   —   for garden ground.

____

11,793,799 total acres.

From the above ftatement it appears, that it would require 3,212,318 fertile acres, to afford four ounces of animal food

---

* The daily confumption of each individual in Paris, is pretty accurately afcertained from the tax on cattle paid at the Barriers, to be about 5$\frac{1}{4}$ oz.; in London it probably more than double.

per day, to every individual in Britain.   But if, at any time, from the increafe of luxury in the nation, every inhabitant was to confume one ounce more per day; in that cafe it would require an additional 803,079 acres of fertile land, one half in rich pafture, and nearly the other half in turnip, to fatten and produce the neceffary quantity; four-fevenths of which, or 458,900 acres, were annually carrying luxuriant crops of corn. But even, computing thefe crops at the low average of two quarters per acre, it would occafion an annual failure of 917,800 quarters, which will account for the difference between the moft flourifhing period of the Corn Trade, and the deficiency of latter times.   Whoever, therefore, confiders with attention the increafed confumption of animal food in Britain, within thefe fifty years laft paft, and particularly fince the peace of 1763, will fee good caufe for the growing fcarcity of corn.

Before I leave this part of my Inquiry, I muft mention another effect of luxury, in adding to the fcarcity both of animal and vegetable food, viz. the great degree of fatnefs to which the people in England now require to have their beef and mutton fed, till, as Milton defcribes the cattle in Paradife,

> ——————————————— On the grafs,
> Couch'd, and now fill'd with pafture, gazing fat,

they can hardly ftand on their legs, or travel a few miles to be flaughtered.   There is reafon to believe, that half the quantity of land would feed cattle moderately fat, that is required to put them in condition for flaughtering in England; and it is more than probable, that the great noife that has been made, of late years, about increafing the fize of live ftock, is a fpecies of quackery which is a real lofs to the nation. Small animals certainly take on more fat, in proportion to their food, than large ones, for two obvious reafons: 1ft, The furface of fmall animals is much greater, in proportion to their weight, than large ones; and as the fat is moftly laid on the furface, they have confequently a larger fpace to lay it on. 2dly, The muf-cular fibres of fmall animals are lefs tenfe than thofe of large ones, and admit more eafily that portion of the fat which is infinuated, in the procefs of fattening, into the interior veficles of the mufcular flefh. I knew an experiment that was tried on the fattening of large and fmall oxen with turnips and hay: The large oxen ate double the quantity of the fmall ones while fatten-ing; they were all fold at the fame time, each large ox brought L. 12 Sterling, but two fmall ones, which confumed no more food, were fold for L. 16. Thus, it is probable, that a con-. fiderable wafte is occafioned in the nation, from increafing the fize of the domefticated animals, and certainly not a little alfo from rendering them extremely fat before they are flaugh-tered.

Nor is the increafed confumption of animal food the only caufe of the fcarcity of corn; the immenfe number of horfes now trained for war, or luxury, or kept for the more necef-fary purpofe of carrying on the largely extended internal commerce of this country; in tranfporting the rude materials. to the fite of manufactures, and returning the manufactured articles to the different markets and ports in the kingdom, in.

carrying the ſtone, brick, wood, and iron, neceſſary for
erecting the numerous buildings throughout the nation.   All
theſe branches of induſtry muſt demand a great number of
horſes, that will not only require a very conſiderable quantity
of corn, but alſo a large portion of land muſt be withdrawn
from cultivation for ſupplying them with hay and graſs,
either to enable them to endure hard labour, or to put on the
pampered ſleek appearance neceſſary for ſhow and luxury.   In
order to form an idea of this conſumption, I ſubmit the following calculation.

From the ſtatement already given, it appears, that it would
require near 12 millions of *fertile* acres, in a high ſtate of
cultivation, to ſupport the population of Great Britain.   But it
is more than probable that it actually requires 24 millions of
acres, of the average quality of arable land; and allowing 5
horſes to every 100 acres in cultivation, that gives of

Horſes uſed in agriculture - -	1,200,000
Do kept for pleaſure, which pay tax -	214,000
Do ſuppoſed not entered - - -	50,000
Do Cavalry, including levies of all deſcriptions -	30,000
Do poſting horſes, mail, and hackney coaches, colts and fillies, not taxed - - -	250,000
Do employed in the carriage of rude materials and manufactured commodities - -	256,000
Total,	2,000,000

Suppoſing each horſe, on an average, to be fed 200 days in
the ſtable, at 20 pounds hay and ¼ pecks Scotch per day, equal

to 4000 lbs. of hay, and $56\frac{1}{4}$ Winchefter bufhels in 200 days, but, with extra feeding, fuppofe

60 bufhels, the produce of   -   1 fertile acre
4000 pounds of hay, or $35\frac{3}{4}$ cwt. the produce of 1 fertile acre
At pafture, 165 days, when he eats the grafs of 1 fertile acre

A horfe therefore confumes the produce of   3 fertile acres; and 2 millions of horfes will require 6 millions of fertile acres to maintain them. Upon this calculation, Great Britain will confume on horfes annually, 15 millions of quarters of grain, of which, about one million is now imported from foreign nations; befides, the produce of 4 millions of acres of fertile land in hay and pafture.

In the period from 1730, to 1750, when Great Britain was exporting the greateft quantity of furplus corn, after fupplying the inhabitants, the tunnage of her fhipping amounted, upon an average of that period only to 475,940 tuns, whereas it now amounts to near three times as much, being in the year 1792, 1,396,003 tuns*. The revenue arifing from the poft-office in the year 1754 amounted to only L. 210,663: it was in 1793, L. 607,268 †; from which it may be fafely inferred, that the internal commerce of Great Britain has been tripled fince the period that the largeft quantity of furplus grain was exported; the increafe of wealth and luxury has alfo been very great, and if we allow that the number of horfes kept for pleafure have increafed in the fame proportion, the additional numbers now employed may be eftimated thus.

* Vide Chalmers' Eftimate of Great Britain.   † Ibid.

Horfes kept at prefent for pleafure   -   264,000

For the carriage of goods, &c.   -   250,000

For pofting, and for mail and hackney coaches   86,000

____

600,000

Deduct one-third in the former period   -   200,000

____

Increafed number of horfes highly fed   -   400,000

Allowing three acres of fertile land for the maintenance of each horfe, this addition to the number of horfes will withdraw 1,200,000 acres of fertile land, from affording fuftenance to the inhabitants of Great Britain.   Here alfo is fufficient caufe for a great deficiency in the production of corn ; and when we alfo take into the account the amazing effect of an increafe in the confumption of animal food, we need not be furprifed at the prefent fcarcity of bread corn, nor at the annual deficiency of one million of quarters of grain, when comparing the quantity now brought into the kingdom, with the quantity formerly exported, even although the population of the country had continued the fame, or had even declined ; notwithftanding the induftry and the capital of the cultivators of the foil have been greatly increafed fince the period when the large furplus quantity of corn was annually exported.

The great increafe of grafs land rapidly extending over the kingdom is obferved by many of the agricultural reporters. I fhall, however, confine myfelf to one fentence, taken from the improved report of the agriculture of the county of Lancafhire ‘ at this period (1795) *the diminution of arable land is likely to*

' *become a ferious calamity to the nation at large.*' It is not by giving an immenfe bounty on the importation of foreign corn, that the legiflature of Great Britain will make up for the annual deficiency in the produce of grain ; for what is this but reforting to the weekly diftribution of ancient Rome, under another form, to relieve the wants of the inhabitants. But it muft be by removing every obftruction to the extention of cultivation over the wafte lands, and every bar to the raifing crops of corn, by the moft productive modes of hufbandry on the fields already improved. As alfo by adopting every judicious regulation which will reduce the price of bread, and encourage the confumption of vegetable food. To effect thefe defirable objects, I humbly fubmit the following regulations to the confideration of the legiflature, as the principles on which laws may be founded ; for encouraging agriculture ; for promoting the intereft of proprietors, cultivators, and manufacturers ; and finally for adding to the wealth, capital, and refources of the ftate.

Regulations for promoting the improvement of the Wafte Lands, for encouraging Agriculture, and for rendering the lands more productive, which are already in a fit ftate for cultivation.

1ft, A general law for dividing commons in England, a meafure now under the confideration of Parliament.

2d*ly*, By heightening the import rate of foreign oats, the crop which can be firft raifed to the greateft advantage on Wafte Lands, in order to fecure to the cultivators, a fufficient return for the labour and capital employed.—*Note*. This regulation would operate as a tax on horfes, in favour of agriculture, by raifing a little the price of oats, without materially increafing the price of the food of the inhabitants. As the fame advancce in luxury, which increafes the confumption of oats in the feeding of horfes, leffens the confumption of oatmeal as the food of man, by the gradual introduction of wheat as bread corn. The expence of cultivating Wafte Land, from the prefent high price of labour and every article of confumption, muft now be very great ; and on the Wafte Lands in Scotland, and a great part of thofe in England, it is by cultivating oats, that a great fhare of the expence may be indemnified.

3*dly*, By a law for fettling on the clergy a fixed revenue in corn, (as grain will always rife in price with the increafing demand for labour, in countries advancing in wealth and profperity under well regulated governments, and when ftationary, it becomes the exact meafure of the real value of every commodity,) and freeing the cultivators from every fpecies of tythe. *Note*. Whilft tythes are drawn, cultivation can never be carried on with fpirit, or approach towards perfection ; and as the country advances in wealth, the paying of tythes will occafion more land being withdrawn from raifing corn, and will prevent old paftures from being ploughed up for cropping, as it now requires greater capitals and exertions of fkill in the cultivators, to replace the rent, expence of cultivation, and profit on ftock, than formerly. Therefore, tythes now fall more heavy on the induftry of the hufbandman, and prove a greater check to his activity.

4thly, By a ſtatute to amend the poor laws* in England, which prevent labourers, mechanics, and manufacturers, who cannot find employment in one pariſh, from removing to another, where they can get work, and burden the farmers with a variable arbitrary tax for their ſupport, to the number frequently in country pariſhes, of one half of the whole inhabitants, and to the amount perhaps of one half, or three fourths of their rent. Where is this evil to ſtop? farmers muſt diſcourage population, and turn their farms into grafs, out of fear of being ruined by poors rates? The rent of land ought to be preciſely aſcertained, for tythes and poors rates operate, like the *taille* under the former government of France, and moſt materially diſcourage cultivation.

5thly, A tax on all lands held by farmers without a leaſe, or any regulation that will encourage landlords to grant leaſes to their tenants; otherwiſe, no ſpirited exertions in agriculture can be carried on in Britain: holding land from year to year may ſuit the cultivation of the vineyards in France, where only labour and a few ſorry tools are neceſſary, but is deſtructive of good huſbandry in this country, where a large capital muſt be inveſted in agriculture.

6thly, A tax on all lands occupied by tenants when reſtricted from cultivation by the landlord. If the ſtate be in want of bread-corn, or any other production which the ſoil affords, the proprietor, who ties up the hands of his tenants from con-

---

* Since writing the above, the poor laws have been brought under the conſideration of Parliament.

tributing a proportional relief, is certainly no friend to his country. Nothing can be more abfurd than the modes of cropping preſcribed by fome landlords to their tenants; for inſtance, obliging them to fallow their lands every third year, preventing them from fubſtituting turnips in place of the fallow; prohibiting them from planting potatoes, or from fowing wheat, after peafe and beans, *reſtraining them from plowing hay or paſture lands**. Grant tenants leafes for twenty years, and let all reſtrictions be aboliſhed, at leaſt till the laſt three or four years of the leafe, allowing them to crop their farms in the manner moſt advantageous for their own and the public intereſt. Relieved from thefe fetters, they will give an advanced †

---

* Mr Arthur Young. In his Tour through France, recommends the allowing the huſbandmen of that country unlimited power to fow and plant what they pleafe, upon the land they farm, in order to render the foil more productive, for fupplying the inhabitants. In his Account of a Diſtrict in Eſſex, in the Annals of Agriculture, he fays, ‘ While I was at Spain's Hall, Mr Ruggles offered to feveral neighbours a large ‘ field of ſtanding grafs, ready to mow for hay, part of it for 25s. per acre, and part at ‘ 35s. and was refufed by all. The ground being excellently good, and the crop large, ‘ I expreſſed my furprife at this, when I was aſſured ſheep would not pay for hay ; that ‘ they would eat 20s. a head in hay, and not be five ſhillings the better for it ; that the ‘ fame remark is applicable to cows, which will never, for any quantity, pay more ‘ than 1s. 6d. per cwt. ; *that there is not a meadow fcarcely in the country, but would be* ‘ *ploughed up, if the landlords would allow it :* whence it is fuſſiciently plain, that they ‘ eſteem corn to be vaſtly more advantageous than grafs, even on land that ſhews ‘ figns of being fingularly adapted to it.' *Vide Annals of Agriculture, vol.* 18. *p.* 410.

† Mr Arthur Young ſhews the advanced rents that are given by tenants, when freed from reſtrictions, even when purfuing the moſt injudicious modes of cultivation, in the following inſtance : ‘ After being pared and burned to fow three ‘ fucceſſive crops of white corn, in confequence of the benefits derived from the

K k

rent, agriculture will become more productive, and the state will reap the benefit of their exertions.

Regulations for lowering the price of Bread, and increasing the con-sumption of Vegetable food.

1*st*, By a law for lowering the duty on beer or ale of a certain description, to enable the labourer, manufacturer, and mechanic, to purchase a nourishing liquor at a moderate price, so as to encourage them to live more on bread and ale, and

' operation, is to rack and exhaust the soil, and following these with rye grass,
' chiefly mowen the first year, and none that I saw close fed, is to continue cropping,
' when the land most needs repose. If, therefore, the practice is really or essentially
' bad, or ruinous, as so many think it, here is one district in which it should be found
' particularly so. But the facts I meet with will not justify such a conclusion : The
' rents of the lands, thus tortured, have risen in twenty years, from 50 to 100 per
' cent. The downs that were let at 2s. 6d. and 3s. an acre, are now at 5s. and 6s.
' Whatever the practice may be, therefore, it cannot materially have hurt the land-
' ler', if it has, in any case, hurt him at all.' *Annals of Agricul. vol* 23. *p.* 358.

In this part of Scotland, where tenants hold their farms generally on leases for 19 or 21 years, they have hitherto been seldom restricted from sowing what they please, during the currency of their leases; but this liberty, so far from lessening the advanced rent given at the renewal of the lease, has certainly had the effect to raise it. Land here is higher rented than in England, in proportion to its quality. There has been lately given for a farm, on a lease for 21 years, L. 3 Sterling per English statute acre, which was severely cropped at pleasure by the preceding tenant, and where no manure can be procured for putting it in order, but from the produce of the farm : Also, for another farm of 140 acres in the same situation, only within reach of Edin-burgh dung, which, however, will cost the tenant from L. 6 to L. 7 to manure an acre, there has been given of yearly rent L. 100 Sterling in money, 63 quarters of wheat, 93 quarters of barley, and 105 quarters of oats.

lefs on butcher meat, as well as to difcourage the pernicious ufe of fpiritous liquors.

2*dly*, By a law for regulating weights and meafures, particularly thofe by which corn is fold; although this is one of the moft important branches of police it is fhamefully neglected, owing to its being left to the management of incorporate bodies in towns. The corn meafures are fraudulently increafed from time to time, and are all of them much larger than the ftandard; the confequence that follows is, that in fixing the price of bread by the affize, it is always rated and fold at a higher price than the law allows in proportion to the real price of wheat by the Winchefter bufhel.

3*dly*, By a law for regulating the affize of bread, after afcertaining the exact quantity of flour produced from wheat of different weights, and the exact quantity of bread produced from a given quantity of flour; not by taking the opinion of corn factors, millers, or bakers, in a committee room of the Houfe of Commons, but after a number of actual experiments, repeatedly made by intelligent men not interefted in the trade*.

---

* By the prefent mode of regulation, the law fuppofes a bufhel of wheat to weigh 56 lbs. and to produce 42 lbs. of flour, only 3-4ths of the weight of the wheat. The law directs this flour to be divided in the bolting. into two equal parts, but of unequal finenefs; of the fine half the wheaten bread is made, and of the coarfe, the houfehold: The law fuppofes, that there are only 12 quartern loaves made out of the produce of a bufhel of wheat; but from Sir George Young's experiments, made in

4thly and *lastly*, By a law for regulating the allowance of millers; obliging them to grind for money, and return the weight of the grain in meal, after deducting the just proportion of waste. I have frequently known poor people take bread

the process of manufacturing wheat into bread, it appears, that a bushel of tythe wheat weighed 60 lbs. which produced 45 lbs. of flour of a medium fineness, of which 60 lbs. of standard wheaten bread was made, and also 9 lbs. of coarse flour, of which 15¼ lbs. of bread was made, making in all 73¼ lbs. per bushel: Whereas the law supposes there are only 52 lbs. 2 ozs. made from the bushel.——But this experiment of Sir George Young only points out part of the evil; it does not detect the frauds that are committed, wherever the assize of bread is regulated by the current prices of wheat, from its produce in flour being divided into a larger portion of fine flour than the law directs. I once sold a parcel of *fine* wheat, the produce of my own farm, the price of which was to be determined by the quantity of flour it produced. The return from the mill was 34 lbs. fine flour, and 20 lbs. household, per bushel, in all 54 lbs. the exact quantity obtained by Sir George Young. Supposing the wheat to be sold at 10s. 6d. per bushel, including the allowance to the baker, it would produce,

	L.		
Of wheaten bread 9 quarterns at 1s.	0	9	0
Ditto 4 twopenny loaves	0	0	8
Of household 5 quarterns at 9d.	0	3	9
Ditto 3 twopenny loaves	0	0	6
	0	13	11
Legal allowance { 6 quarterns wheaten at 1s. / 6 ditto household at 9d. }	0	10	6

Profit to the Baker   L. 0   3   5

per bushel over and above the legal allowance. This extra profit is calculated on the legal estimation, that a sack of flour only produces 80 quartern loaves. But upon my enquiring some time ago, how much bread was made in London, from a given quantity of flour, at an intelligent young man, who had the management of a bakehouse in that city, he answered me, that his master never complained, when they made 86 quarterns out of the sack. Upon comparing this quantity with the propor-

corn to the mill, and get one fifth of the weight abstracted by the miller for grinding.—*Note.* The bill introduced some time ago by Sir Francis Basset, on this subject, seemed well calculated to remedy the complaints of the poor people, and encourage the confumption of bread corn*.

My Supplement to your late Father's Work is now finished; in which I have ventured to fuggest such farther regulations, as have occurred to me, to be necessary for improving the fystem of our Corn Laws, and for rendering the produce equal to the increafing confumption of the kingdom. It was alfo my intention to develope the caufes, which, in addition to the errors in that fystem, have, of late years, occasioned a fcarcity of bread corn in Great Britain; and I have endeavoured to prove, that, in a country rapidly advancing in wealth and refinement, the encouragement of Agriculture is not only neceffary for fecuring the continuance of the national profperity,

---

tional weight of flandard bread, made from the weight of flour, in Sir George Young's experiment, I find them to correfpond exactly, calculating, therefore, the actual produce of bread from the bufhel of my wheat, by the *data* in Sir George's experiment the baker's profit on the bufhel amounted to 4s. 6d. over and above the legal allowance of 1s. 6d. and the value of the bran.

* Since the above fheet went to prefs, a bill has been brought into the Houfe of Commons, from the Committee on Corn, for regulating the allowance to be taken by millers for grinding, &c.

but is the only effectual means of promoting plenty, and of increasing the power and refources of the ftate.

If I have thrown any additional light on this important object, fo as to tend in the fmalleft degree to the advantage of my country, it will prove a fufficient recompence to,

My dear Sir,

Your fincere Friend,

And obedient Servant,

Wm Mackie.

To Lieutenant-Colonel Dirom, of }
Mount Annan, Edinburgh. }

APPENDIX.

A P P E N D I X.

No I.

THE *Principles*, upon which the Ancient Money of England, and of Scotland, is converted into the prefent Sterling Money, are briefly as follows :

I. *Tale or Denomination.*

In England, and in Scotland, at the time of the Conqueft, there were *twenty* fhillings in the Coinage pound of Silver; which continued, with very little variation, in England, till the year 1347; and, in Scotland, till 1306: but now there are *fixty-two* fhillings in the Coinage pound of Silver in both kingdoms; fo that L. 100, at that time, were equal to L. 310 of the prefent money, in point of tale or denomination.

II. *Intereft, or Yearly Value.*

Prior to the fixteenth century, the intereft or yearly value of money, in both England and Scotland, was about *fixteen per cent.* but which is now reduced to *five per cent. per annum.*

EXAMPLE.—Money being raifed or reduced in value according to the yearly legal produce of it, L. 100, bearing intereft at 10 *per cent.* is equal in value to L. 200, bearing only 5 *per cent.* and other fums in proportion : So that L. 100 of ancient money, being equal in value to L. 310, in point of denomination only, and money being now worth only 5 *per cent. per annum;* therefore, the L. 310, with the intereft at 16 *per cent.* was equal to L. 992 of the prefent money.

The following Tables will fhew the value of Money, at different periods, from the Conqueft to the prefent time, both in England, and in Scotland; and, by them, the ancient Money may be converted into the prefent Money, according to the variation in the tale or denomination *only;* or, *alfo,* in proportion both to the tale and the rate of yearly Intereft of money, as done in this Work.

a

TABLE OF THE VALUE OF MONEY IN ENGLAND.

A.D.	Date of Mint Indenture and Monarchs' Reign	Standard of Silver Coin — Fine Silver (oz. pwt.)	Standard of Silver Coin — Alloy (oz. pwt.)	No. of Shillings coined from one pound of silver (s. d.)	Value of the ancient Pound of Accompt, in proportion to the tale or denomination only — Value of one Pound (£. s. d.)	Value of one Shilling (s. d.)	Value of one Penny (d.)	Interest or value of money per annum	Value of the ancient Money, in proportion both to tale and yearly interest of money — Value of one Pound (£. s. d.)	Value of one Shilling (s. d.)	Value of one Penny (d.)
	Before Ed. 3.	11 2	0 18	20 0	3 2 0	3 $1\frac{20}{100}$	$3\frac{10}{100}$	16	9 18 $4\frac{80}{100}$	9 $11\frac{4}{100}$	$9\frac{92}{100}$
1347	20 Edwd. 3.	11 2	0 18	22 6	2 15 $1\frac{33}{100}$	2 9^{7}	2^{75}	16	8 16 4^{80}	8 9^{84}	8^{82}
1354	27 Edwd. 3.	11 2	0 18	25 0	2 9 7^{20}	2 5^{75}	2^{48}	16	7 18 7^{20}	7 11^{16}	7^{93}
1422	9 Henry 5.	11 2	0 18	30 0	2 1 4	2 0^{80}	2^{7}	16	6 12 2^{40}	6 7^{32}	6^{61}
1422	1 Henry 6.	11 2	0 18	37 6	1 13 0^{80}	1 7^{84}	1^{65}	16	5 5 7^{20}	5 3^{36}	5^{28}
1426	4 Henry 6.	11 2	0 18	30 0	2 1 4	2 0^{80}	2^{7}	16	6 12 3^{20}	6 7^{25}	6^{61}
1460	39 Henry 6.	11 2	0 18	37 6	1 13 0^{80}	1 7^{84}	1^{65}	16	5 5 7^{20}	5 3^{36}	5^{23}
1509	1 Henry 8.	11 2	0 18	45 0	1 7 6^{66}	1 4^{51}	1^{33}	14	3 17 0	3 10^{20}	3^{85}
1543	35 Henry 8.	10 0	2 0	48 0	1 5 10	1 3^{50}	1^{29}	14	3 12 9^{60}	3 7^{63}	3^{64}
1545	37 Henry 8.	6 0	6 0	48 0	1 5 10	1 3^{50}	1^{29}	14	3 12 9^{60}	3 7^{68}	3^{64}
1547	1 Edwd. 6.	4 0	8 0	48 0	1 5 10	1 3^{50}	1^{29}	12	3 2 0	3 1^{20}	3^{10}
1549	3 Edwd. 6.	6 0	6 0	72 0	0 17 2^{67}	0 10^{33}	0^{86}	12	2 0 2^{40}	2 0^{12}	2^{1}
1551	5 Edwd. 6.	3 0	9 0	72 0	0 17 2^{67}	0 10^{33}	0^{86}	12	2 0 2^{40}	2 0^{12}	2^{1}
1552	6 Edwd. 6.	11 1	0 19	60 0	0 0 8	1 0^{40}	1^{3}	12	2 9 7^{20}	2 5^{76}	2^{48}
1560	2 Eliz.	11 2	0 18	60 0	0 0 8	1 0^{40}	1^{3}	10	2 1 4^{80}	2 0^{84}	2^{7}
1601	43 Eliz.	11 2	0 18	62 0	0 0 0	1 0	1	10	2 0 0	2 0	2
1625	21 James 1.	11 2	0 18	62 0	0 0 0	1 0	1	8	1 12 0	1 7^{20}	1^{60}
1651	Usurpation	11 2	0 18	62 0	0 0 0	1 0	1	6	1 4 0	1 2^{40}	1^{20}
1714	13 Anne	11 2	0 18	62 0	0 0 0	1 0	1	5	1 0 0	1 0	1

TABLE OF THE VALUE OF MONEY IN SCOTLAND.

Value of the ancient Pound of Accompt, in proportion to the tale or denomination only.

Date (A.D.)	Monarchs' Reign	Fine Silver oz.	pw.	Alloy oz.	pw.	No. of Shillings s.	d.	Value of one Pound £.	s.	d.	Value of one Shilling s.	d.	Value of one Penny d.
	Before Rt. 1.	11	2	0	18	20	0	3	2	0	3	$1\frac{20}{100}$	$3\frac{10}{100}$
1306	1 Robt. 1.	11	2	0	18	21	0	2	19	0^{57}	2	11^{45}	2^{95}
	Uncertain, & for a short time.	11	2	0	18	26	4						
1366	38 David 2.	11	2	0	18	25	0	2	9	7^{20}	2	5^{75}	2^{48}
1369	39 David 2.	11	2	0	18	29	4	2	2	3^{27}	2	1^{35}	2^{11}
1393	3 Robt. 3.	11	2	0	18	32	0	1	18	9	1	11^{25}	1^{94}
1432	27 James 1.	11	2	0	18	37	6	1	13	0^{60}	1	7^{84}	1^{65}
1451	15 James 2.	11	2	0	18	64	0	0	19	4^{50}	0	11^{60}	0^{97}
1456	20 James 2.	11	2	0	18	96	0	0	12	11	0	7^{75}	0^{65}
1475	16 James 3.	11	2	0	18	144	0	0	8	7^{33}	0	5^{17}	0^{43}
1484	24 James 3.	11	2	0	18	140	0	0	8	10^{20}	0	5^{31}	0^{44}
1505	18 James 4.	11	2	0	18	140	0	0	8	10^{28}	0	5^{31}	0^{44}
1529	16 James 5.	11	0	1	0	192	0	0	6	5^{50}	0	3^{87}	0^{28}
1556	14 Mary	11	0	1	0	260	0	0	4	9^{23}	0	2^{86}	0^{24}
1565	23 Mary	11	0	1	0	360	0	0	3	5^{33}	0	2^{7}	0^{17}
1571	5 James 6.	9	0	3	0	334	0	0	3	8^{55}	0	2^{23}	0^{19}
1577	11 James 6.	8	0	4	0	334	0	0	3	8^{55}	0	2^{23}	0^{19}
1579	13 James 6.	11	0	1	0	440	0	0	2	9^{82}	0	1^{69}	0^{14}
1581	15 James 6.	11	0	1	0	480	0	0	2	7	0	1^{55}	0^{13}
1587	21 James 6.	11	0	1	0	480	0	0	2	7	0	1^{55}	0^{13}
1597	31 James 6.	11	0	1	0	600	0	0	2	0^{80}	0	1^{24}	0^{10}
1601	35 James 6.	11	0	1	0	720	0	0	1	8^{67}	0	1^{3}	0^{9}
1633	8 Chas. 1.	11	0	1	0	720	0	0	1	8^{67}	0	1^{3}	0^{9}
1651	Usurpation	11	0	1	0	720	0	0	1	8^{67}	0	1^{3}	0^{9}
1659	Ditto	11	2	0	18	744	0	0	1	8^{40}	0	1^{1}	$0^{8\frac{1}{2}}$
1714	13 Anne	11	2	0	18	744	0	0	1	8	0	1	$0^{\frac{1}{2}}$

Value of the ancient Money, in proportion both to tale and yearly interest of money.

Date (A.D.)	Monarchs' Reign	Interest or value of money per annum.	Value of one Pound £.	s.	d.	Value of one Shilling s.	d.	Value of one Penny d.
	Before Rt. 1.	16	9	18	$4\frac{80}{100}$	9	$11\frac{4}{100}$	$9\frac{92}{100}$
1306	1 Robt. 1.	16	9	9	0	9	5^{40}	9^{15}
	Uncertain, & for a short time.							
1366	38 David 2.	16	7	18	7^{20}	7	11^{16}	7^{93}
1369	39 David 2.	16	6	15	2^{40}	6	9^{12}	6^{76}
1393	3 Robt. 3.	16	6	4	0	6	2^{40}	6^{20}
1432	27 James 1.	16	5	5	9^{60}	5	3^{48}	5^{29}
1451	15 James 2.	16	3	2	0	3	1^{20}	3^{10}
1456	20 James 2.	16	2	1	4^{80}	2	0^{84}	2^{7}
1475	16 James 3.	16	1	7	7^{20}	1	4^{56}	1^{38}
1484	24 James 3.	16	1	8	4^{50}	1	5^{4}	1^{42}
1505	18 James 4.	14	1	4	9^{60}	1	2^{88}	1^{24}
1529	16 James 5.	14	0	18	0	0	10^{80}	0^{90}
1556	14 Mary	12	0	11	4^{80}	0	6^{84}	0^{57}
1565	23 Mary	12	0	8	2^{40}	0	4^{92}	0^{41}
1571	5 James 6.	12	0	9	0	0	5^{40}	0^{45}
1577	11 James 6.	10	0	7	4^{80}	0	4^{44}	0^{37}
1579	13 James 6.	10	0	5	7^{20}	0	3^{36}	0^{28}
1581	15 James 6.	10	0	5	2^{40}	0	3^{12}	0^{26}
1587	21 James 6.	10	0	5	2^{40}	0	3^{12}	0^{26}
1597	31 James 6.	10	0	4	2^{40}	0	2^{52}	0^{21}
1601	35 James 6.	10	0	3	4^{80}	0	2^{4}	0^{17}
1633	8 Chas. 1.	8	0	2	9^{60}	0	1^{68}	0^{14}
1651	Usurpation	6	0	2	0	0	1^{20}	0^{10}
1659	Ditto	6	0	1	11^{20}	0	1^{16}	0^{9}
1714	13 Anne	5	0	1	8	0	1	$0^{\frac{1}{2}}$

THE following Table contains an account of the price of Wheat, in England, with the value in the money of the times, and in the prefent money, calculated on the principles that have been ftated, as far back as it can be obtained upon proper authority, that is from 1223, down to the year 1784.

Prior to the year 1646, the prices have been taken from the collection of Bifhop Fleetwood, from the ftatute books, and other authentic documents.

From that period to the prefent time, we have certain and diftinct accounts of the price of Wheat; which, from 1646 to 1706, have been alfo taken from Bifhop Fleetwood's collection; and the Bifhop has informed us, that they were collected from the audit books of Eton College *.

From 1706 to 1770 inclufive, the prices have been likewife extracted from the audit books of the fame College; and the account is certified by Dr Roberts, the prefent Provoft of the College.

Thefe prices fhew the rates at the market of Windfor, which determine the fum, or converfion in money, to be paid for Wheat to Eton College; they are made up twice in the year, at Lady-day and Michaelmas, and being joined, the medium is taken.

The Wheat payable to Eton College is of the beft kind, and nine bufhels are payable for the quarter; fo that thefe prices muft be higher than the general run of the markets of England.

From 1771 to 1784 inclufive, the prices of Wheat are taken from the Corn regifter eftablifhed by law; and the account of them is attefted by Mr Catherwood.

* Chron. præt. p. 101.

TABLE of the Price of a Quarter of Wheat, in the money of the time, and in the prefent money, from the year 1223 to 1784.

Changes in the value of money.	Anno Dom.	Anno Regis.	Account of the price of the Quarter of Wheat in England at different periods.	Money of the time.			Prefent Money.		
				£	s.	d.	£	s.	d.
	1223	8 Hen. 3	Price of the quarter of wheat	0	12	0	5	19	0
	1237	22 Hen. 3	Price of ditto	0	3	4	1	13	1
	1243	28 Hen. 3	Price of ditto	0	2	0	0	19	10
	1244	29 Hen. 3	Price of ditto	0	2	0	0	19	10
	1246	31 Hen. 3	Price of ditto	0	16	0	7	18	9
	1247	32 Hen. 3	Price of ditto	0	13	4	6	12	3
	1257	42 Hen. 3	Price of ditto	1	0	0	9	18	5
	1258	43 Hen. 3	Price of ditto	0	16	0	7	18	9
	1270	55 Hen. 3	Price of ditto	4	16	0	47	12	4
	1286	14 Edw. 1	Price of ditto	0	3	4	1	13	1
			Price of ditto in the end of the fame year	0	16	0	7	18	9
	1287	15 Edw. 1	Price of ditto	0	3	4	1	13	1
	1288	16 Edw. 1	Price of ditto	0	1	6	0	14	11
	1289	17 Edw. 1	Price of ditto	0	6	0	2	19	6
	1290	18 Edw. 1	Price of ditto	0	16	0	7	18	9
	1294	22 Edw. 1	Price of ditto	0	16	0	7	18	9
	1302	30 Edw. 1	Price of ditto	0	4	0	1	19	8
	1309	3 Edw. 2	Price of ditto	0	7	2	3	11	1
	1315	9 Edw. 2	Price of ditto—a great famine began this year	1	0	0	9	18	5
	1316	10 Edw. 2	Price of ditto—famine	1	12	0	15	17	5
	1317	11 Edw. 2	Price of ditto before harveft—famine	2	4	0	21	16	6
			after harveft	0	6	8	3	6	2
	1336	10 Edw. 3	Price of ditto	0	2	0	0	19	10
	1338	12 Edw. 3	Price of ditto	0	3	4	1	13	0
	1339	13 Edw. 3	Price of ditto	0	8	6	4	4	4
Change in the tale of money in 1347	1346	20 Edw. 3	Price of ditto	0	6	8	3	6	2
	1349	23 Edw. 3	Price of ditto	0	2	0	0	17	8
Change of the tale in 1354	1351	25 Edw. 3	Price of ditto	0	6	8	2	18	10
	1359	33 Edw. 3	Price of ditto	1	6	8	10	11	6
	1363	37 Edw. 3	Price of ditto	0	15	0	5	18	11
	1369	43 Edw. 3	Price of ditto	1	4	0	9	10	4
	1379	—	Price of ditto	0	4	0	1	11	9
	1387	—	Price of ditto	0	2	0	0	15	10
	1390	—	Price of ditto	0	14	0	5	11	0
	1401	—	Price of ditto	0	16	0	6	6	11
	1407	—	Price of ditto	0	3	4	1	6	9
Change of the tale in 1422	1416	—	Price of ditto	0	16	0	6	6	11
	1423	2 Hen. 6	Price of ditto	0	8	0	2	12	10½
	1425	4 Hen. 6	Price of ditto	0	4	0	1	6	5
	1434	13 Hen. 6	Price of ditto	1	6	8	8	16	3
	1435	14 Hen. 6	Price of ditto	0	5	4	1	15	3
	1436	15 Hen. 6	Exportation, when the price of wheat did not exceed	0	6	8	2	4	1
	1439	18 Hen. 6	Price of ditto	1	3	4	7	14	3
	1440	19 Hen. 6	Price of ditto	1	4	0	7	18	8
	1444	23 Hen. 6	Price of ditto	0	4	4	1	8	8
	1445	24 Hen. 6	Price of ditto	0	4	6	1	9	9
	1447	26 Hen. 6	Price of ditto	0	8	0	2	12	10½
	1448	27 Hen. 6	Price of ditto	0	6	8	2	4	1
	1449	28 Hen. 6	Price of ditto	0	5	0	1	13	0

Changes in the value of money.	Anno Don.	Anno Regis.	Price of the Quarter of Wheat in England.	Money of the time £	s.	d.	Present Money £	s.	d.
	1451	30 Hen. 6	Price of the quarter of wheat	0	8	0	2	12	10¼
	1453	32 Hen. 6	Price of ditto	0	5	4	1	15	3
	1455	34 Hen. 6	Price of ditto	0	1	2	0	7	8½
	1457	36 Hen. 6	Price of ditto	0	7	8	2	14	0
	1459	38 Hen. 6	Price of ditto	0	5	0	1	13	0½
Change of the tale this year.	1460	39 Hen. 6	Price of ditto	0	8	0	2	12	10¼
	1463	3 Edw. 4	Importation, when the price of wheat came to	0	6	8	1	15	2½
			Price of the quarter of wheat at London	0	2	0	0	10	7
			in Norfolk	0	1	8	0	8	9¼
	1464	4 Edw. 4	Price of the quarter of wheat	0	6	8	1	15	2¼
	1486	3 Hen. 7	Price of ditto	1	4	0	6	6	8½
	1491	8 Hen. 7	Price of ditto	0	14	8	3	17	5
	1494	11 Hen. 7	Price of ditto	0	4	0	1	1	1¼
	1495	12 Hen. 7	Price of ditto	0	3	4	0	17	7
	1497	14 Hen. 7	Price of ditto	1	0	0	5	5	7
Change of Interest and tale in 1509	1499	16 Hen. 7	Price of ditto	0	4	0	1	1	1¼
	1504	20 Hen. 7	Price of ditto	0	5	8	1	9	11
Change in the tale in 1543	1521	13 Hen. 8	Price of ditto	1	0	0	3	17	0
Change of Interest in 1547	1551	5 Edw. 6	Price of ditto	0	8	0	1	4	9½
	1553	1 Mary	Price of ditto	0	8	0	0	19	10
Change in 1552 of the tale	1554	1 & 2 P.& M.	Price of ditto	0	8	0	0	19	10
	1555	2 & 3 P.& M.	Price of ditto	0	8	0	0	19	10
	1556	3 & 4 P.& M.	Price of ditto	0	8	0	0	19	10
	1557	4 & 5 P.& M.	Price of ditto, in the spring	0	8	0	0	19	10
			Price the same year, before harvest	2	13	4	6	12	3
			The same year, in London, after harvest	0	5	0	0	12	5
			and in the country	0	4	0	0	9	11
	1558	1 Eliz.	Price of the quarter of wheat	0	8	0	0	19	10
	1559	2 Eliz.	Price of ditto	0	8	0	0	19	10
Change of Interest this year	1560	3 Eliz.	Price of ditto	0	8	0	0	16	7
	1561	4 Eliz.	Price of ditto	0	8	0	0	16	7
	1562	5 Eliz.	Price of ditto	0	8	0	0	16	7
	1574	17 Eliz.	Price of ditto in the great dearth at London	2	16	0	5	15	11
			the same year, after harvest	1	4	0	2	9	8
	1587	29 Eliz.	Price of ditto	3	4	0	6	12	6
	1593	35 Eliz.	Exportation, when the quarter of wheat did not exceed	1	0	0	2	1	4
	1594	36 Eliz.	Price of the quarter of wheat	2	16	0	5	15	11
	1595	37 Eliz.	Price of ditto	2	13	4	5	10	5
	1596	38 Eliz.	Price of ditto	4	0	0	8	5	7
Change of tale in 1601	1597	39 Eliz.	Price of ditto	5	4	0	10	15	3
			the same year, after harvest	4	0	0	8	5	7
	1604	2 James 1	Exportation, when the quarter of wheat did not exceed	1	6	8	2	12	4
Change of Interest in 1625	1623	21 James 1	Exportation, when the quarter of wheat did not exceed	1	12	0	3	4	0
	1627	3 Chas. 1	Exportation, when the quarter of wheat did not exceed	1	12	0	2	11	2
	1646	22 Chas. 1	Price of the quarter of wheat	2	8	0	3	16	9
	1647	—	Price of ditto	3	13	8	5	17	9
	1648	—	Price of ditto	4	5	0	6	16	0
	1649	—	Price of ditto	4	0	0	6	8	0
	1650	—	Price of ditto	3	16	8	6	2	6
			Average of these 5 last years	3	12	8	5	16	2

Changes in the value of money.	Anno Dom.	Anno Regis.	Price of the Quarter of Wheat in England.	Money of that time.			Present Money.		
				£	s.	d.	£	s.	d.
Change of Interest this year.	1651	—	Price of the quarter of wheat	3	13	4	4	8	0
	1652	—	Price of ditto	2	9	6	2	19	4
	1653	—	Price of ditto	1	15	6	2	2	7
	1654	—	Price of ditto	1	6	0	1	11	2
	1655	—	Price of ditto	1	13	4	2	0	0
	1656	—	Price of ditto	2	3	0	2	11	7
	1657	—	Price of ditto	2	6	8	2	16	0
	1658	—	Price of ditto	3	5	0	3	18	0
	1659	—	Price of ditto	3	6	0	3	19	2
	1660	12 Chas. 2	Price of ditto	2	16	6	3	7	9
			Average of the last 10 years	2	9	6	2	19	5
	1660	—	Exportation, when the quarter of wheat did not exceed	2	0	0	2	8	0
			Importation, when the quarter of wheat did exceed	2	4	0	2	12	0
	1661	—	Price of the quarter of wheat	3	10	0	4	4	0
	1662	—	Price of ditto	3	14	0	4	8	10
	1663	—	Price of ditto	2	17	0	3	8	5
			Exportation, when the quarter of wheat did not exceed	2	8	0	2	17	7
			Importation, when the quarter of wheat did not exceed	2	8	0	2	17	7
	1664	—	Price of the quarter of wheat	2	0	6	2	8	7
	1665	—	Price of ditto	2	9	4	2	19	3
	1666	—	Price of ditto	1	16	0	2	3	2
	1667	—	Price of ditto	1	16	0	2	3	2
	1668	—	Price of ditto	2	0	0	2	8	0
	1669	—	Price of ditto	2	4	4	2	13	3
	1670	—	Price of ditto	2	1	8	2	10	0
			Average of the last 10 years	2	8	10	2	18	8
			Importation, when the quarter of wheat did exceed	2	13	4	3	4	0
	1671	—	Price of the quarter of wheat	2	2	0	2	10	5
	1672	—	Price of ditto	2	1	0	2	9	2
	1673	—	Price of ditto	2	6	8	2	16	0
	1674	—	Price of ditto	3	8	8	4	2	5
	1675	—	Price of ditto	3	4	8	3	17	7
	1676	—	Price of ditto	1	18	0	2	5	7
	1677	—	Price of ditto	2	2	0	2	10	5
	1678	—	Price of ditto	2	19	0	3	10	10
	1679	—	Price of ditto	3	0	0	3	12	0
	1680	—	Price of ditto	2	5	0	2	14	0
			Average of these 10 years	2	10	8	3	0	10
	1681	—	Price of the quarter of wheat	2	6	8	2	16	0
	1682	—	Price of ditto	2	4	0	2	12	10
	1683	—	Price of ditto	2	0	0	2	8	0
	1684	—	Price of ditto	2	4	0	2	12	10
	1685	1 James 2	Price of ditto	2	6	8	2	16	0
	1686	—	Price of ditto	1	14	0	2	0	10
	1687	—	Price of ditto	1	5	2	1	10	2
	1688	1 W. & M.	Price of ditto	2	6	0	2	15	2
			Exportation, when the quarter of wheat did not exceed	2	8	0	2	17	7
	1689	—	Price of the quarter of wheat	1	10	0	1	16	0
	1690	—	Price of ditto	1	14	8	2	1	8
			Average of the last 10 years	1	19	1	2	6	11

Changes in the value of money.	Anno Dom.	Anno Regis.	Price of the Quarter of Wheat in England.	Money of the time. £. s. d.			Present Money. £. s. d.		
	1691	4 W. & M.	Price of the quarter of wheat	1	14	0	2	0	10
	1692	—	Price of ditto	2	6	8	2	16	0
	1693	—	Price of ditto	3	7	8	4	1	2
	1694	—	Price of ditto	3	4	0	3	16	10
	1695	—	Price of ditto	2	13	0	3	3	7
	1696	—	Price of ditto	3	11	0	4	5	2
	1697	—	Price of ditto	3	0	0	3	12	0
	1698	—	Price of ditto	3	8	4	4	2	0
	1699	—	Price of ditto	3	4	0	3	18	10
	1700	—	Price of ditto	2	0	0	2	8	0
			Average of these 10 years	2	16	10	3	8	3
	1701	1 Anne	Price of the quarter of wheat	1	17	8	2	5	2
	1702	—	Price of ditto	1	9	6	1	15	5
	1703	—	Price of ditto	1	16	0	2	3	2
	1704	—	Price of ditto	2	6	6	2	15	10
	1705	—	Price of ditto	1	10	0	1	16	0
	1706	—	Price of ditto	1	6	0	1	11	2
	1707	—	Price of ditto	1	8	6	1	14	2
	1708	—	Price of ditto	2	1	6	2	9	10
	1709	—	Price of ditto	3	18	6	4	14	2
	1710	—	Price of ditto	3	18	0	4	13	7
			Average of these 10 years	2	3	2	2	11	10
	1711	—	Price of the quarter of wheat	2	14	0	3	4	10
	1712	—	Price of ditto	2	6	4	2	15	7
	1713	—	Price of ditto	2	11	0	3	1	2
Change this year of interest & tal	1714	1 G o. 1	Price of ditto		—		2	10	4
	1715	—	Price of ditto		—		2	3	0
	1716	—	Price of ditto		—		2	8	0
	1717	—	Price of ditto		—		2	5	6
	1718	—	Price of ditto		—		1	18	10
	1719	—	Price of ditto		—		1	14	9½
	1720	—	Price of ditto		—		1	17	0
			Average of the last 10 years		—		2	4	10½
	1721	—	Price of the quarter of wheat		—		1	17	6
	1722	—	Price of ditto		—		1	16	0
	1723	—	Price of ditto		—		1	14	9
	1724	—	Price of ditto		—		1	17	0
	1725	—	Price of ditto		—		2	8	6
	1726	—	Price of ditto		—		2	6	0
	1727	1 Geo. 2	Price of ditto		—		2	2	0
	1728	—	Price of ditto		—		2	14	6
	1729	—	Price of ditto		—		2	7	6
	1730	—	Price of ditto		—		1	16	6
			Average of these 10 years		—		2	2	0
	1731	—	Price of the quarter of wheat		—		1	13	0
	1732	—	Price of ditto		—		1	6	9
	1733	—	Price of ditto		—		1	8	4
	1734	—	Price of ditto		—		1	17	9
	1735	—	Price of ditto		—		2	3	0

Changes in the value of money.	Anno Dom.	Anno Regis.	Price of the Quarter of Wheat in England.	£.	s.	d.
	1736	10 Geo. 2	Price of the quarter of wheat	2	0	4
	1737	—	Price of ditto	1	17	9
	1738	—	Price of ditto	1	15	6
	1739	—	Price of ditto	1	17	6
	1740	—	Price of ditto	2	15	0
			Average of these 10 years	1	17	6
	1741	—	Price of the quarter of wheat	2	7	0
	1742	—	Price of ditto	1	12	1½
	1743	—	Price of ditto	1	5	0
	1744	—	Price of ditto	1	4	11
	1745	—	Price of ditto	1	7	6
	1746	—	Price of ditto	1	19	0
	1747	—	Price of ditto	1	14	10
	1748	—	Price of ditto	1	17	0
	1749	—	Price of ditto	1	17	0
	1750	—	Price of ditto	1	12	6
			Average of the last 10 years	1	13	8
	1751	—	Price of the quarter of wheat	1	18	6
	1752	—	Price of ditto	2	1	10
	1753	—	Price of ditto	2	4	5
	1754	—	Price of ditto	1	14	9
	1755	—	Price of ditto	1	13	9
	1756	—	Price of ditto	2	5	3
	1757	—	Price of ditto	3	0	0
	1758	—	Price of ditto	2	10	0
	1759	—	Price of ditto	1	19	10
	1760	1 Geo. 3	Price of ditto	1	16	6
			Average of these 10 years	2	2	6
	1761	—	Price of the quarter of wheat	1	10	3
	1762	—	Price of ditto	1	19	0
	1763	—	Price of ditto	2	0	9
	1764	—	Price of ditto	2	6	9
	1765	—	Price of ditto	2	14	0
	1766	—	Price of ditto	2	1	6
	1767	—	Price of ditto	3	4	6
	1768	—	Price of ditto	3	0	6
	1769	—	Price of ditto	2	3	1
	1770	—	Price of ditto	2	9	0
			Average of these 10 years	2	7	8
	1771	—	Price of the quarter of wheat	2	7	2
	1772	—	Price of ditto	2	10	8
	1773	—	Price of ditto	2	11	0
			Exportation, when the quarter of wheat was under	2	4	0
			Importation, when the quarter of wheat is at or above	2	8	0
	1774	—	Price of the quarter of wheat	2	12	8
	1775	—	Price of ditto	2	8	4
	1776	—	Price of ditto	1	18	2
	1777	—	Price of ditto	2	5	6
	1778	—	Price of ditto	2	2	0

Changes in the value of money.	Anno Dom.	Anno Regis.	Price of the Quarter of Wheat in England.	Sterling money. £.	s.	d.
	1779	19 Geo. 3	Price of the quarter of wheat	1	13	8
	1780	—	Price of ditto	1	15	8
			Average of the laſt 10 years	2	4	6
	1781	—	Price of the quarter of wheat	2	4	8
	1782	—	Price of ditto	2	7	10
	1783	—	Price of ditto	2	12	8
	1784	—	Price of ditto	2	8	10
			Average of theſe 4 years	2	8	6

An ACCOUNT of the Exportation and Importation of Grain, from and to Great Britain, from the year 1697 to the year 1784 *.

Years.	ENGLAND ALONE.		Exported Quarters.	Imported Quarters.
1697	—	Wheat and Flour — —	14,698	400
		Barley and Malt — —	84,666	211
		Oats and Oatmeal —	295	1
		Rye — —	2,596	—
			102,255	612
1698	—	Wheat and Flour — —	6,886	1,689
		Barley and Malt — —	77,575	150
		Oats and Oatmeal —	172	520
		Rye — —	1,343	3,622
			85,976	5,981
1699	—	Wheat and Flour — —	557	486
		Barley and Malt — —	1,586	—
		Oats and Oatmeal —	302	1,280
		Rye — —	405	350
			2,850	2,116
1700	—	Wheat and Flour — —	49,057	5
		Barley and Malt — —	63,468	—
		Oats and Oatmeal —	391	234
		Rye — —	27,231	—
			140,147	239
1701	—	Wheat and Flour — —	98,324	1
		Barley and Malt — —	72,400	—
		Oats and Oatmeal —	286	20
		Rye — —	43,917	—
			214,927	11
1702	—	Wheat and Flour — —	90,230	—
		Barley and Malt — —	88,137	—
		Oats and Oatmeal — —	90	1
		Rye — —	51,710	—
			230,167	1
1703	—	Wheat and Flour — —	106,615	50
		Barley and Malt — —	194,815	—
		Oats and Oatmeal — —	159	2
		Rye — —	58,439	—
			360,028	52

* The Author mentions, in the memorandum which he left along with his Manuscripts, that the accounts of Export and Import were made up from other documents, before he got the neceffary vouchers from the Cuftom-houfes of London and Edinburgh; and, although the difference be not material, he meant to have reformed them, according to the Cuftom-houfe vouchers, if he had kept his health. *Edit.*

Years.	ENGLAND ALONE.		Exported Quarters.	Imported Quarters.
1704	—	Wheat and Flour — —	90,314	2
		Barley and Malt — —	133,603	—
		Oats and Oatmeal — —	220	—
		Rye — —	29,285	—
			253,422	2
1705	—	Wheat and Flour — —	96,185	—
		Barley and Malt — —	158,783	—
		Oats and Oatmeal — —	100	—
		Rye — —	24,060	—
			279,128	—
1706	—	Wheat and Flour — —	188,332	77
		Barley and Malt — —	151,306	—
		Oats and Oatmeal — —	62	579
		Rye — —	49,892	—
			389,592	656
1707	—	Wheat and Flour — —	74,155	—
		Barley and Malt — —	115,924	—
		Oats and Oatmeal — —	104	12
		Rye — —	34,032	—
			224,215	12

ENGLAND AND SCOTLAND.

Years.				Exported Quarters.	Imported Quarters.
1708	England—	Wheat and Flour — —		83,406	86
		Barley and Malt — —		127,727	—
		Oats and Oatmeal — —		68	70
		Rye — —		4,720	—
1708	Scotland—	Wheat and Flour — —		563	—
		Beer, Barley, Barley Meal, and Malt		16,163	—
		Oatmeal — — —		6,099	—
		Rye — —		12	—
		Hulled Barley — —		—	30
				238,858	186
1709	England—	Wheat and Flour — —		169,680	1,552
		Barley and Malt — —		180,447	606
		Oats and Oatmeal — —		38	1
		Rye — —		166,513	—
		Carried forward		516,678	2,159

Years.	GREAT BRITAIN.		Exported Quarters.	Imported Quarters.
	Brought forward — — —		516,678	2,159
1709	Scotland—	Wheat and Flour — —	1,938	—
		Beer, Barley, Barley Meal, and Malt	15,200	—
		Oats and Oatmeal — —	2,785	—
		Rye — —	6	—
		Hulled Barley — —	—	73
			536,607	2,232
1710	England—	Wheat and Flour — —	13.924	400
		Barley and Malt — —	85,275	576
		Oats and Oatmeal — —	125	253
		Rye — —	12,210	—
1710	Scotland—	Wheat and Flour — —	2,683	—
		Beer, Barley, Barley Meal, and Malt	7,569	—
		Oats and Oatmeal — —	639	—
		Rye — —	21	—
		Hulled Barley — —	—	31
			122,502	1,260
1711	England—	Wheat and Flour — —	76,949	—
		Barley and Malt — —	148,389	—
		Oats and Oatmeal — —	311	—
		Rye — —	37.957	—
1711	Scotland—	Wheat and Flour — —	3,992	—
		Bear, Barley, Barley Meal, and Malt	26,990	—
		Oats and Oatmeal — —	8,595	—
		Rye — — — —	6	—
		Hulled Barley — —	—	19
			303,199	19
1712	England—	Wheat and Flour — —	145,191	—
		Barley and Malt — —	211,463	—
		Oats and Oatmeal —	304	—
		Rye — —	17,735	—
1712	Scotland—	Wheat and Flour — —	3,348	—
		Beer, Beer Meal, Barley, and Malt	36,875	1
		Oats and Oatmeal — —	6,083	—
		Rye — —	83	—
			421,082	1

Year.	GREAT BRITAIN.		Exported Quarters.	Imported Quarters.
1713	England—	Wheat and Flour — —	176,227	—
		Barley and Malt — —	270.518	—
		Oats and Oatmeal — —	1,376	—
		Rye — — —	38.626	—
1713	Scotland—	Wheat and Flour — —	3,742	—
		Beer, Barley, Barley Meal, and Malt	37,867	—
		Oats and Oatmeal — —	8,058	—
		Rye — —	266	—
		Peafe and Beans — —	72	—
			536,752	—
1714	England—	Wheat and Flour — —	174,821	16
		Barley and Malt — —	238.855	—
		Oats and Oatmeal — —	129	21
		Rye — — —	20,455	—
1714	Scotland—	Wheat and Flour — —	5,844	—
		Beer, Barley, Barley Meal, and Malt	34,254	—
		Oats and Oatmeal — —	7,140	—
		Rye — —	23	—
			481,521	37
1715	England—	Wheat and Flour — —	166,490	—
		Barley and Malt — —	108,445	—
		Oats and Oatmeal — —	304	—
		Rye — —	31,161	—
1715	Scotland—	Wheat and Flour — —	6,747	—
		Beer, Barley, Barley Meal, and Malt	28,851	—
		Oats and Oatmeal — —	7,423	—
		Rye — — —	95	—
			349,516	—
1716	England—	Wheat and Flour — —	74,926	—
		Barley and Malt — —	241,474	—
		Oats and Oatmeal — —	720	—
		Rye — — —	40,123	—
1716	Scotland—	Wheat and Flour — —	950	—
		Beer, Beer Meal, Barley, and Malt	33,388	—
		Oats and Oatmeal — —	11,714	—
		Rye — —	1,570	—
			404,865	—

Years.	GREAT BRITAIN.		Exported Quarters.	Imported Quarters.
1717	England—	Wheat and Flour — —	22,954	—
		Barley and Malt — —	269,519	—
		Oats and Oatmeal — —	404	62
		Rye — —	23 032	—
1717	Scotland—	Wheat and Flour — —	2.683	—
		Beer, Barley, Barley Meal, and Malt	38,019	—
		Oats and Oatmeal —	8,850	—
		Rye — —	456	—
		Peafe and Beans —	327	—
			366,244	62
1718	England—	Wheat and Flour — —	71,800	—
		Barley and Malt — —	374,273	—
		Oats and Oatmeal —	869	21
		Rye — —	49,417	—
1718	Scotland—	Wheat and Flour —	2,581	—
		Beer, Barley, Barley Meal, and Malt	54,126	—
		Oats and Oatmeal —	14,010	—
		Rye — —	306	—
			567.382	21
1719	England—	Wheat and Flour —	127.762	20
		Barley and Malt — —	367,148	—
		Oats and Oatmeal —	219	300
		Rye — —	45,502	—
1719	Scotland—	Wheat and Flour — —	2,771	—
		Beer, Barley, Barley Meal, and Malt	49,970	—
		Oats and Oatmeal — —	11,763	—
		Rye — —	187	—
			605 322	320
1720	England—	Wheat and Flour — —	83,084	—
		Barley and Malt — —	258 016	252
		Oats and Oatmeal — —	3,471	2
		Rye — — —	49.241	—
1720	Scotland—	Wheat and Flour — —	1,259	—
		Beer, Barley, Barley Meal, and Malt	43,838	—
		Oats and Oatmeal — —	16,788	—
		Rye — —	353	—
			456,050	254

Years.	GREAT BRITAIN.		Exported Quarters.	Imported Quarters.
1721	England—	Wheat and Flour — —	81,632	—
		Barley and Malt — —	350,551	445
		Oats and Oatmeal —	518	—
		Rye — —	69,698	—
1721	Scotland—	Wheat and Flour — —	1,116	—
		Beer, Barley, Barley Meal, and Malt	45,726	—
		Oats and Oatmeal —	13,535	—
		Rye — —	802	—
		Peafe and Beans —	50	—
			563,688	445
1722	England—	Wheat and Flour — —	178,880	—
		Barley and Malt —	404,257	—
		Oats and Oatmeal —	324	—
		Rye — —	42,579	—
1722	Scotland—	Wheat and Flour —	35	—
		Beer, Barley, Barley Meal, and Malt	22,258	—
		Oats and Oatmeal —	5,905	—
		Rye — —	233	—
		Peafe and Beans —	—	1
			654,471	1
1723	England—	Wheat and Flour —	157,720	—
		Barley and Malt — —	350,853	—
		Oats and Oatmeal —	542	112
		Rye — —	12,738	—
1723	Scotland—	Wheat and Flour —	362	—
		Beer, Barley, Barley Meal, and Malt	3,425	—
		Oats and Oatmeal —	626	—
		Rye —	1	—
		Peafe and Beans — —	—	150
			526,267	262
1724	England—	Wheat and Flour —	245,865	148
		Barley and Malt — —	252,194	—
		Oats and Oatmeal —	516	61,630
		Rye — —	23,441	—
1724	Scotland—	Wheat and Flour —	1,297	—
		Beer, Barley, Barley Meal, and Malt	2,004	10
		Oats and Oatmeal —	621	—
		Rye — —	9	—
		Peafe, Beans, and Buck Wheat	—	10
			525,947	61,798

Years.	GREAT BRITAIN.		Exported Quarters.	Imported Quarters.
1725	England—	Wheat and Flour —	204,413	12
		Barley and Malt — —	307,808	—
		Oats and Oatmeal —	1,447	2,152
		Rye — —	20,540	—
1725	Scotland—	Wheat and Flour —	6,762	—
		Beer, Barley, Barley Meal, and Malt	27,943	—
		Oats and Oatmeal —	8,986	—
		Rye — —	332	—
		Peafe and Beans —	1	23
			578,232	2,187
1726	England—	Wheat and Flour —	142,183	—
		Barley and Malt —	355 943	—
		Oats and Oatmeal —	1,413	20
		Rye — —	18,835	—
1726	Scotland—	Wheat and Flour —	1,443	—
		Beer, Barley, Barley Meal, and Malt	30,795	—
		Oats and Oatmeal —	3,722	—
		Rye — —	1,335	—
			555,669	20
1727	England—	Wheat and Flour —	30,315	—
		Barley and Malt —	250 117	100
		Oats and Oatmeal —	2,205	16
		Rye — —	9,169	—
1727	Scotland—	Wheat and Flour —	715	—
		Beer, Barley, Barley Meal, and Malt	50,052	—
		Oats and Oatmeal —	7,042	1
		Rye — —	435	—
		Peafe, Beans, and Peafe Meal	33	—
			350,083	117
1728	England—	Wheat and Flour —	3,817	71,574
		Barley and Malt — —	195,539	11,745
		Oats and Oatmeal —	1,383	70 070
		Rye — —	14	42,206
1728	Scotland—	Wheat and Flour —	118	—
		Beer, Barley, Barley Meal, and Malt	16,547	—
		Oats and Oatmeal —	1,371	—
		Rye — —	270	—
		Peafe and Beans —	5	—
			219,064	198,595

Years.	GREAT BRITAIN.		Exported Quarters.	Imported Quarters.
1729	England—	Wheat and Flour —	18,993	40,315
		Barley and Malt — —	135,394	17,202
		Oats and Oatmeal —	2,541	184,092
		Rye — —	1,460	132,046
1729	Scotland—	Wheat and Flour —	—	—
		Beer, Barley, Barley Meal, and Malt	9,177	—
		Oats and Oatmeal — —	6,868	—
		Rye — —	17	—
			174,450	373,655
1730	England—	Wheat and Flour —	93,971	76
		Barley and Malt — —	194,429	386
		Oats and Oatmeal —	4,479	95,149
		Rye — —	12,394	—
1730	Scotland—	Wheat and Flour —	559	—
		Beer, Barley, Barley Meal, and Malt	23,882	—
		Oats and Oatmeal —	1,913	—
		Rye — —	165	—
		Peafe, Beans, and Buck Wheat	—	1
			331,812	95,612
1731	England—	Wheat and Flour —	130,025	4
		Barley and Malt — —	191,262	3,503
		Oats and Oatmeal —	1,808	15,893
		Rye — —	21,090	—
1731	Scotland—	Wheat and Flour —	625	—
		Beer, Barley, Barley Meal, and Malt	19,753	—
		Oats and Oatmeal —	2,005	—
		Rye — —	308	—
		Peafe and Beans —	202	—
			367,078	19,400
1732	England—	Wheat and Flour —	202,058	—
		Barley and Malt — —	174,950	—
		Oats and Oatmeal —	,,275	12,044
		Rye — —	15,536	—
1732	Scotland—	Wheat and Flour — —	554	—
		Beer, Barley, Barley Meal, and Malt	15,633	—
		Oats and Oatmeal —	691	—
		Rye — —	40	—
			410,737	12,044

Years.	GREAT BRITAIN.		Exported Quarters.	Imported Quarters.
1733	England—	Wheat and Flour — —	427,199	7
		Barley and Malt — —	240,713	—
		Oats and Oatmeal — —	1,487	9
		Rye — —	28,155	—
1733	Scotland—	Wheat and Flour —	206	—
		Beer, Barley, Barley Meal, and Malt	18,349	—
		Oats and Oatmeal —	2,631	—
		Rye — —	377	—
			719,117	16
1734	England—	Wheat and Flour — —	408,197	7
		Barley and Malt — —	303,349	1
		Oats and Oatmeal —	3,039	9
		Rye — —	10,735	—
1734	Scotland—	Wheat and Flour — —	550	—
		Beer, Barley, Barley Meal, and Malt	27,862	—
		Oats and Oatmeal —	5,570	—
		Rye — —	253	—
		Buck Wheat and Peafe —	—	2
			759,555	19
1735	England—	Wheat and Flour — —	153,344	9
		Barley and Malt — —	277,302	—
		Oats and Oatmeal —	1,921	6,439
		Rye — —	1,330	—
1735	Scotland—	Wheat and Flour — —	1,936	—
		Beer, Barley, Barley Meal, and Malt	26,991	—
		Oats and Oatmeal — —	27,841	—
		Rye — —	203	—
		Peafe and Buck Wheat —	—	1
			490,868	6,449
1736	England—	Wheat and Flour — —	118,171	17
		Barley and Malt — —	199,463	—
		Oats and Oatmeal — —	1,197	268
		Rye — — —	1,221	—
1736	Scotland—	Wheat and Flour — —	47	1
		Beer, Barley, Barley Meal, and Malt	23,091	—
		Oats and Oatmeal — —	16,618	—
		Rye — —	90	—
		Peafe and Beans —	—	—
			359,898	286

Years.	GREAT BRITAIN.		Exported Quarters.	Imported Quarters.
1737	England—	Wheat and Flour — —	461,602	32
		Barley and Malt — —	127,388	—
		Oats and Oatmeal — —	1,922	7
		Rye — — —	7,849	'
1737	Scotland—	Wheat and Flour — —	4,469	—
		Beer, Barley, Barley Meal, and Malt	18,160	1
		Oats and Oatmeal — —	2,729	—
		Rye — —	40	—
		Peafe and Buck Wheat —	—	2
			624,159	42
1738	England—	Wheat and Flour — —	580,597	3
		Barley and Malt — —	259,298	1
		Oats and Oatmeal — —	1,777	21
		Rye — — —	36,159	—
1738	Scotland—	Wheat and Flour — —	7,687	—
		Beer, Barley, Barley Meal, and Malt	32,317	2
		Oats and Oatmeal — —	5,448	—
		Rye — —	166	—
		Buck Wheat — —	—	2
			923,459	29
1739	England—	Wheat and Flour — —	279,543	23
		Barley and Malt — —	246,374	—
		Oats and Oatmeal — —	1,116	32
		Rye — —	29,791	—
1739	Scotland—	Wheat and Flour — —	5,949	—
		Beer, Barley, Barley Meal, and Malt	24,685	1
		Oats and Oatmeal — —	7,927	—
		Rye — — —	503	—
		Peafe, Beans, and Buck Wheat	—	24
			595,838	80
1740	England—	Wheat and Flour — —	54,391	5,469
		Barley and Malt — —	169,565	1
		Oats and Oatmeal — —	2,572	1,333
		Rye — — —	8,980	1,090
1740	Scotland—	Wheat and Flour — —	—	—
		Beer, Barley, Barley Meal, and Malt	7,423	120
		Oats and Oatmeal — —	831	513
		Rye — —	—	—
		Peafe, Beans, and Buck Wheat	—	27
			243,762	8,553

Years.	GREAT BRITAIN.		Exported Quarters.	Imported Quarters.
1741	England—	Wheat and Flour	45,417	7,540
		Barley and Malt	129,972	15,132
		Oats and Oatmeal	1,107	84,822
		Rye	7,622	11,012
1741	Scotland—	Wheat and Flour	—	—
		Beer, Barley, Barley Meal, and Malt	23	374
		Oats and Oatmeal	255	35,722
		Rye	—	—
		Pease, Beans, and Indian Corn	—	3,835
			184,396	158,437
1742	England—	Wheat and Flour	293,260	1
		Barley and Malt	201,008	—
		Oats and Oatmeal	1,380	25
		Rye	63,272	—
1742	Scotland—	Wheat and Flour	2,438	—
		Beer, Barley, Barley Meal, and Malt	31,337	1
		Oats and Oatmeal	7,238	—
		Rye	354	36
		Pease, Beans, and Buck Wheat	10	13
			600,497	76
1743	England—	Wheat and Flour	371,431	3
		Barley and Malt	254,213	—
		Oats and Oatmeal	1,882	13
		Rye	88,273	—
1743	Scotland—	Wheat and Flour	4,548	—
		Beer, Barley, Barley Meal, and Malt	39,778	—
		Oats and Oatmeal	13,988	—
		Rye	361	—
		Pease, Beans, and Buck Wheat	50	8
			774,524	24
1744	England—	Wheat and Flour	231,985	2
		Barley and Malt	239,953	—
		Oats and Oatmeal	1,658	68
		Rye	74,169	—
1744	Scotland—	Wheat and Flour	2,289	—
		Beer, Barley, Barley Meal, and Malt	38,089	—
		Oats and Oatmeal	7,534	—
		Rye	398	—
		Pease and Buck Wheat	—	5
			596,075	75

APPENDIX, No II.

Years.	GREAT BRITAIN.		Exported Quarters.	Imported Quarters.
1745	England—	Wheat and Flour	324,840	6
		Barley and Malt	315,234	—
		Oats and Oatmeal	9,770	5
		Rye	83,966	—
1745	Scotland—	Wheat and Flour	509	—
		Beer, Barley, and Malt	21,840	—
		Oats and Oatmeal	30,737	—
		Rye	160	—
		Buck Wheat and Flour	—	13
			787,056	24
1746	England—	Wheat and Flour	130,646	—
		Barley and Malt	440,744	—
		Oats and Oatmeal	20,203	—
		Rye	45,782	—
1746	Scotland—	Wheat and Flour	459	—
		Beer, Barley, Barley Meal, and Malt	1,001	—
		Oats and Oatmeal	—	—
		Rye	—	—
		Peafe and Buck Wheat	—	4
			638 835	4
1747	England—	Wheat and Flour	266,907	—
		Barley and Malt	464,430	—
		Oats and Oatmeal	2,122	—
		Rye	92,718	—
1747	Scotland—	Wheat and Flour	3,584	—
		Beer, Barley, Barley Meal, and Malt	24,591	—
		Oats and Oatmeal	5,020	14
		Rye	4,010	—
		Peafe and Buck Wheat	—	13
			863,382	27
1748	England—	Wheat and Flour	543,388	6
		Barley and Malt	423,220	—
		Oats and Oatmeal	3,769	—
		Rye	103,892	—
1748	Scotland—	Wheat and Flour	1,852	—
		Beer, Barley, Barley Meal, and Malt	39,151	—
		Oats and Oatmeal	8,377	—
		Rye	251	—
		Buck Wheat, Peafe, and Beans	53	14
			1,123,953	20

Years.	GREAT BRITAIN.		Exported Quarters.	Imported Quarters.
1749	England—	Wheat and Flour —	629 049	3°2
		Oats and Oatmeal — —	1,281	—
		Barley and Malt —	408,091	40
		Rye — —	106,312	—
1749	Scotland—	Wheat and Flour — —	1,958	—
		Beer, Barley, Barley Meal, and Malt	79,669	—
		Oats and Oatmeal — —	23,833	—
		Rye — —	113	—
		Peafe and Buck Wheat —	—	9
			1,250,306	131
1750	England—	Wheat and Flour — —	947,602	28.
		Beer, Barley, Barley Meal, and Malt	555,255	—
		Oats and Oatmeal — —	4,83	20
		Rye — —	99,249	—
1750	Scotland—	Wheat and Flour — —	2,881	—
		Beer, Barley, Barley Meal, and Malt	50,264	—
		Oats and Oatmeal — —	8,203	—
		Rye — —	241	—
		Peafe and Buck Wheat —	—	19
			1,667,778	3'9
1751	England—	Wheat and Flour — —	691,416	3
		Barley and Malt — —	289 245	—
		Oats and Oatmeal — —	2 476	2,291
		Rye — —	71,048	—
1751	Scotland—	Wheat and Flour — —	1 541	—
		Bear, Barley, Barley Meal, and Malt	18,433	—
		Oats and Oatmeal — —	4,365	—
		Rye — — —	—	—
		Peafe and Buck Wheat —	—	14
			1,048 324	2 308
1752	England—	Wheat and Flour — —	429,279	—
		Barley and Malt — —	393,910	—
		Oats and Oatmeal —	1,590	260
		Rye — — —	57,847	—
1752	Scotland—	Wheat and Flour — —	838	—
		Beer, Barley, Barley Meal, and Malt	3,128	56
		Oats and Oatmeal — —	—	14,090
		Rye, Peafe, Buck Wheat, and Hulled Barley — —	12.	223
			886,712	14,629

Years.	GREAT BRITAIN.		Exported Quarters.	Imported Quarters.
1753	England—	Wheat and Flour — —	299,609	—
		Barley and Malt — —	341,474	—
		Oats and Oatmeal — —	7,012	36
		Rye — — .	24,836	—
1753	Scotland—	Wheat and Flour — —	1,145	—
		Beer, Barley, Barley Meal, and Malt	5,066	—
		Oats and Oatmeal — —	4,102	7,013
		Peafe, Beans, Buck Wheat, and Hulled Barley — —	—	17
			683,244	7,066
1754	England—	Wheat and Flour — —	356,270	201
		Barley and Malt — —	369,771	—
		Oats and Oatmeal — —	2 330	52,422
		Rye — —	42,915	—
1754	Scotland—	Wheat and Flour — —	511	—
		Beer, Barley, Barley Meal, and Malt	15,134	—
		Oats and Oatmeal — —	8,706	4,409
		Peafe, Buck Wheat, and Hulled Barley	—	15
			795 697	57,047
1755	England—	Wheat and Flour — —	237,459	—
		Barley and Malt — —	374,404	—
		Oats and Oatmeal — —	1,112	2,883
		Rye — —	43,442	—
1755	Scotland—	Wheat and Flour — —	7	—
		Beer, Barley, Barley Meal, and Malt	7,255	—
		Oats and Oatmeal · —	2,056	3
		Rye — —	4	—
		Buck Wheat — —	—	13
			665,739	2,899
1756	England—	Wheat and Flour — —	101,936	5
		Barley and Malt — —	263,865	5
		Oats and Oatmeal — —	2,310	46,670
		Rye — —	29,969	1,695
1756	Scotland—	Wheat and Flour —	816	—
		Beer, Barley, Barley Meal, and Malt	6,085	—
		Oats and Oatmeal — —	3,189	8,068
		Buck Wheat and Flour —	—	18
			408,170	56,461

Years.	GREAT BRITAIN.		Exported Quarters.	Imported Quarters.
1757	England—	Wheat and Flour —	11,226	132,343
		Barley and Malt —	63,259	5,781
		Oats and Oatmeal — —	4,418	7,759
		Rye — —	907	7,662
1757	Scotland—	Wheat and Flour — —	319	11,219
		Beer, Barley, Barley Meal, and Malt	195	162
		Oats and Oatmeal — —	275	1,601
		Beans and Peafe — —	—	1,617
		Buck Wheat and Indian Corn —	—	957
		Rye — —	57	—
			80,656	167,301
1758	England—	Wheat and Flour — —	9,234	19,040
		Barley and Malt — —	11,419	9,752
		Oats and Oatmeal — —	1,831	13,840
		Rye — —	—	—
1758	Scotland—	Wheat and Flour — —	—	1,313
		Beer, Barley, Barley Meal, and Malt	—	163
		Oats and Oatmeal — —	—	19,782
		Rye — —	—	365
		Peafe, Beans, and Buck Wheat	—	168
		Indian Corn and Hulled Barley —	—	138
			22,484	64,561
1759	England—	Wheat and Flour — —	226,426	82
		Barley and Malt — —	188,942	42
		Oats and Oatmeal — —	3,135	335
		Rye — —	41,480	—
1759	Scotland—	Wheat and Flour — —	1,215	80
		Bear, Barley, Barley Meal, and Malt	19,855	—
		Oats and Oatmeal — —	3,802	1,125
		Peafe and Buck Wheat —	32	24
		Rye — — —	29	—
			484,916	1,688
1760	England—	Wheat and Flour — —	392,710	—
		Barley and Malt — —	258,787	—
		Oats and Oatmeal —	2,338	4
		Rye — — —	52,776	—
1760	Scotland—	Wheat and Flour — —	2,904	3
		Beer, Barley, Barley Meal, and Malt	32,363	—
		Oats and Oatmeal — —	12,158	—
		Buck Wheat and Hulled Barley	—	5
		Rye, Peafe, and Beans —	398	—
			752,434	12

APPENDIX, No II.

Years.	GREAT BRITAIN.		Exported Quarters.	Imported Quarters.
1761	England	Wheat and Flour	440,746	—
		Barley and Malt	376,949	—
		Oats and Oatmeal	2,840	21
		Rye	57,571	—
1761	Scotland	Wheat and Flour	1,210	—
		Beer, Barley, Barley Meal, and Malt	36,942	—
		Oats and Oatmeal	8,450	37
		Buck Wheat and Flour	—	15
		Rye	411	—
			925,119	73
1762	England	Wheat and Flour	294,500	56
		Barley and Malt	385,303	942
		Oats and Oatmeal	1,369	17,400
		Rye	28,410	—
1762	Scotland	Wheat and Flour	885	—
		Beer, Barley, Barley Meal, and Malt	37,761	—
		Oats and Oatmeal	14,623	—
		Rye	219	—
		Buck Wheat	—	34
			763,070	18,432
1763	England	Wheat and Flour	427,074	8
		Barley and Malt	203,884	3,228
		Oats and Oatmeal	1,664	218,474
		Rye	12,934	—
1763	Scotland	Wheat and Flour	2,464	64
		Beer, Barley, Barley Meal, and Malt	11,797	—
		Oats and Oatmeal	1,378	16,425
		Rye	17	—
		Buck Wheat	—	49
			661,212	238,248
1764	England	Wheat and Flour	396,538	1
		Barley and Malt	232,439	5,110
		Oats and Oatmeal	1,101	134,370
		Rye	27,690	—
1764	Scotland	Wheat and Flour	319	—
		Rye	56	—
		Beer, Barley, Barley Meal, and Malt	14,452	—
		Peafe and Beans	13	—
		Oats and Oatmeal	2,851	402
		Peafe, Buck Wheat, and Hulled Barley	—	48
			675,459	139,931

Years.	GREAT BRITAIN.		Exported Quarters.	Imported Quarters.
1765	England—	Wheat and Flour — —	167,036	101,009
		Barley and Malt — —	227,867	3,597
		Oats and Oatmeal —	11,653	82,747
		Rye, Beans, and Peafe —	26,269	5
1765	Scotland—	Wheat and Flour — —	90	3,538
		Beer, Barley, Barley Meal, and Malt	24,060	1,014
		Oats and Oatmeal —	729	25,830
		Rye — —	26	—
		Buck Wheat — —	—	41
		Peafe and Beans —	—	250
			457,730	218,031
1766	England—	Wheat and Flour — —	163,908	9,230
		Barley and Malt — —	95,061	2,611
		Oats and Oatmeal —	10,937	210,129
		Rye · — —	6,045	140
		Peafe and Beans — —	25,048	363
		Indian Corn — —	—	195
1766	Scotland—	Wheat and Flour — —	1,031	1,790
		Barley and Malt — —	54	1,125
		Oats and Oatmeal —	696	20,510
		Peafe and Beans — —	14	1,352
		Buck Wheat and Indian Corn	—	63
			302,794	247,518
1767	England—	Wheat and Flour — —	5,071	481,734
		Barley and Malt — —	18,654	64,895
		Oats and Oatmeal —	10,593	209,403
		Rye — —	53	65,498
		Peafe and Beans —	16,052	16,469
		Indian Corn — —	—	16
1767	Scotland—	Wheat and Flour — —	—	16,172
		Barley and Malt — —	46	9,469
		Oats and Oatmeal — —	12	39,760
		Rye — —	—	259
		Peafe and Beans —	—	3,746
			50,481	907,420

Years.	GREAT BRITAIN.		Exported Quarters.	Imported Quarters.
1768	England—	Wheat and Flour	7,433	333,576
		Barley and Malt	6,508	11,483
		Oats and Oatmeal	12,096	125,014
		Rye	150	57,073
		Beans and Peafe	13,982	5,287
		Indian Corn	—	13,993
1768	Scotland—	Wheat and Flour	—	15,692
		Barley and Malt	79	8,998
		Oats and Oatmeal	8	69,725
		Rye	—	806
		Peafe and Beans	—	7,529
			40,256	649,176
1769	England—	Wheat and Flour	49,892	4,171
		Barley and Malt	37,449	220
		Oats and Oatmeal	13,264	75,376
		Rye	21	22
		Peafe and Beans	16,160	43
		Indian Corn	—	50
1769	Scotland—	Wheat and Flour	—	207
		Barley and Malt	2,376	1
		Oats and Oatmeal	28	34,090
		Rye and Buck Wheat	—	49
		Peafe and Beans	—	44
			119,190	114,273
1770	England—	Wheat and Flour	75,401	34
		Barley and Malt	166,561	28
		Oats and Oatmeal	19,137	109,203
		Rye	642	—
		Beans and Peafe	19,508	9
1770	Scotland—	Wheat and Flour	48	—
		Barley and Malt	3,848	1
		Oats and Oatmeal	9,115	14,942
		Peafe and Beans	6	—
		Buck Wheat	—	9
			294,866	124,225

Years.	GREAT BRITAIN.		Exported Quarters.	Imported Quarters.
1771	England and Scotland—	Wheat and Flour —	10,089	2,510
		Barley and Malt —	34,198	228
		Oats and Oatmeal —	35,233	212,327
		Rye — —	—	2,179
		Peafe and Beans —	17,053	131
			96,573	217,375
1772	England and Scotland—	Wheat and Flour —	6,959	25,474
		Barley and Malt —	14,031	3,068
		Oats and Oatmeal —	23,599	106,820
		Rye — —	—	4,799
		Peafe and Beans —	17,096	490
			61,685	140,651
1773	England and Scotland—	Wheat and Flour —	7,637	56,857
		Barley and Malt —	2,475	63,916
		Oats and Oatmeal —	18,777	329,454
		Rye — —	—	9,255
		Peafe and Beans —	15,181	61,116
			44,070	520,598
1774	England and Scotland—	Wheat and Flour —	15,928	289,149
		Barley and Malt —	2,911	171,508
		Oats and Oatmeal —	16,433	399,499
		Rye — —	2,260	41,427
		Peafe and Beans —	13,567	24,591
			51,099	926,174
1775	England and Scotland—	Wheat and Flour —	91,037	560,988
		Barley and Malt —	51,414	139,451
		Oats and Oatmeal —	26,485	384,942
		Rye — —	2,722	33,574
		Peafe and Beans —	19,349	44,452
			191,007	1,163,407
1776	England and Scotland—	Wheat and Flour —	210,664	20,578
		Barley and Malt —	136,114	8,499
		Oats and Oatmeal —	34,987	378,566
		Rye — —	10,999	3,415
		Peafe and Beans —	56,037	38,843
			448,801	449,901

Years.	GREAT BRITAIN.		Exported Quarters.	Imported Quarters.
1777	England and Scotland—	Wheat and Flour —	87,686	233,323
		Barley and Malt. —	142,725	7,981
		Oats and Oatmeal —	36,614	366,446
		Rye — —	946	18,454
		Peafe and Beans —	47,156	63,829
			315,127	690,033
1778	England and Scotland—	Wheat and Flour —	141,070	106,394
		Barley and Malt —	103,930	42,714
		Oats and Oatmeal —	56,543	201,170
		Rye — —	1,706	9,327
		Peafe and Beans —	37,675	57,933
			340,924	417,538
1779	England and Scotland—	Wheat and Flour —	222,261	5,039
		Barley and Malt —	85,777	7,085
		Oats and Oatmeal —	22,286	348,511
		Rye — —	3,199	1,693
		Peafe and Beans —	44,593	43,745
			378,116	406,073
1780	England and Scotland—	Wheat and Flour —	224,059	3,915
		Barley and Malt —	191,563	352
		Oats and Oatmeal —	27,023	195,224
		Rye — —	6,305	—
		Peafe and Beans —	22,941	25,125
			471,891	224,616
1781	England and Scotland—	Wheat and Flour —	103,021	159,866
		Barley and Malt —	150,468	56
		Oats and Oatmeal —	41,717	109,446
		Rye — —	2,701	10,743
		Peafe and Beans —	19,344	17,753
			317,251	297,804
1782	England and Scotland—	Wheat and Flour —	145,152	80,605
		Barley and Malt —	127,744	13,592
		Oats and Oatmeal —	23,317	38,562
		Rye — —	4,003	—
		Peafe and Beans —	26,128	8,558
			326,344	141,407

Years.	GREAT BRITAIN.		Exported Quarters.	Imported Quarters.
1783	England and Scotland—	Wheat and Flour —	51,943	584,183
		Barley and Malt —	54,065	144,926
		Oats and Oatmeal —	11,826	228,942
		Rye — —	3,355	81,295
		Peafe and Beans —	12,960	31,6.4
			134,159	1,070,960
1784	England and Scotland—	Wheat and Flour —	89,288	216,947
		Barley and Malt —	66,889	77,182
		Oats and Oatmeal —	13,511	266,998
		Rye — —	6,731	24,779
		Peafe and Beans —	10,976	45,816
			187,395	631,722

APPENDIX, No III.

GENERAL ACCOUNT of the Quantities of the different forts of Grain, Exported feverally from England and Scotland, from the Union to the year 1763, when the Great Importation of Foreign Grain commenced.

| SCOTLAND. | | | | | ENGLAND. | | | |
Oats and Meal Quarters.	Barley and Malt Quarters.	Rye, Peafe, and Beans, Quarters.	Wheat and Flour Quarters.	Years	Wheat and Flour Quarters.	Rye, Peafe, and Beans, Quarters.	Barley and Malt Quarters.	Oats and Meal Quarters.
6,099	16,263	12	563	1708	83,426	4,720	127,727	68
2,785	15,200	6	1,938	1709	169,680	166,513	180,447	38
689	7,369	21	2,683	1710	13,924	12,216	85,275	125
8,595	26,090	6	3,992	1711	76,940	37,957	148,339	321
6,083	36,875	83	3,348	1712	145,191	17,735	211,463	304
8,058	37,867	265	3,742	1713	176,227	38,626	270,518	1,376
7,140	30,234	23	5,844	1714	174,821	20,455	238,855	129
7,423	28,851	95	6,747	1715	166,490	31,161	108,445	304
46,872	203,869	512	28,857		1,006,688	329,383	1,371,069	2,665
11,714	33,388	1,570	950	1716	74,926	40,123	241,474	720
8,850	38,019	456	2,693	1717	22,954	23,032	269,519	404
14,010	54,126	306	2,581	1718	71,800	49,417	374,273	869
11,763	49,070	187	2,771	1719	127,762	45,502	367,148	219
16,788	43,838	353	3,259	1720	83,084	49,241	258,016	3,471
109,997	423,210	3,384	39,151		1,387,214	536,698	2,881,499	8,348
13,535	45,726	852	1,116	1721	81,632	69,698	350,551	578
5,905	22,258	233	35	1722	178,880	42,579	404,257	324
626	3,425	1	362	1723	157,720	12,738	350,853	542
621	2,002	9	1,297	1724	245,865	23,441	252,194	516
8,986	27,943	333	6,762	1725	204,413	20,540	307,808	1,447
139,670	524,566	4,812	48,675		2,255,724	705,694	4,547,162	11,755
3,722	30,795	1,335	1,443	1726	142,183	18,835	355,943	1,413
7,042	50,052	468	714	1727	30,315	9,169	250,117	2,205
1,371	16,847	275	118	1728	3,817	14	195,539	1,383
6,868	9,177	17	—	1729	18,953	1,460	135,394	2,541
1,933	23,882	165	559	1730	93,971	12,394	194,429	4,479
160,606	655,019	7,072	51,508		2,545,003	747,566	5,678,584	23,776
2,005	19,753	510	623	1731	130,025	21,090	191,262	1,808
691	15,633	40	554	1732	202,058	15,536	174,950	1,275
2,631	18,349	377	206	1733	437,199	28,155	240,713	1,487
5,570	27,862	253	550	1734	408,197	16,735	303,349	3,039
27,143	26,091	203	1,930	1735	153,344	1,330	277,302	1,921
199,344	763,637	8,455	55,379		3,865,826	824,412	6,866,160	33,306

| SCOTLAND. | | | | | ENGLAND. | | | |
Oats and Oatmeal Quarters.	Barley and Malt Quarters.	Rye, Pease, and Beans, Quarters.	Wheat and Flour Quarters.	Years	Wheat and Flour Quarters.	Rye, Pease, and Beans, Quarters.	Barley and Malt Quarters.	Oats and Oatmeal Quarters.
199,344	763,607	8,455	55,379	1735	3,865,826	824,412	6,866,160	33,306
16,618	23,091	90	47	1736	118,171	1,221	199,463	1,197
2,729	18,160	40	4,469	1737	461,402	7,849	127,388	1,922
5,448	32,327	166	7,687	1738	580,597	36,159	259,298	1,777
7,927	24,685	503	5,949	1739	279,543	29,791	246,324	1,116
831	7,423	—	—	1740	54,391	8,980	169,565	2,572
232,897	869,293	9,254	73,531		5,359,930	908,412	7,868,198	41,890
255	23	—	—	1741	45,417	7,622	129,972	1,107
7,248	31,337	354	2,438	1742	293,260	63,272	201,008	1,380
13,988	39,778	411	4,548	1743	371,431	88,273	254,213	1,882
7,534	38,089	398	2,289	1744	231,985	74,169	239,953	1,658
30,737	21,840	160	509	1745	324,840	83,966	315,234	9,770
292,659	1,000,360	10,577	83,315		6,626,863	1,225,714	9,008,578	57,687
—	1,001	—	459	1746	130,646	45,782	440,744	20,203
5,020	24,591	4,010	3,584	1747	266,907	92,718	464,430	2,122
8,377	39,151	251	1,852	1748	543,388	103,892	423,220	3,769
23,833	79,669	113	1,958	1749	629,049	106,312	408,091	1,281
8,203	50,264	241	2,881	1750	947,602	99,040	555,255	4,283
338,092	1,195,036	15,192	94,049		9,144,455	1,673,467	11,300,318	89,345
4,365	18,233	—	1,541	1751	661,416	71,048	289,245	2,476
—	3,128	123	838	1752	429,279	57,847	393,910	1,590
4,102	5,066	—	1,145	1753	299,609	24,836	341,474	7,012
8,766	15,134	—	511	1754	356,270	42,915	369,771	2,330
2,056	7,255	4	7	1755	237,459	43,442	374,404	1,112
357,381	1,243,852	15,319	98,091		11,128,488	1,913,555	13,069,122	103,865
3,189	6,085	—	816	1756	101,936	29,969	263,865	2,310
275	195	57	319	1757	11,226	907	63,259	4,418
—	—	—	—	1758	9,234	—	11,419	1,831
3,802	19,855	29	1,215	1759	226,426	41,480	188,942	3,135
12,158	33,363	398	2,904	1760	390,710	52,766	258,787	2,338
8,450	36,942	411	1,210	1761	440,746	57,571	376,942	2,840
14,623	37,761	219	685	1762	294,500	28,410	385,303	1,369
399,878	1,377,053	16,433	105,440		12,603,266	2,124,658	14,617,646	122,106

c

TABLE of the Yearly Prices and Averages of Wheat, and of the General Importation and Exportation of Grain, to and from Great Britain, from the year 1697 to the year 1784 inclusive.

	IMPORTATION.			Yearly Prices of the Quarter of Wheat.			Years	Average Prices of the Quarter of Wheat.			EXPORTATION.			
	Sum of Importation. Quarters.	Average Importation. Quarters.	Yearly Importation. Quarters.	£.	s.	d.	Years	£.	s.	d.	Yearly Exportation. Quarters.	Average Exportation. Quarters.	Sum of Exportation. Quarters.	
			612	3	0	0	1697				102,255			
			5,981	3	8	4	1698	-			85,976			
			2,116	3	4	0	1699				2,850			
4 Years	8,948	2,237	239	2	0	0	1700	2	18	1	140,147	82,807	331,228	4 Years
			21	1	17	8	1701				214,927			
			1	1	9	6	1702				230,167			
			52	1	16	0	1703				360,028			
			2	2	6	6	1704				253,422			
			—	1	10	0	1705				279,128			
			656	1	6	0	1706				389,592			
			12	1	8	6	1707				224,215			
			186	2	1	6	1708				238,858			
			2,232	3	18	6	1709				536,607			
10 Years	4,422	442	1,260	3	18	0	1710	2	3	2	122,502	284,945	2,849,446	10 Years
			19	2	14	0	1711				303,199			
			1	2	6	4	1712				421,082			
			—	2	11	0	1713				536,752			
			37	2	10	4	1714				481,521			
			—	2	3	0	1715				349,516			
			—	2	8	0	1716				404,865			
			62	2	5	6	1717				366,244			
			21	1	18	10	1718				567,382			
			320	1	14	9½	1719				605,322			
10 Years	714	71	254	1	17	0	1720	2	4	10½	456,050	449,193	4,491,933	10 Years
			445	1	17	6	1721				563,688			
			1	1	16	0	1722				654,471			
			262	1	14	9	1723				526,267			
			61,798	1	17	0	1724				525,947			
			2,187	2	8	6	1725				578,232			
			20	2	6	0	1726				555,669			
			117	2	2	0	1727				350,083			
			198,595	2	14	6	1728				219,064			
			373,655	2	7	6	1729				174,450			
10 Years	732,692	73,269	95,612	1	16	6	1730	2	2	0	331,812	447,968	4,479,683	10 Years
			19,400	1	13	0	1731				367,078			
			12,044	1	6	9	1732				410,737			
			16	1	8	4	1733				719,117			
			19	1	17	9	1734				759,555			
			6,440	2	3	0	1735				490,868			
			286	2	0	4	1736				359,898			
			42	1	17	9	1737				624,159			
			29	1	15	6	1738				923,459			
			80	1	17	6	1739				595,838			
10 Years	46,909	4,690	8,553	2	15	0	1740	1	17	6	243,762	549,447	5,494,471	10 Years

	IMPORTATION.			Yearly Prices of the Quarter of Wheat.			Years	Average Prices of the Quarter of Wheat.			EXPORTATION.			
	Sum of Importation. Quarters.	Average Importation. Quarters.	Yearly Importation. Quarters.	L.	s.	d.		L.	s.	d.	Yearly Exportation. Quarters.	Average Exportation. Quarters.	Sum of Exportation. Quarters.	
			158,437	2	7	0	1741				184,396			
			76	1	12	1¼	1742				600,297			
			24	1	5	0	1743				774,524			
			75	1	4	11	1744				596,075			
			24	1	7	6	1745				787,056			
			4	1	19	0	1746				638,835			
			27	1	14	10	1747				863,382			
			20	1	17	0	1748				1,123,953			
			431	1	17	0	1749				1,250,306			
10 Years	159,437	15,943	319	1	12	6	1750	1	13	8	1,667,778	843,660	8,486,602	10 Years
			2,308	1	18	6	1751				1,048,324			
			14,629	2	1	10	1752				886,712			
			7,066	2	4	5	1753				683,244			
			57,047	1	14	9	1754				795,697			
			2,899	1	13	9	1755				665,739			
			56,461	2	5	3	1756				408,170			
			167,301	3	0	0	1757				80,656			
			64,561	2	10	0	1758				22,484			
			1,688	1	19	10	1759				484,916			
10 Years	373,972	37,397	12	1	16	6	1760	2	2	6	752,434	582,837	5,818,376	10 Years
			73	1	10	3	1761				925,119			
			18,432	1	19	0	1762				763,070			
			238,248	2	0	9	1763				661,212			
			139,931	2	6	9	1764				675,459			
			218,031	2	14	0	1765				457,730			
			247,518	2	8	6	1766				302,794			
			907,420	3	4	6	1767				50,481			
			649,176	3	0	6	1768				40,256			
			114,273	2	3	1	1769				119,190			
			124,225	2	9	0	1770				294,866			
			217,375	2	7	2	1771				96,573			
12 Years	3,015,353	251,279	140,651	2	10	8	1772	2	7	10	61,685	370,703	4,448,435	12 Years
			520,598	2	11	0	1773				44,075			
			926,174	2	12	8	1774				51,099			
			1,163,407	2	8	4	1775				191,007			
			449,901	1	18	2	1776				448,801			
			690,033	2	5	6	1777				315,127			
			417,538	2	2	0	1778				340,924			
			406,073	1	13	8	1779				378,116			
			224,616	1	15	8	1780				471,891			
			297,864	2	4	8	1781				317,251			
			141,407	2	7	10	1782				326,344			
			1,070,960	2	12	8	1783				134,159			
12 Years	6,940,293	578,358	631,722	2	8	10	1784	2	5	1	187,395	267,182	3,206,184	12 Years

TABLE of the Quantities of the different forts of Grain Exported from Great Britain, and of the Price of Wheat, from the Union to the year 1763, when the Great Importation of Foreign Grain commenced.

Yearly Price of the Quarter of Wheat. £. s. d.	Average Price of the Quarter of Wheat. £. s. d.	Years.	Wheat and Flour Quarters.	Rye, Peafe, and Beans, Quarters.	Barley and Malt Quarters.	Oats and Oatmeal Quarters.
2 1 6		1708	83,969	4,732	143,990	6,167
3 18 6		1709	171,618	166,519	195,647	2,823
3 18 0		1710	16,607	12,237	92,844	814
2 14 0		1711	80,941	37,963	175,329	8,916
2 6 4		1712	148,539	17,818	248,338	6,387
2 11 0		1713	179,969	38,892	308,385	9,434
2 10 4		1714	180,065	20,478	273,109	7,269
2 3 0		1715	173,237	31,256	137,296	7,727
	2 15 4		1,035,545	329,895	1,574,938	49,537
2 8 0		1716	75,876	41,693	274,862	12,434
2 5 8		1717	25,637	23,488	307,538	9,254
1 18 10		1718	74,381	49,723	428,399	14,879
1 15 0		1719	130,533	45,689	417,118	11,982
1 17 0		1720	84,343	49,594	301,854	20,259
	2 0 11		1,426,315	540,082	3,304,709	118,345
1 17 6		1721	82,748	70,550	396,277	14,113
1 16 0		1722	178,915	42,812	426,515	6,229
1 14 8		1723	158,082	12,739	354,278	1,168
1 17 0		1724	247,162	23,450	254,198	1,137
2 8 6		1725	211,175	20,873	335,751	10,433
	1 18 9		2,304,397	710,506	5,071,728	151,425
2 6 0		1726	143,626	20,170	386,738	5,135
2 2 0		1727	31,030	9,637	300,169	9,247
2 14 6		1728	3,935	289	212,086	2,754
2 6 10		1729	18,993	1,477	144,571	9,409
1 16 6		1730	94,530	12,559	218,311	6,412
	2 5 2		2,596,511	754,638	6,333,603	184,382
1 12 10		1731	130,650	21,600	211,015	3,813
1 6 8		1732	202,612	15,576	190,583	1,966
1 8 4		1733	427,405	28,532	259,062	4,118
1 18 10		1734	408,747	10,988	331,211	8,609
2 3 0		1735	155,280	1,533	304,293	29,762
	1 14 0		3,921,205	832,867	7,629,767	232,650

Yearly Price of the Quarter of Wheat.			Average Price of the Quarter of Wheat.			Years.	Wheat and Flour Quarters.	Rye, Pease, and Beans, Quarters.	Barley and Malt Quarters.	Oats and Oatmeal Quarters.
L.	*s.*	*d.*	*L.*	*s.*	*d.*					
Brought forward						1735	3,921,205	832,867	7,629,767	232,650
2	0	5				1736	118,218	1,311	222,554	17,815
1	18	0				1737	465,871	7,889	145,548	4,651
1	15	6				1738	588,284	36,325	291,625	7,225
1	18	6				1739	285,492	30,294	271,009	9,043
2	10	8				1740	54,391	8,980	176,988	3,403
			2	0	7		5,433,461	917,666	8,737,491	274,787
2	6	8				1741	45,417	7,622	129,995	1,362
1	14	0				1742	295,698	63,626	232,345	8,628
1	4	10				1743	375,979	88,684	293,991	15,870
1	4	10				1744	234,274	74,567	278,042	9,192
1	7	6				1745	325,349	84,126	337,074	40,507
			1	11	7		6,710,178	1,236,291	10,008,938	350,346
1	19	0				1746	131,105	45,782	441,745	20,203
1	14	10				1747	270,491	96,728	489,021	7,142
1	17	0				1748	545,240	104,143	462,371	12,146
1	17	0				1749	631,007	106,425	487,760	25,114
1	12	6				1750	950,483	99,290	605,519	12,486
			1	16	1		9,238,504	1,688,659	12,495,354	427,437
1	18	6				1751	662,957	71,048	307,578	6,841
2	1	10				1752	430,117	57,967	397,038	1,590
2	4	8				1753	300,754	24,836	546,540	11,114
1	14	8				1754	356,781	42,915	384,905	11,096
1	13	10				1755	237,466	43,449	381,659	3,168
			1	18	8		11,226,579	1,928,874	14,312,974	461,246
2	5	3				1756	102,752	29,969	269,950	5,499
3	0	0				1757	11,545	964	63,454	4,693
2	10	0				1758	9,234	—	11,419	1,831
1	19	10				1759	227,641	41,509	208,797	6,937
1	16	6				1760	393,614	53,164	291,150	14,496
1	10	3				1761	441,956	57,982	413,891	11,292
1	19	0				1762	295,385	28,629	423,064	15,992
			2	2	11		12,708,706	2,141,091	15,994,699	521,984

TABLE of the Prices and Duties, for the Exportation of Wheat from ENGLAND, prior to the Revolution, *anno* 1688.

	Exportation Prices per Quarter.						Anno Dom.	Anno Regis.	Exportation Duties per Quarter.						
	Present Money.			Money of the Time.					Money of the Time.			Present Money.			
	£.	s.	d.	£.	s.	d.			£.	s.	d.	£.	s.	d.	
Permitted — —	0	0	0	0	0	0	1360	34 Edw. 3.	0	0	0	0	0	0	
——	0	0	0	0	0	0	1393	17 Rich. 2.	0	0	0	0	0	0	
——	0	0	0	0	0	0	1425	4 Hen. 6.	0	0	0	0	0	0	
——	2	4	0	0	6	8	1436	15 Hen. 6.	0	0	0	0	0	0	
——	0	16	6	0	6	8	1554	1 2 P. & M.	0	0	0	0	0	0	
——	1	0	8	0	10	0	1562	5 Eliz.	0	0	0	0	0	0	
——	0	0	0	0	0	0	1570	13 Eliz.	0	1	0	0	2	1	by ftatute
——	0	0	0	0	0	0	—	—	0	2	0	0	4	2	by licenfe
——	2	1	4	1	0	0	1593	35 Eliz.	0	2	0	0	4	2	
——	2	13	4	1	6	8	1604	2 Ja. 1.	0	2	0	0	4	0	
——	3	4	0	1	12	0	1623	21 Ja. 1.	0	2	0	0	4	0	
——	2	11	2	1	12	0	1627	3 Chas 1.	0	2	0	0	3	2	
——	2	8	0	2	0	0	1660	12 Chas 2.	1	0	0	1	4	0	
——	2	17	7	2	8	0	1663	15 Chas 2.	1	0	0	1	4	0	
Without limitation of prices	0	0	0	0	0	0	1670	22 Chas 2.	1	0	0	1	4	0	

SCOTLAND.

	Prices per Boll.						Anno Dom.	Anno Regis.	Duties per Boll.					
	Present Money.			Money of the Time.					Money of the Time.			Present Money.		
	£.	s.	d.	£.	s.	d.			£.	s.	d.	£.	s.	d.
Prohibited — —	0	0	0	0	0	0	1587	20 Jas. 6.	0	0	0	0	0	0
Permitted when under	1	4	0	12	0	0	1663	15 Chas. 2.	0	5	0	0	0	6
——	1	4	0	12	0	0	1669	21 Chas. 2.	0	0	10	0	0	1

TABLE of the Prices and Duties, for the Importation of Wheat into ENGLAND, prior to the Revolution, *anno* 1688.

	Importation Prices. *per* Quarterr.					Anno Dom.	Anno Regis.	Importation Duties. *per* Quarter.					
	Prefent Money.			Money of the Time.				Money of the Time.			Prefent Money.		
	£.	s.	d.	£.	s.	d.			£.	s.	d.	£.	s.	d.
Invited - -	0	0	0	0	0	0	1202	3 John	0	0	0	0	0	0
Invited -, -	0	0	0	0	0	0	1215	16 John	0	0	0	0	0	0
Invited - *	0	0	0	0	0	0	1266	9 Hen. 3.	0	0	0	0	0	0
Invited - -	0	0	0	0	0	0	1297	25 Edw. 1.	0	0	0	0	0	0
Invited - -	0	0	0	0	0	0	1328	2 Edw. 3.	0	0	0	0	0	0
Invited - -	0	0	0	0	0	0	1358	25 Edw. 3.	0	0	0	0	0	0
Permitted - -	1	15	2	0	6	8	1463	3 Edw. 4.	0	0	0	0	0	0
When not above -	2	12	10	2	4	0	1660	12 Chas. 2.	2	0	0	2	8	0
When above that price	0	0	0	0	0	0	—	—	0	6	8	0	8	0
When not above -	2	17	7	2	8	0	1663	15 Chas. 2.	0	5	4	0	6	5
When not above -	3	4	0	2	13	4	1670	22 Chas. 2.	0	16	0	0	19	2
From that price to -	4	16	0	4	0	0	—	—	0	8	0	0	9	7
And when above that price	0	0	0	0	0	0	—	—	0	5	4	0	8	0

SCOTLAND.

	Prices *per* Boll.					Anno Dom.	Anno Regis.	Duties *per* Boll.					
	Prefent Money.			Money of the Time.				Money of the Time.			Prefent Money.		
	£.	s.	d.	£.	s.	d.			£.	s.	d.	£.	s.	d.
Permitted - -	0	0	0	0	0	0	1663	15 Chas. 2.	3	0	0	0	6	0
Prohibited - -	0	0	0	0	0	0	1672	25 Chas. 2.	0	0	0	0	0	0
Prohibited - -	0	0	0	0	0	0	1686	2 Jas. 7.	0	0	0	0	0	0

ABBREVIATION of the Corn Laws, reviewed in this Work, shewing the Prices, Bounties, and Duties, by which the Exportation and Importation of Grain have been regulated in England, and in Scotland, and in Great Britain, down to the year 1773.

Anno Dom.	Anno Regis.	ABBREVIATION OF THE ENGLISH EXPORTATION LAWS.
1360	34 Edw. 3.	Exportation prohibited.
1393	17 Richd. 2.	Allowed, upon payment of the ordinary subsidies and duties.
1425	4 Hen. 6.	The last law confirmed, but reserving power to the King and Council to restrain it.
1436	15 Hen. 6.	Allowed, when Wheat did not exceed 6s. 8d. and Barley 3s. per quarter.
1442	20 Hen. 6.	The last act confirmed for 10 years.
1444	23 Hen. 6	And that act now made perpetual.
1552	5 & 6 Ed. 6.	Prohibited until the prices were at or under 6s. 8d. for Wheat, 3s. 4d. for Barley and Malt, 2s. for Oats, 4s. for Peafe and Beans, and 5s. for Rye, per quarter.
1554	1 & 2 P. & M.	Prohibited, when the prices did not exceed 6s. 8d. for Wheat, 4s. for Rye, and 3s. for Barley, per quarter.
1562	5 Eliz.	Allowed, when the prices did not exceed 10s. for Wheat, 8s. for Rye, Peafe, and Beans, and 6s. 8d. for Barley and Malt, per quarter.
1570	13 Eliz.	Allowed, under the direction of Presidents, &c. upon payment of duties.
1593	35 Eliz.	Allowed, when the prices did not exceed 20s. for Wheat, 13s. 4d. for Rye, Peafe, and Beans, 12s. for Barley and Malt; upon payment of a duty of 2s. for every quarter of Wheat, and 16d. for every quarter of other grain.
1604	2 James 1.	Allowed, when the prices did not exceed 26s. 8d. for Wheat, 15s. for Rye, Peafe, and Beans, and 14s. for Barley and Malt, per quarter; and upon payment of the fame duties.
1623	21 James 1.	Allowed, when the prices did not exceed 32s. for Wheat, 20s. for Rye, 16s. for Peafe, Beans, Barley, and Malt, per quarter; and upon payment of the fame duties.
1627	3 Chas. 1.	Allowed upon the fame terms with the last act.
1660	12 Chas. 2.	Allowed, when the prices did not exceed 40s. for Wheat, 24s. for Rye, Peafe, and Beans, 20s. for Barley and Malt, and 16s. for Oats; upon payment of high duties.
1663	15 Chas. 2.	Allowed, when the prices did not exceed 48s. for Wheat, 32s. for Rye, Peafe, and Beans, 28s. for Barley and Malt, and 13s. 4d. for Oats, per quarter; upon payment of the fame high duties.
1670	22 Chas. 2.	Allowed, without limitation of prices, upon payment of the fame high duties.
1688	1 W. & M.	Not only allowed, when Wheat was not above 48s. Rye 32s. and Barley and Malt 24s. per quarter, but bounties granted.
1699	10 Wm. 3.	Prohibited for one year, from the 10th February 1699.
	11 Wm. 3	Bounty suspended, from 9th February 1699 to 29th September 1700.
1700	11 & 12 W. 3.	The subsidy, and all duties payable upon Corn and Grain, ground and unground, Bread, Biscuit, and Meal, given up and totally removed.

Anno Dom.	Anno Regis.	ABBREVIATION OF THE BRITISH EXPORTATION LAWS.
1706	5 Anne.	Union settled—English bounties adopted over all the kingdom, and extended to Oatmeal, Bigg, and Malt of Wheat.
1709	8 Anne.	Exportation prohibited, until the 29th September 1710.
1729	2 George 2.	Rules laid down for measuring Corn to be exported, and for ascertaining the prices, &c.
1732	5 George 2.	Grand Juries, at Sessions, to present the price of Corn ; and Corn imported, not to be again exported, nor carried coastways.
1741	14 George 2.	Prohibited, until the 25th December 1741.
1751	24 George 2.	Bounties upon Corn exported in Meal, to be paid according to the weight, at the rate of 448 pounds for the quarter.
1753	26 George 2.	Money, due upon Debentures for Corn exported, to bear interest at 3 *per cent. per annum*, if not paid in 6 months after presenting the certificate.
1757	30 George 2.	Prohibited, until the 25th December 1757 ; but with power to the King and Council to take off the prohibition.
1757	31 George 2.	Corn Market established at Westminster ;—and, the same year, an Assize made for Bread.
1766	6 George 3.	Exportation prohibited for a limited time ;—and, same year, an Embargo laid upon ships loaded with Corn, for exportation ;—and, same year, the Mayor and Aldermen of London impowered to determine the prices of Corn in January and July, as well as in April and October.
1767	7 George 3.	Exportation of Grain, and distilling from Wheat or Wheat Flour, prohibited from the 26th September to the 14th November 1767.
1768	8 George 3.	Exportation of Corn, and distilling from Wheat or Wheat Flour, prohibited until 20 days after the commencement of the next Session of Parliament.
1769	9 George 3.	5000 quarters of Bigg allowed to be exported from the Islands of Orkney, yearly ;—and, same year, exportation of Grain, and distilling from Wheat or Wheat Flour, prohibited for a limited time.
1770	10 George 3.	Corn Register established ; and Weekly Returns, from market towns in the several counties, to be made of the prices of Wheat, Rye, Barley, Oats, and Beans, in England ; and of Bear or Bigg, in Scotland. Same year the exportation of Corn, and the distilling from Wheat or Wheat Flour, prohibited till 20 days after the commencement of the next Session of Parliament.
1771	11 George 3.	Exportation of Corn prohibited, and also the distilling from Wheat or Wheat Flour, until 20 days after the commencement of the next Session of Parliament.
1772	12 George 3.	Exportation of Corn, and distilling from Wheat or Wheat Flour, prohibited until 20 days after the commencement of the next Session of Parliament.
1773	13 George 3.	Exportation of Grain, and distilling from Wheat or Wheat Flour, prohibited until the 1st day of January 1774. Same year the former bounties and duties repealed, and a total alteration made in the Corn Laws.
1774	14 George 3.	Alteration of the method of ascertaining the prices of Corn to be shipped for exportation.

f

Anno Dom.	Anno Regis.	Abbreviation of the ENGLISH Exportation Prices.	Money of the time. £.	s.	d.	Present Money. £.	s.	d.
1436	15 Henry 6.	Exportation permitted, when the price of Grain, at home, did not exceed, per Quarter, for						
		Wheat — —	0	6	8	2	4	0
		Barley — — —	0	3	0	0	19	10
1554	1 P. & M.	Permitted, when the price did not exceed, for						
		Wheat — —	0	6	8	0	16	6
		Rye — —	0	4	0	0	9	11
		Barley — — —	0	3	0	0	7	5¼
1562	5 Eliz.	Permitted, when the price did not exceed, for						
		Wheat — —	0	10	0	1	0	8
		Rye, Peafe, and Beans —	0	8	0	0	16	6
		Barley and Malt — —	0	6	8	0	13	10
1593	35 Eliz.	Permitted, when the price did not exceed, for						
		Wheat — —	1	0	0	2	1	4
		Rye, Peafe, and Beans —	0	13	4	1	7	7
		Barley and Malt — —	0	12	0	1	4	10
1604	2 James 1.	Permitted, when the price did not exceed, for						
		Wheat — —	1	6	8	2	13	4
		Rye, Peafe, and Beans —	0	15	0	1	10	0
		Barley and Malt — —	0	14	0	1	8	0
1623	21 James 1.	Permitted, when the price did not exceed, for						
		Wheat — —	1	12	0	3	4	0
		Rye — —	1	0	0	2	0	0
		Barley, Malt, Peafe, and Beans	0	16	0	1	12	0
1627	3 Charles 1.	Permitted, when the price did not exceed, for						
		Wheat — —	1	12	0	3	11	2
		Rye — —	1	0	0	1	12	0
		Barley, Malt, Peafe, and Beans	0	16	0	1	5	7
1660	12 Charles 2.	Permitted, when the price did not exceed, for						
		Wheat — —	2	0	0	2	8	0
		Rye, Peafe, and Beans —	1	4	0	1	8	9
		Barley and Malt —	1	0	0	1	4	0
		Oats — —	0	16	0	0	19	2
1663	15 Charles 2.	Permitted, when the price did not exceed, for						
		Wheat — —	2	8	0	2	17	7
		Rye, Peafe, and Beans —	1	12	0	1	18	4
		Barley and Malt — —	1	8	0	1	13	7
		Oats — —	0	13	4	0	16	0
1688	1 W. & M.	Permitted, when the price did not exceed, for						
		Wheat — —	2	8	0	2	17	7
		Rye — — —	1	12	0	1	18	4
		Barley and Malt —	1	4	0	1	8	9

N. B. Prior to the year 1346, the Exportation of all kinds of Grain, from England, was totally prohibited.

Anno Dom.	Anno Regis.	Abbreviation of the BRITISH Exportation Prices.	Money at the time.			Present Money.		
			L.	s.	d.	L.	s.	d.
1706	5 Anne.	Exportation of Grain permitted, when the price of the quarter did not exceed,						
		For Wheat, ground or unground, or Malt of Wheat	2	8	0	2	17	7
		Rye, ground or unground — —	1	12	0	1	18	5
		Barley, Beer or Bigg, or Malt, ground or unground — —	1	4	0	1	8	9
		Oats — — —	0	15	0	0	18	0
1773	13 George 3.	Exportation permitted, when the prices were under						
		For Wheat — — —	0	0	0	2	4	0
		Rye — — —	0	0	0	1	8	0
		Barley, Beer or Bigg, or Malt thereof —	0	0	0	1	2	0
		Oats — — —	0	0	0	0	14	0

Anno Dom.	Anno Regis.	Abbreviation of the ENGLISH Exportation Duties.	Price of the Quarter of Grain.						Duties per Quarter.					
			Money of the time.			Present Money.			Money of the time.			Present Money.		
			L.	s.	d.	L.	s.	d.	L.	s.	d.	L.	s.	d.
1570	13 Eliz.	For Wheat, when not prohibited —	0	0	0	0	0	0	0	1	0	0	2	0
		Other Grain — — —	0	0	0	0	0	0	0	0	8	0	1	4
		Wheat, exported by licence —	0	0	0	0	0	0	0	2	0	0	4	0
		Other Grain, by ditto — —	0	0	0	0	0	0	0	1	4	0	2	8
1593	35 Eliz.	For Wheat, when the price did not exceed	1	0	0	2	1	5	0	2	0	0	4	0
		Other Grain, as *per* exportation prices	0	0	0	0	0	0	0	1	4	0	2	8
1604	2 James 1.	For Wheat, when the price did not exceed	1	6	8	2	13	4	0	2	0	0	4	0
		Other Grain, as *per* exportation prices	0	0	0	0	0	0	0	1	4	0	2	8
1623	21 James 1.	For Wheat, when the price did not exceed	1	12	0	3	4	0	0	2	0	0	4	0
		Other Grain, as *per* exportation prices	0	0	0	0	0	0	0	1	4	0	2	8
1627	3 Chas. 1.	For Wheat, when the price did not exceed	1	12	0	2	11	2	0	2	0	0	3	$2\frac{1}{2}$
		Other Grain, as *per* exportation prices	0	0	0	0	0	0	0	1	4	0	2	$1\frac{1}{4}$
1660	12 Chas. 2.	For Wheat, when the price did not exceed	2	0	0	2	8	0	1	0	0	1	4	0
		Rye, Peafe, Beans, Barley, Malt, Buck Wheat — — —	0	0	0	0	0	0	0	10	0	0	12	0
		Oats, when not above — —	0	16	0	0	19	2	0	6	8	0	8	0
1663	15 Chas. 2.	For Wheat, when the price did not exceed	2	8	0	2	17	7	1	0	0	1	4	0
		Rye, Peafe, Beans, Barley, Malt, Buck Wheat — —	0	0	0	0	0	0	0	10	0	0	12	0
		Oats — — —	0	13	4	0	16	0	0	0	0	0	0	0
1670	22 Chas. 2.	For Wheat, without limitation of price	0	0	0	0	0	0	1	0	0	1	4	0
		Rye, Peafe, Beans, Barley, Malt, Buck Wheat — —	0	0	0	0	0	0	0	10	0	0	12	0
		Oats — — —	0	0	0	0	0	0	0	6	8	0	8	0

Anno Dom.	Anno Regis.	ENGLISH AND BRITISH BOUNTIES ON EXPORTATION.	Price of the Quarter of Grain.						Bounties *per* Quarter.					
			Money of the time.			Prefent Money.			Money of the time.			Prefent Money.		
			L.	*s.*	*d.*	*L.*	*s.*	*d.*	*L.*	*s.*	*d.*	*L.*	*s.*	*d.*
1688	1 W. & M.	For Wheat, when the price did not exceed	2	8	0	2	17	7	0	5	0	0	6	0
		Rye, ground or unground, when not above — — —	1	12	0	1	18	5	0	3	6	0	4	2¼
		Barley and Malt, ground and unground, when not above — —	1	4	0	1	8	9	0	2	6	0	3	0
1706	5 Anne.	For Wheat, or Malt made of Wheat, ground or unground, when not above	2	8	0	2	17	7	0	5	0	0	6	0
		Rye, ground or unground, when not above — —	1	12	0	1	18	5	0	3	6	0	4	2¼
		Barley, Beer or Bigg, Malt, ground or unground, when not above —	1	4	0	1	8	9	0	2	6	0	3	0
		Quarter of Oatmeal, when Oats not above	0	15	0	0	18	0	0	2	6	0	3	0
1773	13 George 3.	For Wheat, and Malt of Wheat, when the price is under — —	0	0	0	2	4	0	0	0	0	0	5	0
		Rye, when under — —	0	0	0	1	8	0	0	0	0	0	3	0
		Barley, Beer or Bigg, when under	0	0	0	1	2	0	0	0	0	0	2	6
		Oats, when under — —	0	0	0	0	14	0	0	0	0	0	2	0
		And, for every quarter of Oatmeal, confifting of 276 pounds, avoirdupois	0	0	0	0	0	0	0	0	0	0	2	6

Anno Dom.	Anno Regis.	ABBREVIATION of the ENGLISH IMPORTATION PRICES.	Money of the time.			Prefent Money.		
			L.	*s.*	*d.*	*L.*	*s.*	*d.*
1463	3 Edw. 4.	Importation of foreign Grain permitted, when the prices, at home, per quarter, did exceed						
		For Wheat — — —	0	6	8	1	15	2
		Rye — — —	0	4	0	1	1	1
		Barley — — —	0	3	0	0	15	10
1660	12 Chas. 2.	Importation permitted, when the prices did exceed						
		For Wheat — — —	2	4	0	2	12	9
		Rye — — —	1	16	0	2	3	2
		Beans, Barley, and Malt — —	1	6	8	1	12	0
1663	15 Chas. 2.	Importation permitted, when the prices did *not* exceed *						
		For Wheat — — —	2	8	0	2	17	7
		Rye, Peafe, or Beans — —	1	12	0	1	18	5
		Barley, Malt, or Buck Wheat — —	1	8	0	1	13	7
		Oats — — —	0	13	4	0	16	0
1670	22 Chas. 2.	Importation permitted, when the prices did exceed						
		For Wheat — —	2	13	4	3	4	0
		Rye, Peafe, or Beans — —	2	0	0	2	8	0
		Barley, Malt, or Buck Wheat — —	1	12	0	1	18	5
		Oats — — —	0	16	0	0	19	2
1773	13 Geo. 3.	Importation permitted, when the prices were at or above						
		For Wheat — — —	0	0	0	2	8	0
		Rye, Peafe, or Beans — —	0	0	0	1	12	0
		Barley or Malt — — —	0	0	0	1	4	0
		Oats — — —	0	0	0	0	16	0

* This is the act, in which, the infertion of the word *not*, in the importation claufe, entirely altered the intention of the law. See chap. 2. page 57. *Edit.*

Anno Dom.	Anno Regis.	ABBREVIATION OF THE ENGLISH IMPORTATION LAWS.
1202	3 John.	Importation of foreign grain invited.
1215	16 John.	Invited.
1266	9 Hen. 3.	Invited.
1297	25 Edw. 1.	Invited.
1328	2 Edw. 3.	Invited.
1350	25 Edw. 3.	Invited.
1360	34 Edw. 3.	Invited.
1463	3 Edw. 4	Prohibited, until the price exceeded 6s. 8d. for Wheat, 4s. for Rye, and 3s. for Barley, *per* quarter.
1660	12 Chas. 2.	Allowed, upon payment of different duties, according to the prices.
1663	15 Chas. 2.	Allowed, upon payment of lower duties.
1670	22 Chas. 2.	Allowed, upon payment of different duties, according to the prices.
1685	1 James 2.	Regulations to prevent fraudulent importation.
1729	2 George 2.	Regulations for ascertaining the price of Corn, at the time of importation, and for receiving the duties.
1732	5 George 2.	Further regulations anent the prices, and prohibiting Corn imported, to be again exported, or carried coastways.
1757	30 George 2.	Duties, upon the importation of Corn, suspended until the 24th August 1757; and importation allowed, duty free, in ships of foreign nations in amity with Great Britain.
1766	6 George 3.	Importation of Foreign Grain permitted, for a limitted time, duty free.
1767	7 George 3.	Importation permitted, for a limited time, duty free.
1768	8 George 3.	Importation permitted, for a limited time, duty free.
1769	9 George 3.	Importation of Rice permitted, for a limited time, duty free.
1772	12 George 3.	Importation permitted, duty free, to the 1st December 1772.
1773	13 George 3.	Permitted, duty free, to 1st January 1774.—Same year the Old Corn Laws totally altered; and importation of Foreign Grain and Flour permitted, at all times and places, when the price of the quarter was at or above 48s. for Wheat; 32s. for Rye, Pease, and Beans; 24s. for Barley; and 16s. for Oats; and importation of Oatmeal, into Scotland, permitted, duty free, when the price there shall exceed 16s. per boll, weighing 8 stone troy.

Anno Dom.	Anno Regis.	Abbreviation of the ENGLISH Importation Duties.	Price of Grain per Quarter — Money of the time (L. s. d.)	Price of Grain per Quarter — Present Money (L. s. d.)	Duties per Quarter — Money of the time (L. s. d.)	Duties per Quarter — Present Money (L. s. d.)
1660	12 Chas. 2.	For Wheat, when the price did not exceed	2 4 0	2 12 9	2 0 0	2 8 0
		when it exceeded that price —	—	—	0 6 8	0 8 0
		Rye, when the price did not exceed —	1 16 0	2 3 2	1 6 8	1 12 0
		when it exceeded that price —	—	—	0 5 0	0 6 0
		Beans, Barley, and Malt, when not above	1 6 8	1 12 0	1 6 8	1 12 0
		when above that price —	—	—	0 5 0	0 6 0
1663	15 Chas. 2.	For Wheat, when the price did not exceed	2 8 0	2 17 7	0 5 4	0 6 5
		Rye, Peafe, and Beans, when not above	1 12 0	1 18 5	0 4 0	0 4 9
		Barley and Malt, when not above —	1 8 0	1 13 7	0 2 8	0 3 2
		Buck Wheat, when not above — —	1 8 0	1 13 7	0 2 0	0 2 5
		Oats, when not above —	0 13 4	0 16 0	0 1 4	0 1 7
1670	22 Chas. 2.	For Wheat, when the price did not exceed	2 13 4	3 4 0	0 16 0	0 19 2
		when above that price, and not exceeding	4 0 0	4 16 0	0 8 0	0 9 7
		when above that price — —	—	—	0 5 4	0 6 5
		Rye, Peafe, and Beans, when not above	2 0 0	2 8 0	0 16 0	0 19 2
		when above that price — —	—	—	0 4 0	0 4 9
		Barley, Malt, and Buck Wheat, not above	1 12 0	1 18 5	0 16 0	0 19 2
		when above that price — —	—	—	0 2 8	0 3 2¼
		Oats, when not above — —	0 16 0	0 19 2	0 5 4	0 6 5
		when above that price — —	—	—	0 1 4	0 1 7
		BRITISH Importation Duties.				
1773	13 Geo. 3.	When the price of Wheat is at or above —	—	2 8 0	—	0 0 6
		Rye, Peafe, or Beans, at or above —	—	1 12 0	—	0 0 3
		Barley, Bear, or Bigg, at or above —	—	1 4 0	—	0 0 2
		Oats, at or above — — —	—	0 16 0	—	0 0 2
		And for every 100 weight of Wheat-flour	—	—	—	0 0 2

Anno Dom.	Anno Regis.	ABBREVIATION OF THE SCOTCH IMPORTATION LAWS.
1454	17 James 2.	Importation of Foreign Grain invited to be made either by Foreigners or Denizens.
1493	5 James 4.	Invited.
1663	15 Chas. 2.	Allowed from Ireland, upon payment of a duty of L. 3 per boll, when Meal and Barley did not exceed the price of L. 8 per boll at home.
1672	24 Chas. 2.	Importation of Victual from Ireland prohibited under severe penalties.
1687	3 James 7.	Prohibition to import Victual from Ireland renewed, and victual, so imported, ordered to be destroyed.
1703	2 Anne.	Importation of Victual prohibited from foreign parts, until the price of the Boll of Grain exceeds L. 12 for Wheat; L. 8 for Bear, Meal, and Malt; and L. 6 for Oats and Peafe; but with power to the Lords of the Privy Council to sufpend this prohibition when neceffary.
1741	14 Geo. 2.	Importation permitted, when the prices of Grain in the county of Edinburgh exceeded 40s. for Wheat; 20s. for Peafe and Beans; 18s. for Bear and Barley; and 13s. 4d. for Oats, per Quarter; and L. 8 Scots, per Boll, for Oatmeal, upon payment of the duties fixed by the English act of the 22d Charles 2.

Anno Dom.	Anno Regis.	ABBREVIATION OF THE SCOTCH EXPORTATION LAWS.
1555	13 Mary.	Exportation of Grain prohibited under severe penalties.
1587	20 James 6.	Prohibited.
1663	15 Chas. 2.	Exportation of Grain permitted, when the price of Victual at home was under L. 12 for Wheat; L. 8 for Bear and Barley; and 8 merks for Pease and Oats, per boll; upon payment of the usual duty.
1669	21 Chas. 2.	All duties payable upon Grain exported removed, except one merk per chalder upon every kind of Victual.

Anno Dom.	Anno Regis.	SCOTCH IMPORTATION DUTIES.	Price of Grain per Boll. Money of the time L. s. d.	Price of Grain per Boll. Present Money. L. s. d.	Duties per Boll. Money of the time L. s. d.	Duties per Boll. Present Money. L. s. d.
1663	15 Chas. 2.	Duties payable upon the boll of all kinds of Grain imported, when the boll of Barley and Meal did not exceed, at home, —	8 0 0	0 16 0	3 0 0	0 6 0
1703	2 Anne.	A duty of 40s. per boll, besides the former duties, upon each boll of grain from England for seed — — —	—	—	2 0 0	0 4 0
1741	14 Geo. 2.	The same duties to be paid in Scotland, as is payable in England, upon Grain imported by the English Act of the 22d Charles 2.				
		SCOTCH EXPORTATION DUTIES.				
1663	15 Chas. 2.	For Wheat, when the price of the boll, is under — — — —	12 0 0	1 4 0	0 0 5	0 0 6
		Bear or Barley, when the boll is under	8 0 0	0 16 0	0 0 5	0 0 6
		Oats and Pease, when the boll is under 8 merks — — — —	5 6 8	0 10 8	0 0 5	0 0 6
1669	21 Chas. 2.	Duty upon each chalder of Grain, exported, when under the above prices at home —	—	—	0 13 4	0 1 1½
1695	7 William.	Duties upon Exportation ceased, and bounties commenced.				
		SCOTCH EXPORTATION BOUNTIES.				
1695	7 William.	For every chalder of Grain, when the price of the boll of Wheat is at, or under, —	12 0 0	1 4 0		
		Bear, Barley, and Malt, at or under —	8 0 0	0 16 0	5 6 8	0 10 8
		Pease, Oats, and Meal, at or under —	6 0 0	0 12 0		
1706	5 Anne.	The same bounties with England.				

TABLE Explanatory of Sundry Articles in the preceding Work.

Quarters
of Grain
overhead.

Article I.—ENGLAND.

From the year 1700, when the old fyftem of the Corn Laws was completed, until the year 1763, that the great importation of Foreign Grain commenced, the Corn Trade was entirely in the hands of Britain, and importation of Foreign Grain was little known *.

For 55 years after the Union, that is, from the year 1708 to the year 1762 inclufive, there were exported of Grain from England,

Of Wheat and Flour —	12,603,266
Rye, Peafe, and Beans	2,124,658
Barley and Malt —	14,617,646
Oats and Oatmeal —	122,106

Total Exportation from England, in thefe 55 years   —   —   **29,467,676**

By the above proportion of Grain exported, it would appear, that the general crop of England confifts of about eight-twentieth parts of Wheat, and twelve-twentieths of inferior grain.

Yearly average Exportation during thefe 55 years   —   —   535,776

Article II.—SCOTLAND.

During the above 55 years, there were exported from Scotland,

Of Wheat and Flour —	105,440
Rye, Peafe, and Beans,	16,433
Barley and Malt —	1,377,053
Oats and Oatmeal —	399,878

Total Exportation from Scotland, in thefe 55 years   —   —   **1,898,804**

Yearly average Exportation during thefe years   —   —   —   34,524

By the above proportion it would appear, that the general crop of Scotland confifts of one-eightcenth of Wheat, and feventeen-eighteenths of inferior Grain.

Article III.—GREAT BRITAIN.

The Exportation from Great Britain, during the above 55 years confifted

Of Wheat and Flour —	12,708,706
Rye, Peafe, and Beans,	2,141,091
Barley and Malt —	15,994,699
Oats and Oatmeal —	521,984

Total Exportation from Great Britain, in thefe 55 years   —   **31,366,480**

Yearly average Exportation, during thefe years   —   —   570,300

---

* Vide Particular and General Account of Exportation and Importation, Appendix No 2.

TABLE Explanatory—*continued.*

<table>
<tr><td></td><td>Quarters
of Grain
overhead.</td></tr>
</table>

Article III. Brought forward.

During the 55 years mentioned, there were exported from Great Britain, of the several kinds of Grain overhead   —   —   —   31,366,480

And there were only imported, during all that space,   —   1,335,907

Balance in favour of exportation   —   —   —   30,030,573

For the 22 years from 1763 to 1784 inclusive, there have been imported, of foreign Grain, into Great Britain,   —   —   9,937,141

And, in that space, there have been only exported   —   —   5,966,430

Balance in favour of importation   —   —   3,970,711

Article IV.—CONSUMPTION.

If eight millions of people make up the population of Great Britain, and if these require 16 millions of quarters of the several sorts of Grain overhead, yearly, for their subsistence, at the rate of two quarters for each person; and if, of that number of people, two millions and a half of them are employed in husbandry, the true consumption of the kingdom, is the quantity necessary for the support of the other five millions and a half, after maintaining the people and cattle employed in raising the Grain, amounting to   —   —   11,000,000

Article V.—PRODUCTION.

In years when Great Britain supports herself, without receiving or sending out any Grain, or when the quantities exported and imported are equal, the production and the consumption will also be equal, each amounting to   —   —   —   11,000,000

But in years when Great Britain exports more than she imports, her produce must have an increase; and in years when she imports more than she exports, her produce must have suffered a proportional decrease.

During the 55 years already enumerated, the average exportation having been yearly   —   —   Quarters.
570,300

And deducting from thence the average yearly importation   24,289

We have remaining a clear yearly exportation of   —   —   546,011

Which makes the average yearly produce of these 55 years to be   11,546,011

So that our exportation yearly then, was as 1 to 21 ⎫
And the importation as   —   —   1 to 475 ⎬ of the produce.

TABLE Explanatory—*continued.*

Quarters
of Grain
overhead.

Article V. Brought forward.

		Quarters of Grain overhead.
In another point of view we shall again state the consumption —		11,000,000

For the 10 years from 1741 to 1750 inclusive, there were exported yearly, upon an average, — Quarters. 848,660

From which, deducting the yearly importation of — 15,943

We have remaining a clear yearly exportation of — — 832,717

Which extends the yearly average produce of these 10 years to — 11,832,717

And our exportation reached as far as 1 to 14 ⎫
The importation amounted only to   1 to 742 ⎬ of the produce.

We shall again state the consumption being — — 11,000,000

During the 12 years from 1773 to 1784 inclusive, there were imported, of foreign Grain, at an average yearly, no less than — — — Quarters. 578,358

And our average yearly exportation, during these 12 years, only amounted to — — 267,182

This leaves a balance of yearly importation against us — 311,176

Which reduces our yearly average produce, these 12 years, to — 10,688,824

And now the average importation, yearly, is as 1 to 18 ⎫
While our exportation comes only to   1 to 40 ⎬ of the produce.

In the year 1775, there were imported, of foreign Grain, no less than 1,163,407 quarters, while there were only exported, that year, 191,007 quarters, which reduced our produce to 10,027,600 quarters.

This brought the importation nearly as 1 to 8 ⎫
While our exportation was only as   1 to 53 ⎬ of the produce.

Article VI.—Of the Proportional Value of the several kinds of GRAIN.

From the experience of past times, the following appears to be as near the proportions as can be described, without entering into fractions, which in the present case is not necessary.

Wheat, as the superior Grain, must be the standard.
    Rye, Pease, and Beans, two-thirds ⎫
           Barley one-half ⎬ of the value of Wheat.
           Oats one-third ⎭

TABLE Explanatory—*continued.*

Article VI. Brought forward.

According to which computation, Wheat is double in value to the inferior Grain over-
head : For example—

Price or value of a quarter of Wheat fuppofed — —	L. 2	2	0
Two-thirds thereof for the quarter of Rye, Peafe, and Beans L. 1 8 0			
One-half thereof for the quarter of Barley — — 1 1 0			
One-third thereof for the quarter of Oats — 0 14 0			

Amount of all L. 3   3   0

Which, divided by 3, makes the quarter of inferior Grain overhead   1   1   0

Article VII.—Maintenance of each Perfon.

According to the prices in the Corn Regifter, from 1771 to 1784 inclufive, the average prices of the quarter of the feveral kinds of
Grain, are   —   For Wheat   —   L. 2   8   0
                                                                      Barley   —   1   3   8
                                                                      Oats   —   0 16   0
                                                                      Rye   —   —   1 10   3
                                                                      Beans   —   1   8   4

And the average price of thefe feveral kinds of Grain, overhead, *per*
quarter, is   —   —   —   1   9   3

So that the price of two quarters, for the maintainance of each perfon,
now amounts to   —   —   —   L. 2 18   6

And the price of the quarter of Wheat is nearly double the average price
of the inferior Grain overhead.

Thefe are all high prices, and clearly occafioned by foreign
importation taking place of our own cultivation ; for when
our agriculture was in full profperity, the average price of
the quarter of Wheat, for the 10 years from 1741 to 1750
inclufive, was only   —   —   L. 1 13   8

And computing the other Grain, according to the price of
Wheat, and in proportion to the above prices, they amount,
per quarter,   —   For Barley   0 16   7
                                      Oats   —   0 11· 2½
                                      Rye   —   1   1   2
                                      Beans   —   0 19 10

The average price of all thefe feveral kinds of Grain, overhead, being
L. 1 : 0 : 6 ; the price of two quarters for the maintainance of each
perfon, in thefe years, only amounted to ·   —   —   2   1   0

So that the yearly fupport of each perfon, for bread, beer, fpirits, &c.
at prefent, exceeds the former expence in no lefs than   —   L. 0 17   6

TABLE Explanatory—*continued.*

Article VIII. Brought forward.

And if we confider that the prices of Wheat, prior to the eftablifhment of the Corn Regifter, in 1771, are taken from the audite books of Eton, where the Wheat is of the very beft quality, and the meafure nine gallons to the bufhel, the difference muft be confiderably higher.

Article VIII.—Comparative State of the Quantity and Value of the Crops of GRAIN of ENGLAND and SCOTLAND.

From the ftate of the exportation of Grain, from England and Scotland, (Art. 1. of this Table) for 55 years after the Union, it appears that the average yearly exportation, from England, was 535,776 quarters; and that the average exportation, from Scotland, was only 34,524, which is not quite a fifteenth part of the other.

If we are to judge of the production from this ftate of the exportation, we muft conclude that England generally produces fifteen times as much Corn as Scotland.

From the fame ftate it appears, that the crop of England generally confifts of eight-twentieths of Wheat, and twelve-twentieths of the inferior Grain overhead; and that the crop of Scotland generally confifts of one-eighteenth of Wheat, and feventeen-eighteenths of inferior Grain.

By the ftate of the antient revenue of the Scots Clergy it would appear, that the crop of that kingdom confifted of about one-thirteenth of Wheat, and twelve-thir-teenths of inferior Grain.

If we confider that the rents of the clergy were, in general, of better Grain than the ordinary payments of the other rents of the country, and that the exportation was chiefly of inferior grain; if we take the medium of the proportions of the Grain paid to the Clergy, and of that exported, we may conclude with fome degree of certainty, that the crop of Scotland confifts generally of one-fifteenth of Wheat, and fourteen-fifteenths of inferior Grain.

Computing the quarter of Wheat at 40s. and that of inferior Grain overhead, at 20s. we fhall find that, in England, they have

Eight-twentieth parts of Wheat, at 40s.	—	—	L. 0 16 0	
And twelve-twentieths of inferior Grain, at 20s.		—	0 12 0	
		Making	L. 1 8 0	

And, in Scotland, they have only

One-fifteenth part of Wheat, at 40s.	—	—	L. 0 2 8	
And fourteen-fifteenths of inferior Grain, at 20s.	—	—	0 18 8	
		Making	L. 1 1 4	

Thus the quality being about one-fourth better in England than in Scotland, and the quantity being about fifteen times as much, the general value of the crop of England, will be about nineteen times as much as that of Scotland.

TABLE Explanatory—*continued.*

	Quarters of Grain overhead.
Article IX.—Of the Increase of POPULATION from the Extension of Agriculture.	
From the year 1741 to the year 1750 inclusive, the average yearly exportation of Grain amounted to — —	848,661
For the 12 years from 1773 to 1784 inclusive, the average yearly exportation of Grain has only been — —	267,182
The difference is	581,478

quarters of surplus Grain annually raised in Great Britain during that period.

And reckoning twelve people to the raising of every hundred quarters, we must have had 69,768 people then employed in husbandry, more than were necessary to furnish subsistence for the kingdom.

———————

Printed by ALEX. CHAPMAN AND Co.

ERRATA.

Page 10. Line 3. for *are* read *were*.
— 24. — 12. for *a* read *an*.
— 26. Note ‡ for *N*o 6. read *N*o 8.
— 116. Line 15. inftead of *was* read *were*.
— 122. — 9. inftead of *to* read *into*.
— 123. — 13. inftead of 15,193 read 15,943.
— Do. — 15. reference wanted, *Appendix*, No 4. ·
— 196. — 24 read *mercantile*.
— 223. — 6. inftead of *raisd* read *raised*.

www.ingramcontent.com/pod-product-compliance
Lightning Source LLC
Chambersburg PA
CBHW031150120726
47905CB00006B/1894